AN OCEAN VAST OF BLESSING

KALOS

The word *kalos* (καλός) means beautiful. It is the call of the good; that which arouses interest, desire: "I am here." Beauty brings the appetite to rest at the same time as it wakens the mind from its daily slumber, calling us to look afresh at that which is before our very eyes. It makes virgins of us all, and of everything—there, before us, lies something that we never noticed before. Beauty consists in *integritas sive perfectio* [integrity and perfection] and *claritas* [brightness/clarity]. It is the reason why we rise and why we sleep—that great night of dependence, one that reveals the borrowed existence of all things, if, that is, there is to be a thing at all, or if there is to be a person at all. Here lies the ground of all science, of philosophy, and of all theology, indeed of our each and every day.

This series will seek to provide intelligent-yet-accessible volumes that have the innocence of beauty and of true adventure, and in so doing remind us all again of that which we took for granted, most of all thought itself.

SERIES EDITORS:
Conor Cunningham, Eric Austin Lee, and Christopher Ben Simpson

An Ocean Vast of Blessing

A THEOLOGY OF GRACE

. . .

Steven D. Cone

 CASCADE *Books* · Eugene, Oregon

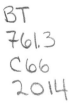

AN OCEAN VAST OF BLESSING
A Theology of Grace

Kalos 1

Cascade Books
An Imprint of Wipf and Stock Publishers
199 W. 8th Ave., Suite 3
Eugene, OR 97401

www.wipfandstock.com

ISBN 13: 978-1-62032-248-2

Cataloging-in-Publication data:

Cone, Steven D.

    An ocean vast of blessing : a theology of grace / Steven D. Cone.

    Kalos 1

    xii + 242 p.; 23 cm—Includes bibliographical references and index.

    ISBN 13: 978-1-62032-248-2

    1. Grace (Theology). 2. Creation. 3. Theological anthropology—Christianity. 4. Sin—Christianity. 5. Jesus Christ—Crucifixion. 6. Salvation—Christianity. I. Series. II. Title

BT761.3 C662 2014

Manufactured in the USA.

For my parents, Robert and Nancy, with thanks and love

Table of Contents

Introduction

O the deep, deep love of Jesus!
Love of ev'ry love the best:
'Tis an ocean vast of blessing,
'Tis a haven sweet of rest.
O the deep, deep love of Jesus!
'Tis a heav'n of heav'ns to me;
And it lifts me up to glory,
For it lifts me up to thee.[1]

Salvation by Christ reveals that God brings this world about and enters into it for the purpose of having eternal communion with us. The transcendent God is thus intimately present and involved in his creation, and, as we shall see, being authentically human means to become like him. The very existence of created being is a relationship with its creator, always depending on both the freedom and transcendence of God in creating.

The ultimate character of human life, then, is known in salvation, not in creation alone, for sin's brokenness and darkness robs humanity of its God-given purpose: growing in God's grace to share the life of the Trinity. The grace of salvation given in and through the cross leads to a healed and elevated—and cruciform—life. In this life, and in its culmination in the world to come, the ultimate purpose and meaning of creation comes to fulfillment, as those whom Christ saves participate in the love and wisdom of God. From the very beginning, the purpose of human life was not to remain merely human. It was to come to share the life of love and wisdom, of personal communion, of true life, that is the life of God (John 17:20–24).

1. Samuel Trevor Francis (1834–1925), "O the Deep, Deep Love of Jesus."

The *Resourcement* of Grace

In Christian theology, the twentieth century saw movements in which, in manifold ways, theology was reborn. Many of these movements self-consciously worked to move forward by listening more deeply to the great voices of the past. In Roman Catholic circles, Henri de Lubac powerfully and controversially championed a *resourcement* of theology, looking beyond the manuals and commentaries authoritative in his day to the still living voice of the Fathers and great Scholastics.[2] Noted Catholic theologian Bernard Lonergan took as his motto, *"vetera novis augere et perficere"*—to enlarge and perfect the old by means of the new.[3] While Eastern Orthodox theology has always looked to its traditional heritage, the great flourishing of Orthodox theology in the twentieth century had much to do with reappropriating this heritage in new ways.[4] In the Anglican communion, Radical Orthodoxy's very name indicates a desire to move forward by rooting itself deeply in the great tradition of the church.[5] In the evangelical world, this *motif* surfaces most explicitly in Thomas Oden's paleo-orthodoxy.[6]

Our intention here is two-fold: first, to present a theology of grace that can add to and clarify current theology; and second, to do so by appropriating the advances of the wider voices in *resourcement*, opening up this array as a resource for today's theology. Our hope is, thereby, to contribute to the generous and historically based orthodoxy that Thomas Oden envisions.[7]

Systematics, Not Doctrines

No one alive today has *"hilasmos"* and *"anakephalaiosis"* as the language of her heart. If we are going to live out what it means for Christ to be our atoning sacrifice (1 John 2:2), and that all of reality is summed up in him (Eph 1:10), we are going to have to transpose these ancient concepts into the world in which we live. The affirmations of doctrine, necessarily, stay close to the language of the revelation. How will we make a good transposition,

2. Witness his co-founding of the primary source collections in *Sources Chrétiennes*.

3. Bernard Lonergan, *Insight*, 768.

4. See, for example, the renewal of Irenaeus by John Behr, David Bentley Hart's dependence on Gregory of Nyssa, and the neo-Palamism of John Meyendorff.

5. See the concern for Thomas Aquinas, especially, in such authors as John Milbank and Catherine Pickstock, and the impressive appropriation of Maximus the Confessor by Conor Cunningham.

6. See his promise of unoriginality, while actually presenting a powerful and constructive theology. Oden, *Classic Christianity*, xv.

7. Oden, *The Rebirth of Orthodoxy*.

retaining the intent of the sacred word, and transforming thereby our present times?

Affirming the classic Christian teaching of salvation by grace, through faith, intrinsically draws us to try and understand what that commitment means. As Paul says, and as all valid Christian teaching affirms,

> For by grace you have been saved through faith, and this is not your own doing; it is the gift of God—not the result of works, so that no one may boast. For we are what he has made us, created in Christ Jesus for good works, which God prepared beforehand to be our way of life (Eph 2:8–10, NRSV).

Anyone, however, who has studied this chapter of Ephesians, or who has the least acquaintance with the secondary literature trying to explain it, will recognize that the commitment one makes in accepting this doctrine opens one up to a further great conversation; but, the conversation thus entered into on the basis of faith is of a different sort than the core affirmation of God's revelation that grounds one in that faith.[8]

To use Bernard Lonergan's terminology, one thereby moves from functional specialty doctrines to functional specialty systematics.[9] "Doctrines," in Lonergan's terms, identifies the judgments of truth that Christians are firmly committed to as a part of Christian identity. "Systematics," then, is the way in which we try to understand how those doctrinal commitments can really be the case, relating them to each other and searching for an inner unity. Doctrines sets forth truths that should be affirmed by Christians with all the certainty of the faith; systematics tries to offer helpful explanations of those undergirding truths.

The second type of conversation—the one that is subsequent to the basic commitment to the truth of the Christian faith—deals with how it *might* be good, how it *may* be helpful, to answer the questions that arise from the affirmation of Christian doctrines. We cannot help wondering how everything fits together, what it all would mean if we could get all the different parts in one big picture. Such a discussion offers *probable* ways to explain the truths affirmed by being in Christ. One hopes they are helpful, and if so, that is well and good. If not, the truths of the faith remain.

Although systematics deals with merely probable affirmations, it is of great importance for how we live out the truths of the faith. We *will* make the translation from the biblical world to our own, somehow. If it is done thoughtlessly, we will likely be dominated by the voices of our culture,

8. See Lonergan, "The Supernatural Order," 63.

9. Lonergan, *Method*, 295–354. Functional specialties explain the distinct but related operations that theologians perform while doing theology.

reading the logic of the present age into the revelation. The work of systematics is to try to subject this transposition to some kind of worthwhile theoretical control. The understandings it offers are merely probable, but their intention is to communicate to us the truths of the Christian faith in a way that transforms our present horizons.

Thanksgiving

This work would not exist without my having received much help. I would like, first of all, to thank my family: my wife, Violeta, and my children, Anna and Stella. Their love and grace have carried me through this process. I would also like to thank my parents, Robert and Nancy, and my wife's parents, Pavel and Snejana, for their selfless generosity and support.

I would also like to thank the administrators of my university for supporting my research, particularly Academic Dean James Estep, Provost Clay Ham, and President Keith Ray. May this work bless many, within the university and outside of it. I also thank my colleagues, Christopher Simpson, John Castelein, and Robert Rea; over fifteen years you have put up with me and edified me in my search to understand grace.

This work has evolved in conversation with a number of interlocutors. I would like to thank Danielle Cerqueira, Katlyn Chambers, Elisabeth Nelson, Matthew Welch, Ryan Hemmer, Joe Gordon, Justin Schwartz, and Jodie Merritt. I would also like to thank my professors at Boston College, especially the readers of my dissertation, Fred Lawrence, Charles Hefling, and M. Shawn Copeland; additionally, I would like to thank Louis Roy, Stephen Brown, and Matthew Lamb. Finally, to my friends Jeremy Wilkins, Jamie Beasley, and R. J. Snell, my heartfelt thanks. Chris, Jamie, Matthew, Danielle, Katlyn, Ryan, and Joe, in particular, read either the whole of this work or substantial parts; any errors in it are likely my own, but their careful reading and interaction covered over a multitude of errors and contributed to whatever degree of excellence the work has.

Above all, thanks be to God, who gives us the victory in our Lord Jesus Christ. In him there is no condemnation, and the law of the Spirit of life sets us free from the law of sin and death (Rom 7:25—8:2).

1

Nature Bright with Grace

CREATION

Tossing his mane of snows in wildest eddies and tangles,
Lion-like March cometh in, hoarse, with tempestuous breath,
Through all the moaning chimneys, and 'thwart all the hollows and
    angles
Round the shuddering house, threating of winter and death.

But in my heart I feel the life of the wood and the meadow
Thrilling the pulses that own kindred with fibres that lift
Bud and blade to the sunward, within the inscrutable shadow,
Deep in the oak's chill core, under the gathering drift.

Nay, to earth's life in mine some prescience, or dream, or desire
(How shall I name it aright?) comes for a moment and goes—
Rapture of life ineffable, perfect—as if in the brier,
Leafless there by my door, trembled a sense of the rose.[1]

Because God creates this universe, making sense of grace inextricably calls us to examine the basic nature of this world. This pairing may seem strange; creation often seems to us an event, while grace can be relegated to a legal standing merely applied to us. However, reimagining the doctrine of creation more adequately teaches Christians that the natural world is intimately related to God and interpenetrated by his grace. The relation of the world to God is an asymmetrical one; relatedness to God is constitutive of the created world's being, yet the converse is not true with respect to God's

1. William Dean Howells, "Earliest Spring," 812.

1

being. It is exactly this radical contingency of the natural order, however, that leads to its goodness, for created being is the intentional work and gift of God.

The Christian understanding of creation, therefore, has nothing to do with a two-storied universe in which supernatural or spiritual being is an optional or dispensable accompaniment to the natural world. Rather, the supernatural order and the natural order are both sets of relations that essentially have to do with God. "Secularity," a so-called neutral ground of autonomy insulated from religious concepts or relations, must thus be considered a sub-Christian understanding of reality. Yet neither do the natural and the supernatural orders collapse into or elide each other, for the strictly supernatural relations creatures enter into depend on and validate the relations that God has established as the state of nature.

One may see the grand sweep of these notions in the powerful creation theology of Maximus the Confessor. His cosmic theology forms a significant resource for this work of reimagining, and the modern form of this discussion helps clarify and update his theology. Maximus sets forth a coherent vision in which the ages of the created world are ordered to distinct ends; the first age of creation moves toward the incarnation, the second toward the incorporation of those Christ has saved into the very life of God. In this positive understanding of the natural universe—made to receive the Son of God and destined for glorification in him—one may also see the significance and place of human beings in the cosmic story. For the movement of this universe, of which humans are a microcosm, has as its *telos* the eternal rest of the Creator God.

The Distinction

One of the great challenges—and essential keys—in creation theology is articulating the relation of creature and Creator in a way that does justice to each. Essentially, creation is a relationship; yet, the terms in this relation are of such different sorts.

Robert Sokolowski proposes an essential insight into this relation in what he terms, "the distinction." "The distinction," as he terms it, names the asymmetrical relation of absolute dependence in which the creature's being is defined and exists only in relation to the Creator. The Creator, though, is self-sufficient, self-existent, and not modified at all by relation to the creature.[2]

---

2. Sokolowski, *Faith and Reason*, 31; Sokolowski, *Christian Faith*, 38–39.

As David Burrell's excellent work interpreting and expanding upon Sokolowski explains, "the distinction" expresses a relation that appears in the world but that does not name something in it.[3] God does not appear in the world, but he is the source of the world's meaning.[4] The world—the entire created cosmos itself, all that is not God—is placed as one of the terms in this relation, yet in a subordinate way; God is more foundational and fundamental than the distinction.[5] His preeminent existence allows "the distinction" to occur.

This relation does not change God's being, and the asymmetrical nature of this relation is fundamental to Christian revelation and theology. It is not that Christianity considers relation to created being as unimportant to God; rather, God relates to the world by a depth of generosity, wisdom, commitment, and love that we cannot comprehend. This is, however, the relation of the only God to those he has brought into existence in the freedom of wisdom and love. Our existence depends on, and does not constitute, his.[6]

In discussing the names of God, for example, Thomas Aquinas analyzes names such as "Lord," wondering if God's lordship indicates an aspect of God's being. If so, it would seem that the existence of someone to be lord over (i.e., a creature) would be a real modifier of God's being. He concludes:

> Since therefore God is outside the whole order of creation, and all creatures are ordered to Him, and not conversely, it is manifest that creatures are really related to God Himself; whereas in God there is no real relation to creatures, but a relation only in idea, inasmuch as creatures are referred to Him.[7]

What Aquinas here indicates is that the relation of God to the created world is of a fundamentally different nature than the relation of the Father to the Son. The inter-Trinitarian relations are eternal and constitutive of God's being.[8] The created world does not modify God's eternal being; created being

3. Burrell, *Unknowable God*, 20.

4. Ibid., 1.

5. Ibid., 31–33.

6. See also Christopher Ben Simpson's elucidation of the philosophical theology of Irish philosopher of creation William Desmond, saying that, "Beyond this, the theistic God of creation is, for Desmond, the God beyond the whole. As beyond the whole of the world, this God possesses an absoluteness (*ab–solo*—from itself alone), and asymmetric and 'idiotic' infinity that is beyond any need for completion and so opens the space for otherness apart from itself." Simpson, "Theology, Philosophy," 275; see Desmond, *God and the Between*, 159, 163, 241, 304.

7. Aquinas, *Summa Theologica* (hereafter abbreviated as *ST*), I, 13.7.

8. *ST* I, 28.2.

is only possible because of God's eternally complete being and does not become an element in it.[9] On the other hand, relation to God is a modifier of—or rather, the basis of—creaturely existence.[10]

Sokolowski draws out the way that "the distinction" is occasioned by the core doctrines of the Christian faith and helps to explain them.[11] The way for the fully Christian doctrine of creation is opened up by the doctrines affirmed, especially, by the first four ecumenical councils.[12] These councils set definitive limits for answers to questions such as, "When we say the Father is 'God' and the Son is 'God,' is the word 'God' used in the same sense?" and, "What does that mean in relation to the Son as a human being?" In affirming Christ's consubstantiality with the Father as something radically different from his consubstantiality with us, and yet in affirming both as true and united in the person of Christ, the solutions of Nicaea, Constantinople, Ephesus, and Chalcedon served as a great pedagogy on the transcendence of God and his work of creation.[13] Created reality is affirmed as real and significant, else the humanity of Christ would be insignificant. Yet, the full greatness of God, also affirmed of Christ, is neither part of this world nor conditioned by it.[14] In that the ecumenical councils crystallize and explain the message of Scripture, they reflect the pedagogy and progress of revelation present in Scripture.[15] For, the sum and culmination of the message of Scripture is Christ, the first fundamental question of this world, whose words and actions reach beyond its confines (John 5:39–46, Luke 24:25–27, Col 1:15–20, and Rev 1:17–18).[16]

While this theology of creation does serve to affirm the transcendence of God, it also paradoxically has the effect of validating the goodness and significance of created being in all of its finitude and particularity.[17] In this vein, Burrell sketches out a tri-partite analogy in the work of Aquinas, in which the relation of matter to form is analogous to the relation of essence

9. See also *ST* I, 28, 1ad3.

10. Ibid.

11. Sokolowski, *Christian Faith*, 38–39.

12. Ibid., 43.

13. Ibid., 44; Sokolowski, *Faith and Reason*, 35–36.

14. Sokolowski, *Christian Faith*, 45. See also Lewis, "Dogma and the Universe," 41–42.

15. Sokolowski, *Faith and Reason*, 123, 126–29.

16. Ibid., 145.

17. Note Chalcedon's affirmation that the particular characteristics (*ideomata*) of both natures are preserved, with Christ's human nature neither contaminating nor swallowed up in his divine nature.

to *esse* and to the relation of potency to act.[18] The key term the analogy pivots on and attempts to explain is *esse*, the verb "to be."[19] Aquinas' point is the priority of individual existing things. Matter without form is indeterminate, essence without *esse* is non-existent, and potency without act is merely potential. The particular, actual, and real have priority.

In this way, Burrell (*via* Aquinas) confirms the stability and dignity of the "ontological units" present as created being.[20] Because God gives the *esse* of created beings, God affirms them in their existence.[21] Yet, this *esse* of created being has a "density" to it that our understandings strain to grasp.[22] The affirmation of created being by God is not the relation of one thing to something like it; rather, it is the way that every existent thing is related to the absolutely transcendent ground of all possible existence.

The Christian doctrine of creation is an advance, and to understand its import, one must look at the theology of emanation that it competed against and adapted. Emanation is an analogy that concerns the relation of the world we experience to its source. It proposes that relation to be something like the light that emanates from the sun, or an echo that proceeds from clapping hands. So, for example, the intelligible (and in some cases intelligent) nature of the world reflects a higher, more basic and unified, intelligibility that is its source.[23] Emanation theory has roots in Plato and Aristotle and is a hallmark of Neoplatonic thought. It is also one of the most significant analogies Christians have used to understand creation across the length and breadth of church history.

Sokolowski and Burrell agree in describing the theology of emanation as the natural and spontaneous way in which pagans understand the world.[24] As classically voiced by Plotinus, for example, its key point is as follows:

> The divine and the nondivine form parts of a larger whole. The divine may be recognized as the exemplary, the controlling, the best, and even in some sense the origin, but it is not normally

18. Burrell, *Unknowable God*, 29–30.

19. See ibid., 60.

20. Ibid., 36.

21. Ibid., 32–34.

22. Sokolowski, *Christian Faith*, 41.

23. See McGrath, *Christian Theology*, 221, for an explanation of emanation relative to creation theology, including a discussion of its advantages and limitations.

24. Sokolowski, *Christian Faith*, 40–41; Burrell, *Unknowable God*, 9–10.

conceived as that which could be, in undiminished goodness and excellence, even if everything else were not.[25]

Creation, in the sense fundamental for Christianity, does not seem to have been an issue for pagans.[26] In fact, one may even describe the doctrine of creation as offensive, for without the example of Christ how could one ever believe that the mere particulars of created being have value over and against a truly transcendent One?[27]

Burrell and Sokolowski know very well the extent to which Aquinas and other landmark Christian theologians have used the analogy of emanation; one, in fact, *should* use it. Properly understood it illuminates the relation of creature to Creator, and the heart of the doctrine of creation is, after all, relationship.[28] Burrell and Sokolowski carefully note the way in which Aquinas uses this model.

In Aquinas, the function of the emanation model is to secure and express the analytic power of "the distinction," and significant changes are introduced to allow the model to express a relation of which Plotinus had little idea.[29] Creation, for example, is a personal transaction.[30] It is something to which there is a beginning; and, although the "beginning" is less important than the relation of total dependence of creature to Creator, the fact of a beginning emphasizes the freedom of the creative act.[31] Creation also emphasizes the care of the Creator for each individual.[32] The God thus affirmed is also responsive to his creation.[33]

The point where "the distinction" most deeply alters the classical understanding of emanation is with respect to the radical contingency of the created order. All that is, aside from God, might not be; and, it would not change in any way the being, blessedness, or joy of God should all of created reality not exist. Plotinus, and other classical exponents of emanation,

25. Sokolowski, *Christian Faith*, 40. See Plotinus, *The Enneads*, Books I–II. See also Gerson, "Plotinus," for a good but brief introduction to Plotinus.

26. Sokolowski, *Faith and Reason*, 12–13; 45. Examples such as the *Euthyphro* myth serve to explain the nature of what is already here, not to explain the complete contingency of the entire world that we know.

27. Lewis notes the offensive nature of the doctrine of creation to classical ears in "Dogma and the Universe," 40.

28. Burrell, *Unknowable God*, 72–73.

29. Ibid., 34–35. Sokolowski, *Faith and* Reason, 48–50. See *ST* I, 65. 3 and 4.

30. Sokolowski, *Christian Faith*, 43.

31. Burrell, *Unknowable God*, 75.

32. *ST* I, 22.1, 2, and 3.

33. Burrell, *Unknowable God*, 105–6. See also Goris, "Divine Foreknowledge," especially 100–103, 112–15.

do realize that our being has being only by participation in the being of the One, and, therefore, there is an analogy when using the word "being" about both the One and us. Christian theology, however, radicalizes this analogy to include both creation by choice out of nothing and the absolute transcendence of God.[34]

"To be (*esse*)," for us, therefore formulates our relation to the Trinity.[35] Our existing results from the graciously chosen action of the Creator and has no other source.[36] The reason that existence itself, including the depths of our own true selves, is unfathomable to us is that the source of our being is the unfathomable God, and this relation is constitutive for all of created reality.[37] This relation also indicates an intimacy of our being (*esse*) with God.[38] For, our act of existence does not exclude relationship with God, but rather includes it. We have being because of God, with God, in a way that differs from our relationship with any created being.[39]

The consequence of the complete contingency of creation, again, is its goodness.[40] Through the materiality of the world, God gives an indication of his being and life.[41] In the Seventh Ecumenical Council (Nicaea II), through the vicissitudes of the iconoclastic controversies, the church affirmed the dignity of material reality as revelatory and receptive of God's life. There is, therefore, intrinsic importance to history, as well, and an expectation of the interpenetration of the transcendent Creator with history.[42] For, the world of space and time is created from nothing, and its every place, every object, and every moment must reflect divine causality.

The excellence of creation is therefore the glory of God. As Thomist scholar Bernard Lonergan puts it:

> To conceive God as originating value and the world as termi-
> nal value implies that God too is self-transcending and that the

34. Sokolowski, *Christian Faith*, 41, 46–47; Burrell, *Unknowable God*, 15–16; *ST* I, 45.5.

35. Burrell, *Unknowable God*, 30. See *ST* I, 45.6; see also Simpson's analysis of Desmond's creational Trinitarianism in Simpson, "Theology, Philosophy," 275–78.

36. Burrell, *Unknowable* God, 32; Sokolowski, *Christian Faith*, 43.

37. Burrell, *Unknowable God*, 21–24.

38. Ibid., 49.

39. Sokolowski, *Faith and Reason*, 42. See *ST* I, 4.2. See also Kierkegaard's point in *Sickness unto Death* that our selves intrinsically include relation to the one who brings us into existence; see Kierkegaard, *Sickness*, 13–14.

40. Sokolowski, *Faith and Reason*, 34, 42.

41. Sokolowski, *Christian Faith*, 50.

42. Ibid. Contrast the positive Christian evaluation of history as revelatory of God with the expectations of the pagan *mythoi*; see Lewis, "Dogma and the Universe," 45.

world is the fruit of his self-transcendence, the expression and manifestation of his benevolence and beneficence, his glory. As the excellence of the son is the glory of the father, so to the excellence of mankind is the glory of God. To say that God created the world for his glory is to say that he created it not for his sake but for ours. He made us in his image, for our authenticity consists in being like him, in self-transcending, in being origins of value, in true love.[43]

Creation is an act of freedom and love.[44] In that we have being only by God's wisdom and will, we will achieve the purpose of our being, and our own true nature, only insofar as we imitate him.

The culmination and most fitting expression of humanity, then, will be to live like Jesus Christ. In this way, we see that the purpose of created reality was never to stay chained within the immanent causal nexus of the world. For, human action imitating Christ is not merely human.[45] By imitating Christ—participating in his life—we are able to imitate the generosity of the Creator (Matt 16:25; Mark 8:35; Luke 9:24).[46]

Because the completion of human reality is to imitate a divine person, again, one can see the way that relation to God interpenetrates our history and destiny.[47] The materiality of the world, in all its history and particularity, therefore expresses and expects an existence that is sacramental. For, sacraments exactly involve the creation's need—*our* need—for actions and events that relate us to the God who is not part of this world.[48] A sacrament's power and meaning lies in its inherent connection to the promises and life of Jesus.

The Problem with Pure Nature

Rather than expressing "the distinction," some Christian (and subsequent non-Christian) understandings of creation have underscored only the separation of creature and Creator. Instead of seeing creatures as always—and in every way—constituted by relation with their creator, this sub-Christian theology sees nature as a realm that is apart from the action of God, aside from the event of his having brought nature into existence. This putative

---

43. Lonergan, *Method*, 116–17. See *ST* II–II, 132. 1ad1.

44. Sokolowski, *Christian Faith*, 4.

45. Sokolowski, *Faith and Reason*, 145.

46. Ibid.

47. Burrell, *Unknowable God*, 89.

48. Sokolowski, *Faith and Reason*, 147–49.

natural realm makes space for human autonomy by being emptied of the divine.

This view's difference from "the distinction" appears clearly in the contrasting understandings of both the natural and the supernatural. As understood by Aquinas, both the natural and the supernatural are "orders," that is, they are sets of relations.[49] The relations of the natural order concern the condition and capacities humans and other creatures exist in or have according to the gift of created being. The relations of the strictly supernatural order have to do with coming to be a part of the life of God. Because the relations of the Trinity constitute God's being, the supernatural is an order of persons, three of whom are the divine persons of the Trinity, whose community of wisdom and love we come to share by supernatural grace.[50]

Both of these orders intrinsically include relation to God.[51] The moral apogee of the natural order is practical wisdom, the knowledge by which we live excellently in this world. The peak of the supernatural order is the love that makes us friends with God.[52] To live excellently in this world, one must, as a matter of first importance, fulfill one's duty to God. Because of the gift of God's Spirit, being friends with God means coming to love God, and thereby coming to love as Jesus loves (Rom 5:5).[53] These orders are related to each other: the supernatural perfects the natural order, but depends on it as well.[54] With respect to either order, one has being because one has relation to God and only rightly lives unto God. With respect to the supernatural order, humans receive relations that complete and fulfill human nature, but which depend on the free gift of God that exceeds the proportion of this world.[55]

John Milbank has ably described the development of a competing understanding of reality quite hostile to "the distinction." Its root lies in the devolution of Christian theology in the centuries following Aquinas, and its fruit is the positing, not of a natural order, but of a secular world.

---

49. See *ST* I–II, 111. 1ad2. See also Lonergan, *Grace and Freedom*, 14–20, Stebbins, *Divine Initiative*, 78–84, and Cone, "Transforming Desire," 144–53.

50. I thank Charles Hefling for this insight. One may see metaphors for the supernatural order operative in Scripture: the kingdom of God (a political order), the body of Christ (an organic order), the bride of Christ (a relational order).

51. See Snell and Cone, *Authentic Cosmopolitanism*, 87–91, 105–8.

52. See Schockenhoff, "Charity," 244–58, and Keenan, "Prudence," 259–71, for discussions of charity and practical wisdom (or prudence). See also Porter, "Right Reason," 167–91, on the right relation of natural morality to God.

53. See Stebbins, *Divine Initiative*, 120–22.

54. *ST* I–II, 62.1, 2; I–II, 65.3; I–II, 67.1, 2.

55. *ST* II–II, 1.5; and II–II, 23.2. See Wieland, "Happiness," 57–68.

> Once, there was no "secular." And the secular was not latent,
> waiting to fill more space with the steam of the "purely human,"
> when the pressure of the sacred was relaxed. Instead there was
> the single community of Christendom, with its dual aspects of
> *sacerdotium* and *regnum*. The *saeculum*, in the medieval era, was
> not a space, a domain, but a time—the interval between fall and
> *eschaton* where coercive justice, private property and impaired
> natural reason must make shift to cope with the unredeemed
> effects of sinful humanity.[56]

This secular world, by contrast, understands human freedom as natural autonomy, made possible by the absence of God.[57] True religion may exist, but
it is only a matter for the individual heart.[58] Christianity, rather than rightly
permeating society and leavening every discourse, becomes a private matter
that retreats from the world.[59]

As the medieval world developed in the centuries following Aquinas,
the center of theological discussion moved from questions of God's wisdom
and his right ordering of the universe, to questions of the possible uses of
God's power.[60] Often the intention of this move was to speak of God's freedom and omnipotence in relating to his creation.[61] Authors such as William
of Ockham thereby emphasized God's love for the creation he freely chose.[62]

Milbank, however, lays out the cost of this decision.[63] Power is competitive, and an ontology or ethics based on power will inevitably devolve
into alienation and violence.[64] Witness the imperialistic attitude toward
nature after Descartes, Bacon, Machiavelli, and Hobbes, in which the purpose of science is not simply to understand the universe, but to render it
exploitable for human benefit.[65] Witness also the development of a political
theory of sovereignty whose first attribute is not justice but control.[66] The

---

56. Milbank, *Social Theory*, 9.

57. Ibid., 11, 13.

58. Ibid., 9.

59. Ibid., 17–18.

60. See, for example, Scotus, "Ordinatio I, dist. 44;" Aquinas, of course, believed
in God's omnipotence, but his discussion of God's power starts in Question 25 of the
Prima Pars of the *Summa Theologica*, after the questions on God's existence, wisdom
and goodness.

61. See Burrell, *Unknowable God*, 108.

62. See Leff, *Ockham*, 14–17.

63. See also Cunningham, "*Natura Pura*," 243–54.

64. Milbank, *Social Theory*, 257–326. See also Hart, *Beauty of the Infinite*, *passim*.

65. Sokolowski, *Faith and Reason*, 22.

66. Milbank, *Social Theory*, 13–17.

secular realm must be lacking God's presence and power because, otherwise, human presence and power would have no significance; control, not right relationship, comes to be of fundamental significance.

According to "the distinction," by contrast, the way that our being depends on God's being, and therefore participates in it, must also be understood as a participation in the divine creativity, "which reveals itself as ever-new through time."[67] The diversity and difference of the world of space and time results from, and is grounded in, the divine unity by which it exists.[68] Christian theology, therefore, can deal with the historical and individual nature of the beings in the universe according to relations of wisdom and goodness, while the "secular" social sciences tend toward reducing all sets of relations to power.[69] Christianity is able to codify the transcendental difference as peace, not an original violence.[70] Christian theology must recover a right discourse about creation, then, out-narrating a view whose upshot is a two-story universe: the lower story a secular realm of pure nature, the upper story a supernatural realm that is essentially an (all too detachable) add-on.[71]

67. Ibid., 308. See also Sokolowski, *Faith and Reason*, 43–44.

68. Milbank, *Social Theory*, 336–37.

69. Ibid., 260.

70. Ibid., 5–6. Again, see also Hart, *Beauty of the Infinite, passim*. Any position that hangs its hat on opposing another view runs the risk of itself becoming a parody of that view, and it can be tempting to read Milbank in this way. By so opposing the secular, has he not given in to an unbridled supernaturalism that, instead of upholding the natural order, negates it? Based on the preface to *Theology and Social Theory*'s second edition, one may see that this is not really the case. He there argues that his attitude toward secular reason was never purely negating, because secular reasoning is never taken on its own terms (xiv). Rather, it is taken as something that either depends on the positivity of Christianity or that seeks it; therefore it either still shows or at least desires positivity. Also, in Milbank's interaction with Henri de Lubac, he recognizes a "problematic balance" in de Lubac's thought, concerning the universe, before glorification, between natural and supernatural (xxiv). The natural, therefore, has provisional validity, even if it is not an end in itself. Milbank's defense of Eckhardt likewise shows a desire to reconcile Eckhardt's mystical teachings with an ontology that is participatory, or world-affirming, not pantheistic (xxvi–xxviii). Milbank's argument in "Only Theology Overcomes Metaphysics" seems of similar import: his disagreement with Jean-Luc Marion exactly turns on the import and significance of a participatory ontology that honors both the contingency and validity of created being (Milbank, *Word Made Strange*, 36–52). The later Milbank, at least, seems on the side of "the distinction," even if he would articulate it in a different way than Sokolowski and Burrell.

71. Such a "two-story" position actually has to do with the Neo-Scholasticism that became characteristic of Catholic theology in the nineteenth century, claiming Aquinas' name but indebted to the nominalism and voluntarism that developed after his death.

Maximus on Creation

The creation theology of Maximus the Confessor forms a powerful resource for this theological re-narration. Maximus sets forth a grand architectonic of created reality in two acts. In the first act, or age, of the universe, the universe's purpose is God's becoming a human being; in the second, human beings come to share in the divine life. Based on this salvific ontology, Maximus presents a strongly positive understanding of the created universe.

The Drama of Created Being

Any analogy has possible pitfalls, and Maximus' dramatic presentation is no exception. To set proper limits for understanding creation, he argues that one must preserve nine elements in a truly Christian creation theology: first, creation out of nothing; second, creation resulting from God's will, not necessity; third, creation depending on God's benevolence; fourth, creation is by the Word (*Logos*); fifth, creation results from God's prudence; sixth, creation reflects the divine condescension; seventh, creation introduces the element of motion and does not result from it; eighth, every created being is a composite of substance and accident; and ninth, God creates particular beings, who have qualities and who need God's providence, not qualities that are independent of beings.[72] Many of these elements serve to correct the Origenist creation theology of his day, which he saw as inadequate both in terms of honoring this universe of change and leading toward God's final rest.[73] They also serve to purify the theology of emanation he received, reconciling it more adequately with Christian faith.[74]

During the first act, or age, of creation, Maximus sets forth the meaning of the universe as God's preparation for the incarnation.[75] This is Act One of the Grand Drama of Incarnation and Salvation:

> By his gracious condescension God became man and is called man for the sake of man and by exchanging his condition for ours revealed the power that elevates man to God through his love for God and brings God down to man because of his love

72. Thunberg, *Microcosm and Mediator*, 49.

73. See Louth, *Maximus*, 64–69, on the Origenist cosmologies Maximus partially adapted and significantly opposed.

74. See Thunberg, *Microcosm and Mediator*, 49–94.

75. Maximus, *Ad Thalassium* 22.

for man. By this blessed inversion, man is made God by divinization and God is made man by hominization.[76]

Christ is creation's center and star, and he is the meaning after which Maximus quests.[77] In the economy of salvation—the economy of creation—the
mystery of Jesus provides the key to the cosmos.[78]

The analogy Maximus uses for salvation is *theōsis*. While this chal-
lenging term is sometimes translated as "divinization," it does not indicate
literally "becoming God" in any way. Rather, it is an analogy that speaks of
the way that saved human life is transformed so as to resemble—as far as is
possible for a mere creature—the transcendent life of God.[79] The point of
the metaphor is that salvation means we are called to grow into the full measure of the maturity of Christ, who is a divine person.[80] Truly, to be saved
means to be transformed by grace, to be like him (Eph 4:1–13).[81] Humans
never become the divine substance, for one cannot become something infinite and eternal; only God is ever God. The change we experience by being
saved, though, deserves the strongest of language. It will outlast time. We
will be like God, because we will see him as he is (1 John 3:2).[82]

To use the traditional Thomist categories, humans have five "causes"
that explain their existence: efficient, material, formal, final, and exemplar.
Briefly, an efficient cause is that which makes or fashions something; a material cause is that out of which it is made; a final cause is that for the sake
of something is made; and, an exemplar cause is that according to which
something is made. Formal cause is the intelligible way that something exists; this is closely tied to the definition, or meaning, of a thing. One could
say that formal cause tells what something is, while efficient, material, final,
and exemplar causes tell how and why it came to be that way.

76. Maximus, *Ambiguum 7*, 2.

77. Blowers and Wilken, *Cosmic Mystery*, 17.

78. Ibid., 26, 28.

79. See Pseudo-Dionysius, *Ecclesiastical Hierarchy*, 1.3, in *Complete Works of Pseudo-Dionysius*. For the standard discussion of divinization in the Eastern tradition, see Rus-sell, *Deification*.

80. For both Eastern and Western understandings of divinization, see Christensen and Witting, *Partakers in the Divine Nature*; see also Williams, *Ground of Union*; Steb-bins, *Divine Initiative*, 35–65; and Cone, "Aquinas' Sanctifying Grace and Lonergan's Religious Conversion."

81. Aden, "Justification and Sanctification," gives a helpful discussion of the relation between the Lutheran doctrine of justification and the Orthodox teaching of deification.

82. See also 2 Pet 1:4, Rom 8:15–19, and John 8:34 (quoting Ps 82:6).

With respect to human beings, Thomas identified three of the five causes as God: efficient, final, and exemplar.[83] God makes us, and is therefore our efficient cause. Our destiny is union with God, and God is therefore the final cause for whose sake we are made. We are made according to the wisdom of God; God himself is therefore the exemplar in whose image we are made. Human material and formal causes are not God. Our material cause is flesh and blood, and our formal cause is the Image of God. Significantly, matter and form constitute a substance (an individual existing thing), and therefore created being has its own being and its own goodness; it is not God.

Christian theologians are often rightly concerned with the teachings of pantheism and panentheism. One way of explaining pantheism, to use Thomas' framework, is that pantheists understand all five of the causes of the universe to be God; God's infinity is construed to exclude any other existence or causality but his.[84] Panentheism often is explained in terms of God being the soul of the universe. Since the soul is the form of the body, in Thomas' terms panentheists would understand the formal cause of the universe to be God, while the material cause is not necessarily so. In either case, the universe does not have a complete and real existence of its own because either matter or substance or both are not sufficiently distinguished from God.

Traditional dualist creation formulations also struggle adequately to capture this nexus of causes, however. In a traditional dualist formulation, creation is one thing, and God is another. The two uses of the word "is" in that sentence, however, are not univocal. "Is" as referring to creation inherently includes relation to God; "is" as referring to God includes relation to nothing whatsoever. It is difficult to speak of being as a category, then. Our being is a relationship with God; God's being is simply himself.

While the language of Eastern theologians has often understandably given Protestants pause concerning whether implicitly or explicitly it is embracing pantheism, it seems better to see the Eastern tradition, exemplified by Maximus, as trying to put "the distinction" into words. The Eastern tradition strongly affirms that creation and God are different. But they will not use sets of language that construe our being to be non-dependent on God's, and our destiny to be anything other than a life of unimaginable communion with God.

83. *ST* I 44.

84. Whether or not these account adequately explain pantheism or panentheism, they do help explain positions a Christian theology must deny. See Burrell, "Analogy, Creation, and Theological Language," 85–95.

One of the most eloquent modern Western exponents of divinization is C. S. Lewis:

> Morality is indispensable: but the Divine Life, which gives itself to us and which calls us to be gods, intends for us something in which morality will be swallowed up. We are to be remade. . . . [W]e shall find underneath it all a thing we have never yet imagined: a real man, an ageless god, a son of God, strong, radiant, wise, beautiful, and drenched in joy.[85]

Lewis, as with Maximus, does not intend to denigrate any aspect of the Christian life, such as sanctification, justification, or immortality.[86] His message is that the point of each of these aspects is only found in the higher calling to receive a life like God's and share in his blessedness forever (Rev 22:1–5).

Divinization is Act Two of the cosmic drama. It is possible only because of Act One, during which the eternal and divine Son of God, in the fullness of time, entered into personal union with a human nature while remaining always and completely God.[87] To explain the difference this culmination of the first age of creation made for the universe, Maximus synthesized and adapted a long line of biblical and patristic tradition concerning the analogy of divinization.[88]

In this act of the drama, one sees the grand dynamic of existence that follows from creation out of nothing, either to proceed to a true union with being or to fall back into the non-being whence it came.[89] In this age of salvation, the natural knowledge and longing of our soul set the stage for incorporation into the knowledge and joy of God.[90] Created being in all its materiality and particularity, therefore, finds its true meaning, for part of it comes to share the life of its Creator.[91]

Hans Urs von Balthasar's work on Maximus in many ways opened up this Eastern theologian to Western readers. Balthasar argued that the way Maximus presents divinization is particularly well adapted to participatory

---

85. Lewis, "Man or Rabbit," 85; Lewis refers to John 10:34–35, in which Jesus quotes Ps 82:6.

86. See also Lewis, *Mere Christianity*, 174–75.

87. Louth, *Maximus*, 72. One can here see an example of the Chalcedonian nature of all of Maximus' thought. See Thunberg, *Microcosm*, 21–22.

88. See Russell, *Deification*, 262–95.

89. Louth, *Maximus*, 64–65. See Pieper, *Virtues of the Human Heart*, 9–10.

90. Balthasar, *Cosmic Liturgy*, 58–62.

91. See Thunberg, *Microcosm*, 97–100.

ontology.[92] One might add that such is especially the case if that participatory ontology centers on "the distinction."

Balthasar notes that the relations Maximus uses to illuminate divinization are classic examples used to explain *perichōrēsis* (*circumincession* or interpenetration, literally "dancing with"): light suffusing air and fire suffusing iron.[93] Because created being depends on God absolutely in every aspect of its existence, there is an intimate unity of embodied being in God. We are necessarily, also, related to each other; the completion of our being will come when we find true life, together, in him.[94]

The point of Maximus' theology, of creation and of everything else, is to reconcile all things in Christ.

> For Maximus, however, a synthetic understanding of Christ became a theodicy for the world: a justification not simply of its existence but of the whole range of its structures of being. All things, for him, had become organic parts of ever-more-comprehensive syntheses, had themselves become syntheses pointing to the final synthesis of Christ, which explained them all.[95]

Because Christ (the Word) made every aspect of created being in all its differentiation, all of those differences are significant, as is the progress of cosmic history that brought them about. However, because all of these differences have their being only by depending on Christ (the Word), none of them can affect a final separation that fundamentally pits person against person, being against being. Rather, *because of the way we have being,* our relationship with each other and with the created universe is one of "creative unity," in which, "unconfused and inseparable," we are only truly ourselves when we live for each other and for God.[96]

One may well note the Chalcedonian language in this formulation. Maximus suffered as a defender of Chalcedon, and the great council's

---

92. Balthasar, *Cosmic Liturgy*, 56. Participatory ontologies, such as Plotinus' emanation and Sokolowski's "the distinction," emphasize the way that the existence of contingent beings depends on and comes from a higher, necessary being. In other words, they emphasize coming into existence and having existence as a relationship (of dependence), not merely an event.

93. Ibid., 63–64.

94. Ibid., 66.

95. Ibid., 66. See Maximus, *Mystagogia*, 7.

96. Maximus, *Mystagogia*, 7. See also Balthasar, *Cosmic Liturgy*, 68–71. Maximus thus makes room for a purified notion of *apokatastasis* (the restoration of all things in Christ) within the canon of Christian orthodoxy; he also enriches the patristic understanding of recapitulation as a model of salvation.

solution suffuses his theology.[97] Chalcedon clarified our confession of the Christ, one person to be acknowledged in two natures, without confusion, change, division, or separation (*en dio physesin asunchytōs, atreptōs, adiairetōs, achōpistōs*).[98] In this formula, which explicates Christ's being, Maximus found a great tutelage on our salvation, that is, *our* being in Christ.

> A good example of this aspect is found in *Ambiguum 5* where the penetration (Maximus uses the verb *perichōrein*) of human nature into the *totality* of divine nature is said to be the fruit of that union without confusion (*asynchytōs*) with the divine nature which has already taken place in Christ. In this way, says Maximus, absolutely nothing of what is human is separated from the divine, with which it is hypostatically united.[99]

What Christ is by nature, we are called to become by grace, insofar as is possible for a created being. Christ is a personal (that is, hypostatic) union of human and divine natures. We never cease being human—in fact, we find what it truly means to be human—and our true human personhood is revealed as we are subsumed and transformed by the gift of God's life.[100]

When faced with the immensity of the universe, ancient and modern believers alike can find difficulty in believing that one particular person, situated in space and time, could constitute the meaning of the entire universe, or that one particular book could tell its story in an authoritative way. In actuality, the problem runs the opposite direction. Jesus Christ is God, and God is infinite. The universe, in all its immensity, is finite; next to infinity, even the greatest finitude is as nothing. How can any finite universe, however immense, have meaning compared to the infinite God? The ancient gnostics had this question right, though not its answer.[101] Seeing the incomparable excellence of the hidden Spiritual Father, they considered this material world as evil and irrelevant.

On the basis of Chalcedon, Maximus is able to answer this more significant question.[102] The finite and contingent universe has meaning because

---

97. See Thunberg, *Microcosm and Mediator*, 433.

98. See Schaff, *Symbolum Chalcedonense*.

99. Thunberg, *Microcosm and Mediator*, 28, emphasis original and Greek transliterated.

100. See Balthasar, *Cosmic Liturgy*, 70. See also Maximus, *Ambiguum 71*, on the virgin birth as demonstrating that an entirely new way of being human has come in Christ.

101. See Jonas, *Gnostic Religion*, and Pearson, *Ancient Gnosticism*, on the myriad of ancient religious viewpoints that fall under the heading "gnostic."

102. See Thunberg, *Microcosm and Mediator*, 49, on the way that Christology leads to cosmology for Maximus.

it is created to receive the advent of the Christ. God made this universe so that, in the person of the Son, he would be personally united with it, also sharing his life with us through the work of Christ and the gift of the Holy Spirit.[103]

In common with much Orthodox theology, Maximus saw these truths powerfully declared in the revelatory moment of Christ's transfiguration (Matt 17:1–13; Mark 9:2–13; Luke 9:28–36).[104] In the transfiguration, Maximus saw a deepening of the incarnation, in which all the forms of God's revelation are summed up and become understandable.[105] Because Christ is the interpretive key to Scripture, and because all Scripture truly speaks of him, God's revelation in Scripture is truly known through the Incarnate One. Because Christ is the Wisdom of God (the Word) according to which the world was made, the true nature of created reality becomes clear through him. However, we come to know Scripture and the universe only if we know Christ as he truly is: both God and human, a divine person united with a human nature. The glorious nature of God's condescension in Christ becomes clear to us as we see his divinity radiant through his human form.

The cosmic imagination of Maximus in this way gives powerful voice to the systematic precision of "the distinction." The Christian understanding of salvation as divinization has consistently tended toward what "the distinction" formalizes.[106] Maximus gathered together the strands of biblical and patristic tradition and presented an ontology and cosmic plan in which the created and completely dependent universe is interpenetrated (*perichōrein*) with God's own majesty in order that we might be divinized in Christ.

The Goodness of Created Being

Maximus' view of creation and salvation laid the foundation for his highly positive understanding of the natural world. He saw human beings as the microcosm of the universe, its fit representatives as those who are being saved. He also set forth a highly inventive participatory ontology in which the meanings by which we exist are related to the Word. Finally, Maximus

---

103. Maximus, *Ad Thallassium* 22; see also Lewis, "Dogma and the Universe," 41.

104. Louth, *Maximus*, 70–71; see also Thunberg, *Microcosm and Mediator*, 108–9.

105. Thunberg, *Microcosm and Mediator*, 70–71.

106. Witness Hilary of Poitier's statement, "The assumption of our nature was no advancement for God, but His willingness to lower Himself is our promotion, for He did not resign His divinity but conferred divinity on man." Hilary, *On the Trinity*, IX.4–5.

saw the whole grand scope of the movement of the world as tending toward final rest in God.

The understanding of humans as microcosm extends at least back to Plato.[107] Maximus saw human beings as a second cosmos, and therefore rightly at the center of the cosmos' meaning and struggle.[108] Having linked our deification so strongly to the incarnation, he likewise links our deification to the transformation of the world.[109] The intellectual or spiritual world is strongly linked to the material world in this process: both have their being in Christ and are made for existence with each other.[110]

The unity and consummation of the universe is rightly found in its microcosm. Maximus saw clearly the manifest disunity of the entities that compose the universe. Humans, also, exist in a fragmented, separated, and complex way; such is the case partially because of the nature of created being and partially because, by being fallen, humans do not live up to what God created them to be.[111]

The nature of human disunity, moreover, participates in each of the great divisions that are present in and constitute the created world.[112] First, there is the most basic division, that separation of created from uncreated being. The second division has to do with the difference of "that which is perceived by the mind and that perceived by the senses."[113] Third, the nature perceived by the senses is divided between heaven and earth. Fourth, earthly existence is divided between the life of paradise and the life we know (the life of the oikoumenē, the inhabited world). Finally, the life we know is divided between male and female.[114] Humans share in all of these divisions and are, in fact, "the laboratory in which everything is concentrated."[115]

107. Plato, Timaeus, 30b; 37c–47e; one could also consider the Republic's treatment of the city as a larger version of the soul. See Louth, Maximus, 63–64.

108. Maximus, Ambiguum 7, 4; Louth, Maximus, 72. See Thunberg, Microcosm and Mediator, 132–37, for Christian uses of this concept before Maximus.

109. Thunberg, Microcosm and Mediator, 142.

110. Maximus, Mystagogia, 7. See Thunberg, Microcosm and Mediator, 137–42.

111. Maximus, Ambiguum 41.

112. Ibid.

113. Ibid.

114. Maximus believed that God equally created male and female human beings, and that both were present in the life of paradise. However, he believed the division between the genders to be something that God graciously gave to us because he knew that we would fall. The genders, therefore, and the relations between them, exist as providential assistance to salvation. That this division is overcome in Christ does not mean that the genders will disappear, no more than our materiality will disappear. Our relations as male and female are, however, transformed by being in Christ. Thunberg, Microcosm and Mediator, 50–57, 151–53.

115. Maximus, Ambiguum 41.

All of these divisions are overcome in Christ, the true human being, and in those who come to share God's life in him. By being born as a human being, entering into and experiencing all of our division, but without sin, Christ sums up and places under one head all of created existence.[116] The mediation of human beings eliminates division on the moral level, but preserves it and makes the disparate things cohere on the ontological level.[117]

The universe, therefore, finds its unity in Christ, and in those who are being divinized, for in Christ and the saved ones there is a synthesis of the cosmos, a cosmic liturgy in which the elements of division no longer alienate but bless.[118] This recapitulation (summing up under one head) fulfills the purpose of the universe, for it is made for the worship of God and the display of his glory.[119] By stressing Christ's salvific mediation of disparate elements that both fulfills and preserves each extreme, Maximus is able to protect the dignity of creation from a rampant supernaturalism; both natural and supernatural reality are made in Christ and have validity because of him.[120]

To express the ontological basis of this cosmology, Maximus speaks of the relation between the Word (*Logos*) and the words (*logoi*).[121] By the *Logos*, Maximus means the Only-begotten by whom the universe was made (John 1:1–18). The *logoi* are the individual meanings that inform each created existence.

In his use of *Logos*, Maximus is not merely echoing biblical language; he is indicating that God's inexhaustible and eternal wisdom is the principle of being according to which each aspect of the universe has existence, and that this wisdom is God himself. The *logoi*, the individual meanings that reflect and depend on the *Logos*, themselves are eternal because they are aspects of the wisdom of God.

> If by reason of wisdom, a person has come to understand that what exists was brought out of non-being into being by God, if he intelligently directs the soul's imagination to the infinite differences and variety of things as they exist by nature and turns his questing eye with understanding toward the intelligible model (*logos*) according to which things have been made, would

116. Louth, *Maximus*, 74.

117. Thunberg, *Microcosm and Mediator*, 57.

118. Maximus, *Ambiguum 41*; see Louth, *Maximus*, 73–74, and Balthasar, *Cosmic Liturgy*, 137.

119. Maximus, *Ambiguum 7*, 4.

120. Balthasar, *Cosmic Liturgy*, 71–72.

121. Blowers and Wilkins, *Cosmic Mystery*, 54–55.

he not know that the one Logos is many *logoi*? This is evident in the incomparable differences among created things. For each is unmistakably unique in itself and its identity remains distinct in relation to other things. He will also know that the many *logoi* are the one Logos to whom all things are related and who exists in himself without confusion, the essential and individually distinctive God, the Logos of God the Father. He is the beginning and cause of all things *in whom all things were created, in heaven and on earth, visible and invisible, whether thrones or dominions or principalities or authorities—all things were created from him and through him and for him* (Col 1:15–17; Rom 11:36). Because he held together in himself the *logoi* before they came to be, by his gracious will he created all things visible and invisible out of non-being. *By his Word and his Wisdom he made all things* and is making all things, universals as well as particulars, at the proper time.[122]

The meanings that structure and cause the entire universe are always held together in God.[123] In his incarnation, the *Logos* is able to recapitulate the entire universe because all of its meanings preexist in him; therefore, the universe has being and comes to completion because it participates in him.[124]

In this ontology, Maximus adapts the work of the author who wrote under the name of Dionysius the Areopagite.[125] Dionysius' writings show a significant influence from Neoplatonism, and they became important for

122. Maximus, *Ambiguum 7*, 2; italics original indicating quotation of Col 1:15–17, Rom 11:36, and Wis 9:1–2; there is of course reference to John 1:1–18 throughout.

123. Thunberg, *Microcosm and Mediator*, 72–72. Significant overlap exists between Maximus' *Logos-logoi* ontology and the moderate realism of Aquinas. One must not think of the *logoi*, or of the Ideas Aquinas speaks of, as bits of meaning floating around inside God. Rather, God, in his eternal and incorporeal wisdom, knows the ways he is imitable and the plans he has to bring created being about. God is the exemplar cause of the world, and therefore constitutive of the being of each created thing; all things are made according to his wisdom, which is not different from his being. This does not mean that the meaning and goodness of the individual created things exists only in God and not in the individual things. Rather, individual created things exist in meaningful and significant ways, and God gives these meanings, and the rest of their existence, to them. See *ST* I, 15.1, 2; I. 44.3. See Burrell, *Unknowable God*, 62, 68.

124. Maximus, *Ambiguum 7*, 2.

125. This author is sometimes referred to as Pseudo-Dionysius the Areopagite, or following medieval tradition, as Denys (or Pseudo-Denys). The reference is to the Athenian convert of Paul named in Acts 17:34, but the author here in question wrote during the fifth or sixth century of the Christian era. The present work will refer to him as Dionysius. John Scotus Erigena translated his writings into Latin in the ninth century, and Aquinas also repeatedly refers to them.

the theological development of both Eastern and Western theology. Of interest here are the changes Maximus made to Dionysius; they illustrate the way that an ontology that fully recognizes "the distinction" must adapt even a Christianized Neoplatonism.[126]

Dionysius' cosmology pictured the created universe as the radiant display of God's glory, rightly ordered by worship of him.[127] He, in fact, spoke of a celestial "hierarchy," a word that he coined, and whose meaning differs significantly from the modern use.

> In my opinion a hierarchy is a sacred order, a state of understanding and an activity approximating as closely as possible to the divine. . . . The goal of a hierarchy, then, is to enable beings to be as like as possible to God and to be at one with him. . . . Hierarchy causes its members to be images of God in all respects, to be clear and spotless mirrors reflecting the glow of primordial light and indeed of God himself. It ensures that when its members have received this full and divine splendor they can then pass on this light generously and in accordance with God's will to beings further down the scale.[128]

A "cosmos" is, first and foremost, an "arrangement." The purpose of the universe itself, then, reaches toward the divinization of the saved ones, for God has ordered its every moment and its very being toward this end. The worship of the church reflects this order and contributes to it, for the purpose of the sacraments and services of the church is to mediate the grace and glory of God within this cosmic order.[129] In the cosmos, therefore, was a divine community reaching from heaven to earth.[130]

In many ways, Dionysius' cosmic vision provided the framework in which Maximus operated.[131] Maximus could not, however, accept every aspect of Dionysius' vision with sanguinity. Dionysius' vision of cosmic movement was circular: the end is like the beginning.[132] Maximus replaces Dionysius' primordial circular movement with movement onward toward

126. See Simpson, "Theology, Philosophy," 264–66, on the Christian tradition of Neoplatonism.

127. See Louth, *Maximus*, 28–31.

128. Dionysius, *Celestial Hierarchy*, 3.1–2, in *Complete Works of Pseudo-Dionysius*.

129. Louth, *Maximus*, 72–74.

130. Ibid., 75. Balthasar, *Cosmic Liturgy*, 58–60.

131. Louth, *Maximus*, 31.

132. As did Origen, and much more destructively, the Origenist theology Maximus opposed. See ibid., 64–66.

a final rest.[133] Just as Dionysius had referenced the worship of the church in his *Celestial Hierarchy*, so also does Maximus in his correction. The liturgy of the church, though cyclical, has culminating parts and intrinsically points to an end.[134]

Maximus thereby expels from Dionysius' system the latent pantheism that still managed to inhere within it. "He has noticed the questionable points of the system; with unquestionable discretion, he transforms the Dionysian system of emanations into the framework of an ecclesial metaphysic."[135] Maximus here emphasizes the lasting and dignified nature of the temporal world, for rather than being a temporary accommodation for spiritual reality, it is the very ground of supernatural life.[136]

For Maximus, all of reality has a meaningful nature, which is directly connected to the reality of Christ. Rather than disparaging the fragmented and contingent nature of created reality, he sees in it elements that will contribute to and be subsumed in eternal life.[137] In this way, Maximus can be considered the most world-affirming of the Greek theologians.[138] Guided by the positive evaluation of created reality in Chalcedon—for the human nature of the Christ is a created entity—Maximus affirms the goodness of contingent being.[139] In Jesus, all the fullness of deity dwelt in bodily form. Just as he looked beyond the shame of the cross to the glory of the resurrection and ascension, we, too, may see in these humble clods of flesh the elements of eternal life (Col 1:19; Phil 2:5–11; 3:7–11).

The movement of creation is, therefore, one that always and in every way intends final rest in God. In the vast reaches of space and the intricacies of human life, one finds a cosmic drama in which the ages of creation are not lost and meaningless but part of a direction. The arrangement of this universe, then, displays the judgment and providence of God.[140]

---

133. Ibid., 73–74. See Lowery, *Revelation Rhapsody*, 121–44, for the spiral structure of time, moving toward crescendo, set forth in Christian revelation.

134. Maximus, *Mystagogia*, 7.

135. Balthasar, *Cosmic Liturgy*, 60.

136. Ibid., 61.

137. Thunberg, *Microcosm and Mediator*, 95.

138. Balthasar, *Cosmic Liturgy*, 63.

139. Cf. Aquinas' declaration that contingent being is good by its own goodness, and not by God's. Things are in one respect declared to be good because of their relation of dependence on the divine goodness, yet they have been given existence—and thereby goodness—of their own. This gift is a gift of being intimately related to God, as "the distinction" makes clear. Yet, creation is not God, and if it has existence of its own must have goodness of its own, too. God has made no being without value. *ST* I, 6.4.

140. Thunberg, *Microcosm and Mediator*, 105.

The question of movement reveals one of Maximus' greatest disagree-
ments with the Origenist theology that he, in many ways, drew on. Origen
saw the universe cyclically: human souls were created at rest with God, developed movement away from God in their fall, and would be restored to
final rest with God at the end by the work of Christ.[141] Maximus, however,
argued that it is impossible to create beings who are at final rest; creation
itself is a movement, a move from non-being to being.[142]

Rather than periods of rest interrupted by a decadent period of change,
Maximus argued that creation brings into existence beings who fundamentally are set in motion. The meaning of the universe's motion is summed up
by divinization; the movement God makes is not purposeless, but rather
it finds its final goal in life with him.[143] Progress was therefore expected of
Adam, for his creation was a call to seek final rest in his Creator.[144] Fallenness consists of movement not in accord with this goal, that is, in movement
that does not cohere with the *Logos* by whom all things are made.[145] Because
of the grace of Christ, the grace of the *Logos*, though all of reality may seem
subject to purposeless movement, it may be restored to its original purpose
by participating in him.[146]

The eschatological consummation of reality has therefore already begun. The meaning of this present age is to find the peace that Christ has
already declared.[147] Having given the universe being, God is not content
until the "well-being" that one sees in rightly ordered existence is brought
to completion in being that is eternal.[148]

One sees this inaugurated eschatology present in baptism and in the
Lord's Supper. The baptized one experiences a two-fold divine birth in which
we are adopted into God's family and our wills are regenerated to cohere
with the movement toward God's rest.[149] The full grace of adoption is given
in baptism, along with propulsion toward our final goal: already, but not yet,
we have received salvation.[150] In Holy Communion, one finds a celebration

141. Louth, *Maximus*, 66.

142. Maximus, *Ambiguum 7*, 1.

143. Ibid.

144. Louth, *Maximus*, 67.

145. Maximus, *Ambiguum 7*, 2.

146. Maximus, *Ad Thalassium 2*; Louth, *Maximus*, 74.

147. Balthasar, *Cosmic Liturgy*, 141–42.

148. Maximus, *Ambiguum 7*, 2.

149. Maximus, *Ad Thalassium 6*; Maximus here interacts with John 3:5–6 and
1 John 3:9.

150. Blowers and Wilkins, *Cosmic Mystery*, 38–43, 103n1. Cf. *ST* III, 69.5.

and recapitulation of the incarnation.[151] We remember the person of Jesus and declare his death, until he comes (1 Cor 11:23–26). In the Communion liturgy, then, we proclaim the grace by which we are part of supernatural life and participate in the gift of that life, leading toward our eternal home. For, it is fitting that the restoration of all things comes by the gift, the action, and the very being of the one by whom all things were made.[152]

Maximus, in his wide-ranging and visionary cosmology, thus presents a theology entirely consistent with "the distinction." In the way he relentlessly reshaped his sources, and in the way he suffered to oppose a heresy that proposed a false fusion between the human and the divine, Maximus sets forth an ontology and soteriology that declares both the absolute dependence of created reality on God and the real significance of the reality God creates.[153] One sees this dependence and significance most clearly in Christ: one person acknowledged in two natures, both the God who gives creation being and the human whose death gives creation divine life.

Why Not Augustine?

It is fair to ask why this work follows Maximus, not Augustine, as the resource for its architectonic theology of creation. Assuredly, I have garnered many insights from Eastern theologians, but I do not pretend to be one. Why turn away from the Western doctor of grace at this essential beginning point? No one has ever written a greater and more comprehensive vision of the universe and its unfolding than the *City of God*.

The reason for this choice is two-fold. First, Augustine lived and wrote before Chalcedon. His theology is deeply consonant with the great council, as seen especially in the Christology of *The Trinity*. It is no fault of his, though, that the magisterial definition (one person acknowledged in two natures: without confusion, without separation, without division, without change) provides fecundity and precision for Christian reflection that he did not fully have. Maximus sucked the marrow out of this rich joint, even to the point of suffering unjust trial and mutilation, bearing witness in his flesh to God.

Just as significantly, though, there seems to be a darkness that tinges Augustine's later works flowing from his doctrine of original sin. Moving from the anti-Pelagian controversies, into the *Literal Commentary on Genesis*, and culminating in the *City of God*, there seems an attraction that bends

151. Louth, *Maximus*, 72.

152. Maximus, *Ambiguum 41*.

153. See Balthasar, *Cosmic Liturgy*, 48.

his theologizing downward under the gravity of that dark star. As indebted to Augustine as this work is—and that debt is very great—one struggles to see the astonishment and overwhelming character of the universe's origin in God, worked out in his cosmic symphony of justice, at least not in the way one sees it in Maximus' cosmic liturgy of love.

Conclusion

At its heart, this work argues that the transcendent God is intimately present and involved in his creation, and that truly being human means to become like him. This chapter has set forth a rationale by which we may recognize the foundation of this teaching in a way that is fully theistic: neither deistic, concentrating mainly on the event or beginning of creation, nor pantheistic, in which the free, personal, and dependent nature of creation disappears. Rather, creation's widest horizon is a gratuitous relationship that has the *telos* of eternal life.

The basis of supernatural life is the embedding of creation in dependence on its Creator, and the non-reciprocal freedom of and transcendence of God in creating. In this way, creation theology intimately links the meaning of this world and its being. As Maximus' theology of the two acts of creation emphasizes, the kind of existence this universe has results from and includes the incarnation, in which God becomes present in it and saves it. Reality is neither formless nor empty, because graciousness and reality have come to it in Jesus Christ (Gen 1:2; John 1:17).

The right declaration of the being of the Christ, therefore, grounds and illuminates the right explanation of created reality, for creation brings about a natural world able to receive personal union with the fullness of deity in Jesus of Nazareth. An adequate ontology, then, will be perichoretic, expecting the coming of the Christ because it already and always has the foundation of its being in him. Christ comes to his own, even if they do not receive him; created being cannot have being apart from relation to him (John 1:3, 11). The Christ who comes to creation, then, is both the long-expected one and the most intimate stranger: expected, for he is the completion of creation's intention; stranger, for he is a divine person and therefore unexplainable within the structures and beings of this world; intimate, because this divine excess is the one by whom we live and move and are (John 1:14; Acts 17:28).

This perichoretic ontology, however, must not just preserve but flow from "the distinction" between creature and Creator. We rightly worship Jesus because he is a divine person, acknowledged in two natures. We must not worship even divinized creation because in divinization our created natures are not replaced by a divine nature; rather, we graciously receive entry into a supernatural order of relations in which our humanity finds its true meaning through intimate communion with the Father, the Son, and the Holy Spirit (John 17:20–23).

Because this meaning is a constitutive element in the being God makes, the existence of this universe can be both grounded and summed up (Col 1:15–20; Eph 1:3–10). The *Logos*, who is both the Wisdom of God and God himself, creates us. We are, therefore, made *according to* the *Logos*; that is, because there is no other source for meaning in the universe, the finite natures of this universe must reflect the inexhaustible creativity of the divine Wisdom. The meanings that make us what we are, then, have intrinsic relation to the Wisdom of God, to God's own self. Created being finds in him its fitting consummation as Christ gives flesh to the divine intention (John 1:14–17).

The movement of the ages of this world, therefore, shows in all its immensity and complexity the stamp of the Son of God. Its *telos* is the revelation of the sons and daughters of God in the bodily resurrection (Rom 8:14–24). As the fitting representatives of created reality, those who are being saved will testify to the rightness and unifying power of God's redemptive work. The divine intention in creation, incarnated in Christ, will bring forth a redeemed community whose existence rightly deserves the name "eternal life." That is to say, the lives and existence of the redeemed ones will be like that of Jesus, as far as is possible for a created being; and the glory of God declared in and as them can scarcely be conceived (1 Cor 2:6–10).

The life of Christian worship, therefore, declares and participates in the meaning of creation. The sacraments and the worship of the church declare and make present the supernatural life for which the world was always intended. The gospel they declare is the true meaning of the world, for in their every authentic moment, they speak of Christ (1 Cor 11:26, Rom 6:3–4, and Rev 4–5).

2

The Image and Likeness of God

ANTHROPOLOGY

This universe, therefore, exists so that part of it may enter into union with its Creator, a relationship and transformation the universe has no ability to bring about on its own terms. Coming to understand the realm of created being, and our place in it, will then require us to come to terms with being that has inherent dignity, validity, and reality, but whose very existence is ordered from and toward another. The being of this universe is given with a purpose inherent in its existence.

God, through creating and saving this universe, takes us from the way we are and makes us who we are supposed to be, through the ministry of Jesus Christ. As the first chapter has explored the nature of this being and its character as ordered toward a supernatural end, this chapter will examine the dynamics of transformation by which contingent beings come to share the life of the Uncreated One. In each case, the key is to understand the beauty and goodness of created being as it reaches (and is moved) toward its culmination. The very goodness of the universe coheres with the way it is ordered toward its final rest. Thomas' understanding of potency and Kierkegaard's explanation of sublation are powerful conceptual tools to understand the change wrought in salvation.

The theology of Irenaeus of Lyons also provides a powerful historical model in which we can see the implications of this universal vision for human existence and nature. Irenaeus, at the very beginning of Christian systematic theology, explains the character of the universe through a complex analogy of an "economy," in which humans are both created good and essentially moved toward growth and change. This analogy enriches

Maximus' cosmic vision by showing in human terms that progress toward the life of God is inherent in what it means for this universe to exist. Creation, therefore, as an ongoing and cumulative relationship, conditions and participates in the meaning and being of humanity's final end.

Potency

Aristotle proposed the distinction of potency (*dynamis*) and act (*energeia* or *entelecheia*) to solve the besetting problem of stability and change that his philosophical tradition bequeathed him.[1] His insight rests on the clarification that "being" can have more than one sense, and that things can have being in more than one way. In particular, Aristotle distinguishes between "being-in-act" and "being-in-potency." It is not right to say, simply and statically, that something either exists or does not exist. Being certainly follows the principle of non-contradiction; that is, in absolute terms something must either exist or not. Non-contradiction, however, does not tell the whole story about being, for the kind of being that material things have is inherently ordered to certain avenues of change.

Therefore, when speaking of a material substance such as a match, one is right to say that it exists as a piece of wood. This is the actual being the match has, but it is also right that the same match simultaneously has the potential (or potency) to exist as a fire. That is, the being-in-act of a match is as wood, and its existence also includes the being-in-potency of fire, because that is the kind of being that particular piece of wood has.[2]

Movement from one state to another, then, does not involve the extinguishing of one thing and its replacement by another; nor does it involve a world of ceaseless flux. Rather, in any change, there is something that passes away (such as the match simply as a piece of wood), something that comes to be (the match as fire), and something that stays the same (the identity of the match itself). The being that comes to exist through the process of change is that which was already existing potentially with the being-in-act.

It is important to note that potency toward something and actuality of something are not ingredients in things or components of them. Rather, they are ways of expressing the intelligible and active way that the things in

---

1. The classical *loci* for potency and act in Aristotle's corpus are *Physics*, 1 and 2, *Metaphysics* Theta, and *Nichomachean Ethics*, 10. For key moments in the Greek philosophical tradition leading up to Aristotle discussing stability and change, see Graham, "Heraclitus," and Palmer, "Parmenides."

2. For the most comprehensive level of discussion on this point in Aristotle, see *Metaphysics* Theta. For a brief secondary discussion, see Kelly, *Basics of Western Philosophy*, 82–84.

the world of our experience have being.³ Acorns turn into oak trees, if given the chance; barring the miraculous, they do not turn into tigers. This does not mean that there is a little oak tree in the acorn, nor that "potency for oak-tree-ness" is one of its parts. It means that the kind of being the acorn has evidences a regular intelligibility whose fruition leads to particular kinds of change (and not to others).

Being, for Aristotle, has an active character. Things exist most fully, and are most themselves, when they are at work in the most excellent way.⁴ Hence, *eudaimonia* (happiness or flourishing) is the *energeia* (act) of humans as human; *eudaimonia* is human excellence in action.⁵ In other words, "human being" does not indicate an inert object, but rather the kind of existence in which we excel in the life of virtue. Lacking such excellence does not indicate a lack of humanity in a person, for even humans who can perform no actions whatsoever are still fully and completely human; *eudaimonia* indicates the ultimate fulfillment of the kind of nature that we have, not the condition for having that nature. The virtues, tellingly, are not extrinsic standards to which humans must measure up, but the immanent norms of what it means to be rational and political animals.⁶ For, by living lives of friendship marked by wisdom and justice, we bring fully into existence (into act) the humanity we have potential toward.

Aquinas interpreted and expanded Aristotle's insight with a view toward eternal life. Act is the *completion* of being, and the kind of being any human has is one ordered to everlasting friendship with God.⁷ Aquinas' introduction to the Second Part of the *Summa Theologica* indicates the way that our distinctly human operations are ordered to freedom, providing the essential basis in our created being for our finding completion by knowing and loving God:

> Since, as Damascene states (*De Fide Orthod.* ii.12), man is said to be made to God's image, in so far as the image implies *an intelligent being endowed with free-will and self-movement*: now that we have treated of the exemplar, *i.e.*, God, and of those things which came forth from the power of God in accordance

3. See Blanchette, *Philosophy of Being*, 337–39.

4. Aristotle, *Physics*, 3.1–3.

5. Aristotle, *Nicomichean Ethics*, 1; see Snell and Cone, *Authentic Cosmopolitanism*, 138–40. "Happiness," according to Aristotle does not indicate a transient emotional state but rather a life of excellence in action. With respect to the properties that are most especially human, to be "happy," according to Aristotle, is to live those out in the most meaningful and maximal way.

6. See Snell and Cone, *Authentic Cosmopolitanism*, 131–45.

7. Blanchette, *Philosophy of Being*, 343–45.

with His will; it remains for us to treat of His image, *i.e.*, man, inasmuch as he too is the principle of his actions, as having free-will and control of his actions.[8]

Aquinas knew that human beings are not just rational and political animals, but that our most proper definition is the image of God. Because human beings are rational, our minds seek out the First Truth; because we have freedom of the will, our rational nature desires the Greatest Good. Human beings, therefore, find the completion of their being in knowing and loving God and, thereby, being transformed.

Actual (fully real) human existence, then, is human existence as sublated in a supernatural relationship with the Trinity. That such is the case does not deny the humanity of all who are still in development, who so far fall short of that goal; to be a developing human is still to be human, and we have need of exactly this completion precisely because we are human. Whereas Aristotle saw human beings as having potency toward *eudaimonia* (happiness) whose principles are wisdom and justice, Aquinas sees the larger perspective of an *eudaimonia* whose blessedness flows from friendship with God. The act of being human, for Aquinas, includes and signifies both to receive and freely to choose eternal life.

That Thomas insists on human intelligence and free will does not compromise the gratuitous nature of salvation.[9] One can briefly see the conjunction of human and divine activity Thomas intends through two seemingly contradictory factors. First, knowing and loving God in the way needed for salvation (the completion of human being) is not possible for human beings by means of their natural powers.[10] Second, achieving our final end must come as a result of human operations.[11]

The natural powers we have as human beings can achieve only results that are natural and human. What we need is to come to share in the life of God, and this life of wisdom and love exceeds the proportion of anything in the created world.[12] Conversely, if the end of human existence does not involve free human operations, it will not be the *act* of our human being. Being is active, and the operations by which we know and love God must be *our* actions, else, they cannot be the completion of *human* being; salvation is not an extrinsic add-on to human nature, but the true and final flourishing of Adam's race. Without being ordered to this completion, humans would

8. *ST* II–I, *Introduction*, italics original.

9. See the discussion of predestination in chapter 4.

10. *ST* II–I, 5.5.

11. *ST* II–I, 5.7.

12. *ST* II–I, 5.1, 5, and 6; see Cone, "Transforming Desire," 142–58.

then not rightly be designated as the image of God, for the active existence we have receives its true specification from our goal, or end.[13]

Part of the solution to this seeming impasse is the medieval distinction between natural and obediential potency.[14] Humans have potency toward divinization—eternal friendship in union with God—else we could never receive it or achieve it.[15] The transition in something from potency to act, however, is always brought about by something that is already in act. For example, a youth wanting to learn how to play basketball will need to learn how from someone who actually understands basketball, not from someone who only potentially has an understanding of the game. The youth is potentially knowledgeable about playing basketball, for she possesses the desire and is capable of learning. The actual knowledge possessed by a good basketball coach, whether gained from experience or from theoretical analysis, helps this potential to be realized; quite a different result would come about should the trainer be ignorant of basketball (that is, herself only a potential basketball teacher and not an actual one).

Not every potency is of the same sort, however. Depending on what kind of act is to be brought about by actuating the potency, different kinds of active sources of change can be required. Learning how to play basketball is proportionate to human nature. That is, learning how to play basketball does not require a supernatural act; ordinary human knowledge and abilities suffice for accomplishing it. Hence, the potency of the young basketball-player-to-be is a natural potency.

In an obediential potency, however, the result sought is not proportionate to natural human capacity. Because divinization—our life of salvation—involves sharing the life of the infinite God, it requires a source of actuation that is actually infinite. That is, it requires the operation of the Creator, who is the infinite source of this contingent world. God is not part of this present world, and knowing him as he truly is exceeds the capacity of this universe; the completion of human being is the active life of knowing and loving him.[16]

That our potency to salvation is obediential does not indicate that it is not really our potency. If we did not have potency to salvation, God would have to change us into a different kind of being in order to save us.[17] It rather

13. *ST* II–I, 1.3, 7.

14. For a helpful explanation of obediential potency, see Stebbins, *Divine Initiative*, 143–49.

15. *ST* II–I, 5.1.

16. *ST* II–I, 2.8, 3.8, and 5.6.

17. See Lonergan, *Insight*, 718–19.

indicates that we are finite beings called to eternal life. Because eternal life is to know God, only the infinite God himself can bring this potency into act. The potency remains, however, the potency of our being. It is our human operations—our knowledge and love—that must come to know and love the infinite God; although God must actuate the potency, only free actions are, properly speaking, the operations of human beings.[18]

Although the final completion of our being—our being brought completely into act as who we really are—awaits the parousia, eternal life begins with this present life in those who are being saved. In faith, hope, and charity, we begin to live the heavenly life now. Faith is "a habit of the mind, whereby eternal life is begun in us, making the intellect assent" to divine truth.[19] By hope, we lean on God's assistance to achieve eternal life, "which consists in the enjoyment of God Himself."[20] Charity is the friendship of humans for God based on the communication of God's own happiness, that is, the real gift to us of his blessedness.[21] By charity we also come to love our fellow human beings, coming to know them as they really are: those whose destinies are also in God.[22]

In faith, hope, and charity—the theological virtues—we find the greater completion of our being knowable through Christian revelation. These operations define the active being by which true humanity comes fully to exist. Our *eudiamonia* (flourishing or happiness), the act of being completed as human, consists in living a life that is eternal. We cannot achieve this life on our own terms, but we must receive this actuation by the gift of God. The grace, however, that brings about this blessedness does not annul our human being, but rather brings about the fulfillment of it.

Now, one could question whether understanding our salvation in terms of potency leads to the conclusion that all humans are somehow owed salvation. It is also strange to speak of a potency, whose actuation comprises a being's very meaning, but that cannot be achieved by that being's own powers. This brings one unease, because in the first case, salvation would be a debt that is paid by God, not the free gift of his grace. In the second case, it would seem that God's creation of us is somehow insufficient and incomplete.[23]

18. *ST* II–I, 1.1, 4.3 and 4. See also Augustine, *On Free Choice of the Will*, 3.15–16. The major distinction is that operations that occur only according to an external source are violent to a nature and not natural for it.

19. *ST* II–II 4.1.

20. *ST* II–II 17.2.

21. *ST* II–II 23.1.

22. *ST* II–II 25.1.

23. For a fuller discussion of these questions, see Snell and Cone, *Authentic*

This entire universe, though, exists only by the gracious will of God in the first place. As explained above in "the distinction," any contingent being at all depends on the gift of a God who does not gain by the giving, but who acts in pure unmerited love.[24] So, whatever the relation of humans to God, it cannot be a situation in which God is our debtor.

The relation God has with his creation continues to reflect the eternal act that brings them into being; that is, God's holy disposition toward the beings he creates continues to be one of unmerited love. In fact, it may be appropriate to ask whether and how God would make salvation possible (or even actual) for all those he creates. The right answer to that question, however, will proceed not on the basis of obligation, but according to the dynamics of personal love.

One could raise, on another basis, the question as to whether, having chosen to create in this way, God is required to complete this work and save those he creates.[25] Just as a partially baked cake is not a completed cake, and therefore lacking what it means to be a cake, so also humans made in God's image are lacking what it means to be fully human without the completion of divinization. This question is closely related to the question of whether God's creation of us is incomplete if we cannot, on our own terms, achieve our proper end; both questions see the incompleteness of natural human being and propose it as unbefitting the work of God.

Aquinas, again, is able to illuminate God's creative activity as wise, providing for, and completing his creation in multiple ways. He does so by reflecting on the philosophical maxim that, "Nature fails in nothing necessary." In other words, God's work of creating this world has validity and goodness, such that the beings that exist in it are able to come into act as the beings they truly are.

> Just as nature does not fail man in necessaries, although it has not provided him with weapons and clothing, as it provided other animals, because it gave him reason and hands, with which he is able to get these things for himself; so neither did it fail man in things necessary, although it gave him not the wherewithal to attain Happiness: since this it could not do. But it did give him free-will, with which he can turn to God, that He may make him

Cosmopolitanism, 92–95.

24. See chapter 1.

25. Karl Barth's paradox that salvation precedes creation seems to have this import. For a nuanced explanation of Barth's understanding of salvation, see Hunsinger, *Disruptive Grace*, 242–49.

happy. "For what we do by means of our friends, is done, in a sense, by ourselves" (Ethic. iii, 3).[26]

The happiness (act) that we can achieve in this life is, then, necessarily penultimate; but it is neither entirely lacking nor an empty set. This life has validity and meaning, but the kind of being we have been created as then requires a fulfillment in eternal life.[27] In friendship with God, brought about by his grace and freely chosen by our will, we find the completion of who we are and who we are called to be.

Sublation

German philosopher G. W. F. Hegel proposed the notion of sublation (*aufheben*) because of the excessive nature of the truths and realities we find most significant.[28] Whereas some truths (such as those of arithmetic) seem obtainable through tidy deductive categories, which give well-defined results with no remainder, Hegel thought that the most important truths we seek have a different character. He sought to clarify the nature of these realities through an innovation in the way we understand our reason to function.

Aufheben is a difficult word to translate, the most common choices being "sublation" or "suspension." In its native German, the word has the disparate connotations of raising up, abolition, and preserving.[29] Ralph Palm explains the difficulty in Hegel this way:

> We can begin to explain its importance by quoting the first lines of the second paragraph: "'To 'sublate' has a twofold meaning in the language: on the one hand it means to preserve, to maintain, and equally it also means to cause to cease, to put an end to." Now, a word with more than one meaning is by no means remarkable in and of itself. Any dictionary is full of them. Hegel, however, considers both of these meanings to function *simultaneously*. He does not mean this simultaneity as a metaphor, or a pun, or in any figurative sense whatsoever. The question is thus how one is to comprehend such a "literal double meaning," and therein lies the essence of sublation's complexity.[30]

26. *ST* I–II 5.5 ad. 1.

27. For a wide-ranging argument for this position, see Lonergan, "Finality, Love, Marriage," 17–52.

28. See Reese, "Hegel," 286–87. Hegel's most significant discussion of sublation's meaning is in his *Science of Logic*, 107.

29. Inwood, "Sublation."

30. Palm, "Hegel's Concept of Sublation," 9, emphasis original. The text quoted is

The meaning that Hegel intends cannot be captured in a static understanding of logic or metaphysics, for what he points to is the way that the being of this universe itself has elements of change. Change, according to Hegel, is not just something that happens to the beings in this world; rather the process of change is constitutive for the reality we know and the kinds of beings that we are.

Hegel's exact meaning for *aufheben* is a subject of considerable controversy.[31] Examples Hegel offered that illuminated sublation were the change from acorn to oak, embryo to birth, and flower to fruit.[32] At the least, the term carries the positive denotation of preserving something while (or by) removing it from its immediate context.[33] Along these lines, Walter Kauffman gives the example of picking up something that has fallen on the floor; the thing itself is preserved exactly because it has been removed from its immediate context (the floor).[34] By way of negative definition—what *aufheben* is not—it does not mean annulling or abolishing something, nor does it mean the merely external unity of a synthesis in thought that fails to express a truly changed reality.[35] A sublated reality, then, is not one in which the former way of being has simply gone out of existence to be replaced by something new; it is, though, one whose being is really different.

Within the horizon of Christian theology, Søren Kierkegaard appropriated and transformed Hegel's conceptual breakthrough. As Christopher Ben Simpson brings out, Kierkegaard saw Christian theology as a "guiding vision for human life (a *theologia viatorum*)," the perspective from which the manner of human existence comes to fulfill the true longings of humanity in a real and trustworthy way.[36] Such is the case because only Christian theology declares to us most fully and truly the eternal reality by which we can become our true selves.[37]

Kierkegaard lays out a series of stages—aesthetic, ethical, and religious—in which he explains what it means for Christian theology, and the Christ it declares, radically to order and transform our lives.[38] The question

---

from Hegel, *Science of Logic*, 107. Palm's dissertation, a book-length treatment of the subject in English, directed by William Desmond, is well worth reading.

31. See Redding, "Hegel," for a brief summary of the interpretive trends present in post-Hegelian philosophy.

32. Westphal, *Becoming a Self*, 21.

33. Palm, "Hegel's Concept of Sublation," 8–11.

34. Walter Kaufmann, *Hegel*, 144.

35. Palm, "Hegel's Concept of Sublation," 16–20.

36. Simpson, *Truth is the Way*, 68–69.

37. Ibid., 69–70.

38. The discussion of the stages is spread across much of Kierkegaard's

of each stage, and its difference from each other stage, has to do with the way that what is of central importance to us orders and orients our lives.[39] In the ethical stage, we make questions of conscience, and of good and evil, the most significant factors in the way that we make decisions and understand the nature of the world. In the religious stage, the ordering factor is our relation to God. Merold Westphal argues that the best way to understand the aesthetic stage is as a lack of the other two, because neither questions of conscience nor of God have final authority. People in the aesthetic stage live according to what is interesting to them at the moment.[40]

One can see the relation of Christian theology to the stages Kierkegaard explains, and thus to human existence, in Kierkegaard's rich understanding of truth. Simpson brings out this relation quite powerfully in his comment on Kierkegaard's pseudonym in *Concept of Anxiety*.

> Thus, Vigilius Haufniensis writes: "Viewed intellectually, the content of freedom is truth, and truth makes man free. For this reason, truth is the work of freedom, and in such a way that freedom constantly brings forth truth" (CA 138). Truth is not the same thing as reality. Truth is the right relationship to reality (classically, a relationship of correspondence). Freedom is involved inasmuch as the subject judging the truth is actively relating to the given reality (for one could judge the truth to be otherwise). However, beyond such a merely intellectual or "objective" truth (as a relation of correspondence between one's thought and, say, external being), "truth is for the particular individual only as he himself produces it in action. . . . [T]he question is whether a person will in the deepest sense acknowledge the truth, will allow it to permeate his whole being, will accept all its consequences" (CA 138).[41]

---

pseudonymous authorship. *Stages on Life's Way* obviously deals with them. The most significant discussions of the relation of the aesthetic and the ethical stages, however, is in *Either/Or*, while *Fear and Trembling* deals with the relation of the aesthetic and the religious stages. *Concluding Unscientific Postscript*, additionally, makes a significant revision and refinement of the religious sphere, both in its relation to the ethical and in its internal constitution.

39. This concept is closely connected to what Lonergan means by a "principle" or "orientation" according to which our lives are lived. See Cone, "Transforming Desire," 153–62.

40. Westphal, *Becoming a Self*, 20–32. One could, again, make a profitable comparison to Lonergan's understanding of moral and religious conversions. See Cone, "Transforming Desire," 221–79; see also Snell and Cone, *Authentic Cosmopolitanism*, 105–27.

41. Simpson, *Truth Is the Way*, 63. For a discussion of Kierkegaard's use of pseudonyms, see Westphal, *Becoming a Self*, 8–18, and Simpson, *Truth Is the Way*, 19–22.

Christian theology, then, guides the truly human life because it provides the truth we could not conceive on our own but which reveals who we really are. The extent to which we accept Christian truth, and thereby find union with Christ, is the same extent to which we become our own true selves. This acceptance, and union, must be lived—enacted—starting in this age and culminating in the world to come.[42]

Christianity is the culmination of the religious stage of existence (Religiousness B), and one may ask what its real relation is to the other stages.[43] That is, how does Christianity, in fact, constitute the summation and actuation of everything we humans are? The answer has to do with the way that Kierkegaard understands subsequent stages to suspend (or, one might say, sublate) the earlier ones.[44]

The stages are each ways of life. In the aesthetic stage, which is a kind of "baseline human" existence in which ethical and religious commitments have no abiding place, one pursues a life in which the ultimate evil is being bored. One is trying to choose one's own good in a way that the self one has is fulfilled by pursuit of interesting things.

The ethical critique of the aesthetic life given by Kierkegaard's pseudonym, Judge William, does not center on the dubious acts the thorough aesthete commits, but rather on the way this person, by choosing a merely aesthetic way of life, is failing to achieve the very values he is setting himself to achieve.[45] The aesthete fears boredom and pursues the interesting, but because he has no frame of reference beyond the moment's interests, he is unable to understand the meaning of his life and have an explanation for it.[46] His soul finds rest in moments of amusement and pleasure, yet the very character of the momentary is to slip away. Always, there must be something else, another moment, another interest, to sustain—or, better, to anaesthetize—his spirit.[47]

---

42. For the way that right relation to God constitutes our being, see Kierkegaard, *Sickness unto Death*. For our need for a savior and our inadequacy to come to this truth on our own terms, see Kierkegaard, *Philosophical Fragments*.

43. See Kierkegaard, *Postscript*, 1.556–61.

44. Westphal, *Becoming a Self*, 25.

45. See Kierkegaard, *Either/Or*, 2, 177–79.

46. One could, again, fruitfully compare Kierkegaard's point with the Lonergan's understanding of the relation of intellectual and moral conversions, as well as his notions of individual and general biases. See Cone, "Transforming Desire," 188–220, 232–79.

47. See Kierkegaard, *Either/Or*, 2, 184–86. Compare Pascal's notion of *divertissement*; Pascal, *Pensées*, 139.

Judge William, who typifies the ethical stage, is able to understand the goals and limitations of the aesthetic stage precisely because he has a higher way of life. To suspend (or sublate) something is simultaneously to preserve it and to put an end to it. Someone who truly lives in the ethical stage preserves the human pursuit of interest and beauty, but she has put an end to "momentary interest" as an all-consuming life by pursuing a better way of existence. This ethical way of life is more fully human, and thereby more satisfying, than a merely aesthetic way of existence; the human spirit presses beyond the merely momentary and seeks to know what is truly good.

In this discussion of the suspension of the aesthetic by the ethical way of life, Kierkegaard has followed Hegel's lead fairly closely.[48] This consonance ends with the relation of the ethical and religious stages.[49] Kierkegaard agrees with Hegel in linking our understanding of ethics closely with the way our reasoning is embedded in the societies in which we live. As *Fear and Trembling* brings out, though, the revelation by which we know God, and the relationship that revelation makes possible, can neither be accounted for by our societies nor contained within their terms.

Fear and Trembling reflects on the biblical character of Abraham, the Father of Faith, especially in his decision to follow God's call to sacrifice his son, Isaac. Abraham's decision makes no sense—is absurd—by the standards of ethical human society.[50] That is, there is no sufficient reason, from the viewpoint of society, to justify the decision; no greater benefit would accrue to society on the basis of the sacrifice, and no societal duty is fulfilled by it. Abraham answers not the requirements of his human society, but the call of faith in God.

As Westphal brings out, it is important to see the relation here illustrated between the ethical and religious stages as one of suspension.[51] Abraham's actions are absurd (unethical) only from the point of view of human society that does not take God properly into account. Just as the mere aesthete cannot understand the way that "the interesting" is truly sought in a better way when one pursues an ethical way of life, so a merely ethical viewpoint cannot understand relation to the eternal God. The laws and customs of our human societies will never comprehensively contain and

---

48. Even with respect to the suspension of the aesthetic stage by the ethical, Kierkegaard differs from Hegel in that he does not consider any of the suspensions to be necessary, clearly logical, progressions. The aesthetic can stay merely aesthetic, and often does. Neither does its progress to become ethical result purely from dynamics inherent in it.

49. Westphal, *Becoming a Self*, 25–31.

50. See Kierkegaard, *Fear and Trembling*, 16–17; Westphal, *Becoming a Self*, 27.

51. Westphal, *Becoming a Self*, 25–31.

fulfill God's revelation and standards. The reason for that is not that God's revelation is unreasonable, but because it is reasonable in a way that our merely human societies cannot account for.

Each of the stages is a way of life ordered by something considered to be of ultimate value. From the standpoint of each lower stage (aesthetic to ethical and religious, ethical to religious, merely religious to truly Christian), the priorities and precepts of the higher stage do not make sense. The mere aesthete will not be able to understand the ethical commitment of marriage, with its true blessedness, without transcending the merely aesthetic point of view. The often complacent and self-satisfied "religion" of our ethical human societies does not comprehend the absolute commitment of someone who has had his life transformed by God. None of the world's merely religious viewpoints, finally, can account for "The Way, the Truth, and the Life" (John 14:6).

From the viewpoint of the higher stages, the lower stages are understandable.[52] In fact, they are known according to their true nature, and all the essential forms and content of the lower stages are not only preserved, but also fulfilled by being suspended in the life of the higher stages. Because each of the stages is animated by a core human concern, each of them is not just an indication of one's priorities, but a way of being human. The most human way of life will be that which can account for and include each of these human concerns and capacities. Therefore, existing in the higher stages does not just indicate possessing superior viewpoints, but becoming more fully human, becoming one's own true self.

Take as an example of this suspension a marriage ceremony. The wedding will likely include music, poetry, decorations, special clothing, a pleasing setting, dancing, and tasty food and drink. It will also include the centrally ethical commitment of one person to another of love and fidelity. In a good wedding, the aesthetic elements (music, poetry, and the like) serve the purpose of the wedding, the joining of two lives together in a committed bond. It is important that they each are aesthetically valid; no one wants to listen to bad wedding music or eat a bad cake. The purpose of a wedding, however, cannot be contained within the bounds of what makes a good musical or culinary performance. On the other hand, the importance of the ethical commitment of the wedding makes it perfectly appropriate that the aesthetic elements be incorporated in the celebration. It can also give order to what is appropriate and truly best with respect to these elements; it would be foolish to pursue a wedding that beggared the bride and groom (or their families) and thereby prevented a happy start to married life.

52. Simpson, *The Truth Is the Way*, 69–73.

The Apostle Paul teaches us, however, that when he speaks of a rightly ordered married life he is really declaring the holy mystery of Christ and the church (Eph 5:32). In a truly Christian wedding, one will likely find elements, such as prayers, a sermon, and celebration of Holy Communion, that speak to the way that this ethical commitment is not everything it is supposed to be until it is part of the shared life of Christ. The ethical promises made by the bride and groom of love and fidelity do not become less binding or important by becoming also vows made before God. Their true import, however, becomes visible as the relation of Christ and the church redefines what the ethical commitment of marriage should be.

The life of the world to come, to which marriage's joys point and for which life together is a precursor, cannot be explained from within the logic of any ethical commitment, or any social arrangement, among human beings.[53] It is only from the perspective of eternal life that the whole progression and nature of this world will finally make sense. Because eternal life suspends our human existence, we become who we truly are, the image of God, by knowing Christ and receiving his life.

Irenaeus and the Economy

Irenaeus of Lyons' understanding of the nature of created being, and humanity's nature, offers a helpful historical model illuminated by the systematic distinctions of potency and sublation.[54]

The Economy of Creation and Salvation

In speaking of the "economy," Irenaeus explains the way that God's action with respect to created being forms one consistent narrative.[55] Irenaeus' usage is distinctive, and it shows the way he understood the particular things and individual actions and meanings present in the world to cohere in Christ.

> "Economy" originally meant simply an intelligent plan (a law: *nomos*) for ordering things properly, especially a household (*oikos*). . . . Theologians prior to Irenaeus, including Gnostics, used it to describe the plans or purposes of God. Irenaeus, too, uses the word in this sense, and speaks of the various economies

53. See Lonergan, "Finality, Love, Marriage," 41–48.

54. This section owes a substantial debt to John Behr's excellent work.

55. Holsinger-Friesen, *Irenaeus and Genesis*, 35–36. For a foundational statement about the economy, see Irenaeus, *Against Heresies*, 1.1.10.

of God. But he also uses it in the singular to describe the single, unified purpose or plan which God has for the whole of his creation.[56]

The temporal nature of this world, then, is part of an intelligible order, as God's eternal plan unfolds in time.[57]

This economy mainly concerns the creation and salvation of human beings, with the rest of the universe being included because of its connection with them.[58] Irenaeus thus describes three stages in the economy: from creation to the incarnation, from the incarnation to the *parousia*, and from the *parousia* into eternal life.[59] In the economy, one may discern the order of God's saving plan, in which the divine wisdom makes sense of history and pulls the various world orders God has established together into unity; the economy, thus, gives meaning to the story of humankind through God's revelation and action.[60]

Both creation and salvation are included in the economy, for the nature of creation is to grow into union with the eternal and changeless God.[61] Irenaeus would in some cases speak of two aspects of human creation: a first creation out of mud, and a continual formation of human beings through the economy of God.[62] Augustine's masterful discussion of creation and salvation in his *Confessions* mirrors this technique, blending together the language of creation and the language of salvation; the waters over which the Spirit broods in Genesis flow together with the waters of baptism graced by Christ, while the light that God made by his Word lives in our hearts by faith (Gen 1:2–3; John 1:4–5, 9, 31–33).[63] Neither Irenaeus nor Augustine would say that creation and salvation are the same; they proceed from the same economy but are not equivalent to each other.[64] In salvation, however, we see a true human being, as those whom God has made grow into the fullness of the maturity of Christ (Eph 4:13).

To return to the language of potency and sublation, one may understand that humans are made with potency to receive divinization. The

56. Minns, *Irenaeus*, 56.

57. Behr, *Irenaeus and Clement*, 40–44; see also McGrath, *Christian Theology*, 236–37.

58. Minns, *Irenaeus*, 57.

59. Ibid.

60. Osborn, *Irenaeus*, 20–21.

61. Behr, *Irenaeus and Clement*, 37–38n12, 42.

62. Ibid., 78n137.

63. Augustine, *Confessions*, 13.

64. Behr, *Irenaeus and Clement*, 47.

economy Irenaeus speaks of expresses the way that our intelligible relation to change becomes actuated by the cooperation of human freedom and the work of God (all by God's plan). Because creation and salvation are distinct but not separate processes, we may also see that the created reality is not abrogated by salvation, but rather its true meaning is fulfilled as it is sublated by eternal life.

The economy, if taken in this way, has an essentially pedagogical nature.[65] Irenaeus describes the manifold ways that God, through the course of human history, teaches us:

> Thus it was, too, that God formed man at the first, because of His munificence; but chose the patriarchs for the sake of their salvation; and prepared a people beforehand, teaching the headstrong to follow God; and raised up prophets upon earth, accustoming man to bear His Spirit [within him], and to hold communion with God: He Himself, indeed, having need of nothing, but granting communion with Himself to those who stood in need of it, and sketching out, like an architect, the plan of salvation to those that pleased Him. And He did Himself furnish guidance to those who beheld Him not in Egypt, while to those who became unruly in the desert He promulgated a law very suitable [to their condition]. Then, on the people who entered into the good land He bestowed a noble inheritance; and He killed the fatted calf for those converted to the Father, and presented them with the finest robe. Thus, in a variety of ways, He adjusted the human race to an agreement with salvation.[66]

The maturity of human beings, according to Irenaeus, is to see God and be joined with him in divinization.[67] Because we are made like God, having choice and freedom, our free choices are both constitutive of what it means for us to be human and also significant for our salvation or damnation.[68] The meaning of temporal existence, therefore, is educating and persuading human beings for eternal life, while also serving God directly through worship.[69]

---

65. Ibid., 50.

66. Irenaeus, *Against Heresies*, 4.14.2. See also Behr (*Irenaeus and Clement*, 49–53; 53n65), who suggests that the last phrase of this section has a musical reference and should be translated "he harmonized the human race to the symphony of salvation."

67. Behr, *Irenaeus and Clement*, 45–46.

68. Ibid., 42–43.

69. Irenaeus, *Against Heresies*, 3.16.7. See also Minns, *Irenaeus*, 61–62. Briggman, *Irenaeus and the Holy Spirit*, 172.

The Economy of Christ

The economy of human existence is created, known, and defined by Jesus Christ. Irenaeus could, in fact, use the word specifically to refer to the incarnation and to Jesus Christ himself.[70] The plan of God to save us, in all its historical fullness, comes fully in Jesus Christ and can only be known in him.[71]

> For there is the one Son, who accomplished His Father's will; and one human race also in which the mysteries of God are wrought, "which the angels desire to look into"; and they are not able to search out the wisdom of God, by means of which His handiwork, confirmed and incorporated with His Son, is brought to perfection; that His offspring, the First-begotten Word, should descend to the creature (*facturam*), that is, to what had been moulded (*plasma*), and that it should be contained by Him; and, on the other hand, the creature should contain the Word, and ascend to Him, passing beyond the angels, and be made after the image and likeness of God.[72]

God's absolute transcendence, paradoxically, leads to his intimacy with creation, for it is according to his handiwork that we his creatures should be united to him in Christ.[73]

The Evangelist declares, then, the master key for understanding creation in Christ's prayer for his disciples, before he was betrayed, in John 17.[74] The intention of God in bringing about this universe is that the life of love and wisdom possessed eternally by the Trinity should be shared with his creatures by knowing Christ and following him (John 17:20–26). God's identity as Creator is decisive for understanding Jesus Christ, and the meaning of his act of creation is declared through the cross.[75]

---

70. See, e.g., Irenaeus, *Against Heresies*, 1.6.1; see also Unger and Dillon's note in Irenaeus, *St. Irenaeus of Lyons*, 164n5.

71. Behr, *Mystery of Christ*, 88.

72. Irenaeus, *Against Heresies*, 5.36.3.

73. Behr, *Irenaeus and Clement*, 20; one may see here clear overtones of Irenaeus' implicit understanding of "the distinction."

74. Ibid., 36.

75. Holsinger-Friesen, *Irenaeus and Genesis*, 121; Behr, *Mystery of Christ*, 179. One may see here parallels with Luther's insistence that we know God and participate in his purposes not by so-called theologies of glory but only through the cross. Luther, "Heidelberg Disputation," Theses 19–20, in *Selected Works of Martin Luther*.

The economy declared and summed up in Christ is Trinitarian.[76] The Spirit prepares us for the Son, the way to the Father, who grants us incorruption and eternal life.[77] Each member of the Trinity, then, has a distinct role in the economy: "The Father plans and orders, Son executes these orders and performs the work of creating, and the Spirit nourishes and increases, while man makes continual progress."[78] In this plan of creation and salvation, the hiddenness of the Father moves us to humility before God's transcendence and surpassing greatness, yet the revelation and gift of the Father's glory keeps us from ceasing to exist.[79]

Writing against gnostic opponents, Irenaeus repeatedly emphasizes the material nature of creation and its dignity as being created by God and summed up in Christ.[80]

> We should not say that flesh and blood will take hold of the Kingdom, but rather that the Spirit will take hold of flesh and blood and lift them up to the Kingdom. Our flesh will not take possession of the Spirit, rather, the Spirit will take possession of our flesh and so transform it that, without ceasing to be flesh, it will be radiant with the glory of God (AH V.9.4; 10.2).[81]

Irenaeus agrees with the traditional views he inherited that the image of God in us indicates our rationality and freedom; he adds, however, an insistence that God's image also embraces our material nature.[82] He believed, in fact, that Adam's body was made in the image of the body of Christ, and that the gift of the Holy Spirit would share with our material bodies the gift of God's immortality and incorruptible nature.[83]

---

76. One would not expect of Irenaeus the totality of the conceptual development concerning the Trinity that the church achieved in the councils of Nicaea, Constantinople, Ephesus, and Chalcedon. A Trinitarian understanding, however, is clearly present in Irenaeus' polemic against the gnostics. See Lashier, *Trinitarian Theology of Irenaeus*, for a thorough and balanced explanation of Irenaeus' Trinitarian theology. See also Irenaeus, *Demonstration of the Apostolic Preaching*, 3–5, for a seminal discussion in Irenaeus' own words.

77. Behr, *Irenaeus and Clement*, 56.

78. Ibid., 38.

79. Ibid., 56.

80. See Briggman, *Irenaeus and the Holy Spirit*, 42–44, for Irenaeus' contention that, although God is spirit, his creation is through material things.

81. Minns, *Irenaeus*, 77.

82. Ibid., 60–61. On Irenaeus' insistence on the importance of human freedom and its connection to the image of God, see Behr, *Irenaeus and Clement*, 87, 90.

83. Irenaeus, *Against Heresies*, 5.6.1, 7.2, and 8.1. See Minns, *Irenaeus*, 60–61.

Jesus Christ himself, then, is the foundation of our potency to diviniza-tion and the means by which our natural human lives are sublated by a life that is divine. While we do not, of course, become Sons of God by nature, we are given by grace a relationship with God that Christ's existence prefigures and makes possible. Because human beings are made in the image of God, Jesus Christ becomes the principle of actuating our human potency and the type of what created existence will be like when fully sublated in eternal life.

Christ gives us God's life—actuates this potency—by recapitulating human history (and thereby human nature) in his incarnation.[84] Reca-pitulation has to do with drawing things together and summing them up.[85] Irenaeus, through his teaching of recapitulation, provides an influential and far-reaching analogy for understanding the way that created being is saved in Christ.[86]

At one level, recapitulation can take the form of a fairly simple ty-pology. Israel wandered forty years in the desert, and Christ was tempted forty days in the desert; Israel passed through the Jordan to take the land of promise, and Christ was baptized in the Jordan to begin his public minis-try; the first Adam became apostate through a tree, but Christ, the second Adam, saves through a tree—the cross. At a deeper level, recapitulation teaches that such types signify that by entering into human history Christ fundamentally redefines and transforms it. The human story becomes his story, for he is its central character, and human history becomes his history, no longer ending in death, but having the promise of resurrection. Christ recapitulates humanity's struggle against evil, and by doing so achieves the victory that we could not achieve on our own; rather than succumbing to temptation and being conquered by death, he lives out and brings fully into existence the image of God.[87]

Recapitulation indicates the way that change is the sign of the un-changing God's creating and saving activity.

> All finds meaning in the person and work of Jesus Christ, who
> is the first principle of truth, goodness, and being. So far from
> transcendent simplicity, his work involves joining the end to the
> beginning and changing reality in a radical way, so that the word

84. I will further discuss Irenaeus' analogy of recapitulation in chapters 5 and 6.

85. The most direct biblical root of Irenaeus' theology of recapitulation is Eph 1:10, in which, according to God's eternal plan, he moves "to gather up" all things in Christ (NRSV). "To gather up" translates "*anakephalaiosis*," which has connotations of bring-ing things together under one head.

86. See Irenaeus, *Against Heresies*, 3.18.1 and 5.21.1.

87. Hart, *Beauty of the Infinite*, 326.

becomes flesh, Alpha is joined to Omega, and death becomes life.[88]

By recapitulating human history in himself, Christ changed the meaning and reality of it. The complex and varied strands of this universe's progress and failure are drawn together by Christ in redemption.

The Hypothesis in Scripture

Scripture rightly communicates this divine economy in which there consists the salvation of the world. Irenaeus uses the word "hypothesis" to explain the unity of Scripture in telling this plan. Ancient dramatists and rhetoricians sometimes used "hypothesis" to connote the plot of a play or argument of a speech that makes it hold together.[89] Just as a coherent plot gives unity to the disparate scenes in a play, so the message of Scripture gives coherent meaning to the progress and regress of the world.[90]

Human intelligence is only effective at discovering the universe's true nature within the hypothesis declared by Scripture.[91] Irenaeus' complaint against the gnostics did not only expose the abstruse nature of their theology, but centrally turned on their false interpretation of Scripture.[92] Because heretics read Scripture according to the wrong hypothesis, they are unable to come to a valid understanding of the world.[93]

> A very large part of Irenaeus' scriptural argument against his opponents is given over to demonstrating that Old and New Testaments do not reveal each a different God, but only different stages of the relationship between the one and only God and his creation. What begins as a fairly mechanical, and, at times, rather naïve, anti-heretical strategy develops into an extraordinarily rich and influential theological theme: a theology of history built upon the belief that it is the God-given destiny of humankind to grow into perfection by gradual stages, and that

88. Osborn, *Irenaeus*, 20–21.

89. Behr, *Irenaeus and Clement*, 32.

90. See Grant, *Irenaeus*, 29–40, for a summary of Scripture and post-scriptural Christian authors known to Irenaeus.

91. Behr, *Irenaeus and Clement*, 34–35. Clement of Alexandria agrees with Irenaeus on the nature and importance of Scripture as a hypothesis but adds a positive parallel role for philosophy. Ibid., 19.

92. Irenaeus, *Against Heresies*, 1.8.1 and 1.9.4.

93. Behr, *Irenaeus and Clement*, 34–35.

God guides this development in a loving, infinitely patient, ever-vigilant, and non-coercive manner.[94]

Irenaeus therefore likened the gnostics (and all heretics) to those who rearrange the tiles of a mosaic of the king to display a fox or dog instead; the words of Scripture are still there, but they have been rearranged by the gnostics to disfigure their true meaning.[95] As known through reading Scripture rightly, the economy of salvation declares to us the true God and the true nature of the world.

The right reading of Scripture coheres with the apostolic preaching of what the prophets declared, which has become reality in Jesus Christ.[96] As a disciple of Polycarp (the disciple of John), and as a European bishop in the second century, Irenaeus was able to appeal against the gnostics both to his own and others' memories of those who had personally heard the apostles; he could also appeal to the history of public preaching in congregations with apostolic foundation.[97] One could know the hypothesis of Scripture by listening to the still-echoing voices of its human authors through the teaching they passed down.

The apostolic preaching itself was valid because it existed within the hypothesis of the Old Testament writings, which themselves declared Christ. In our times, the New Testament seems the more solid and settled document, and our preaching and teaching often finds the Old Testament more problematic. It is clear that Irenaeus knew many of the New Testament writings and considered them Scripture.[98] The polemical context in which he wrote, however, valued the antiquity and solidity of the Old Testament writings, and often when Irenaeus refers to "the Scriptures," he primarily means them.

In the Old Testament, Irenaeus saw Christ; in this interpretation he agreed with the great majority of the early church.[99] In his *Demonstration of the Apostolic Preaching*, for example, Irenaeus embarks on a succinct, but ambitions, journey through the key moments of the Old Testament, showing how in every case God, through the Old Testament writers, was

94. Minns, *Irenaeus*, 56.

95. See Behr, *Irenaeus and Clement*, 34–35, for very relevant comment.

96. Ibid., 28–31.

97. See Irenaeus, *Against Heresies*, 2.2.1.

98. Irenaeus, *Against Heresies*, 3.1.1.

99. See, for example, Heine, *Reading the Old Testament*, for a well-researched and accessible account of the ways that the ancient church saw Christ in all of Scripture. See also Heine, *Origen*, 63–82, for Irenaeus' influence on Alexandrian Christianity specifically with respect to the reading of Scripture.

declaring the economy of Christ.[100] Irenaeus understood himself hereby to follow the teaching of Christ himself, who, opening the disciples' minds to understand the Scriptures, declared to them,

> "How foolish you are, and how slow to believe all that the prophets have spoken! Did not the Messiah have to suffer these things and then enter his glory?" And beginning with Moses and all the Prophets, he explained to them what was said in all the Scriptures concerning himself. (Luke 24:25–27, NRSV)

Just as Jerome declared that he believed Isaiah wrote more a gospel than a prophecy, and Ignatius of Antioch maintained that to him the Old Testament was Christ, so also Irenaeus saw each element of the scriptural narrative and each moment of God's salvation history to declare Jesus.[101]

Irenaeus did not claim that Abraham and Moses and Isaiah completely understood the reality of the incarnation, but that what God was revealing through them was Jesus Christ. After the coming of the Christ, we are able to look back and see what God was doing all along. We also have the ability, because of this revelation, to understand and participate in God's plan to bring this universe to final fruition by our salvation. Scripture itself is therefore intrinsic to the economy, because becoming the beings we are supposed to be requires the participation of our intelligence and free will.

The right reading of the Old Testament itself, then, is known only through the cross and resurrection of Christ.[102] The interpretive key of Scripture is Jesus Christ himself. As we learn to see him in the Scriptures, we discover the divine intention; as we follow the apostolic message and are inscribed within this scriptural narrative, we take as our foundation our Savior and Lord. In this way we come to know the truth of the world and live more fully as our own true selves, for we are made in the image of God, that is, in the image of Jesus Christ.

Therefore, through Scripture, God makes our potency to divinization known to us, and he works to enact it. The message of Scripture communicates to us Jesus Christ. Because our intelligence and will are involved in divinization, Scripture provides an account of God and the universe, of human nature and God's work within it: a plan we can understand—at least in part—and commit ourselves to. It also communicates to us the truth about Jesus, and his goodness and love, so that we may come to know him and be transformed.

100. See Behr, *Irenaeus and Clement*, 29–31. Irenaeus' method of exposition here coheres, in many ways, with that of the great sermons of Acts.

101. Jerome, *Epistle 53*, 8; Ignatius, *Philippians*, 8.2.

102. See Behr, *Mystery of Christ*.

It is not surprising, then, that Irenaeus' explanation of the economy of God often had special reference to the creation accounts of Genesis 1 and 2.[103] While some of this interest was probably occasioned by the destructive speculations of Irenaeus' gnostic opponents, he saw in Gen 1:26 and 2:7 teachings necessary for understanding the total and complete nature of the salvation wrought by God through the economy.[104] Humans, made in the image of the Trinity, are fashioned from the mud of the ground and enlivened. Irenaeus emphasized through these passages God's personal involvement in creating human beings as well as their material nature.[105]

The meanings of creation and salvation begin in the Garden, but they do not end there. Irenaeus saw Scripture to declare an economy that progresses through history. What was made (and, to an extent, lost) in Adam's creation and apostasy is restored as we are given the gift of eternal progress into the perfection of God.[106] "If Christ's recapitulation of 'all things' (Ephesians 1.10) has soteriological value for humanity, it must involve his summing up of a humanity that, according to Genesis, was meant to be embodied."[107] This divine pedagogy, therefore, works to extend the inner life of the Trinity to those material beings whom God has made in his image.[108] Christ's new covenant abrogates the rule of the decalogue and the old covenant by fulfilling them, and the gift of God's Spirit extends and fulfills the natural precepts resulting from creation as God implants his love in our hearts (Rom 5:5 and 8:1–2).[109]

We are nourished by Scripture in the church and prepared for immortality there by the Eucharist.[110] Eden prefigured the church, for it is the place in which we are to live as we grow into God's purposes.[111] In the church, as part of a worshipping community, we receive instruction and nourishment communicating to us true human life.

> For the glory of God is a living man; and the life of man consists in beholding God. For if the manifestation of God which is made by means of the creation, affords life to all living in

103. See, for example, Irenaeus, *Against Heresies*, 4.20.1.

104. Holisinger-Friesen, *Irenaeus and Genesis*, 2, 26.

105. Briggman, *Irenaeus and the Holy Spirit*, 119–23.

106. Ibid., 150.

107. Holsinger-Friesen, *Irenaeus and Genesis*, 37.

108. Behr, *Irenaeus and Clement*, 56.

109. Ibid., 70–71.

110. Ibid., 70.

111. Ibid., 66.

the earth, much more does that revelation of the Father which
comes through the Word, give life to those who see God.[112]

As Behr comments concerning this passage, "Rather than seeing human life
governed by an injunction to glorify God, for Irenaeus it is God who seeks
to glorify man, bringing him to share ever more fully in his own glory."[113]
Working through the economy of his divine will, as declared to us in Scripture, as ministered to us in the Eucharist, as constituted of us in the church,
as fully realized in Jesus Christ, God brings into existence and saves human
beings suited to be divinized and share his life.[114]

Conclusion

To be human means to have potency to be sublated by a fully transforming relation to God in eternal life (1 Cor 15:50–54). Human nature is not a
static fact, but rather a creation by God that finds its fulfillment through a
particular history of change. The being that we are given, by being created
as human, has a *telos* in salvation (Acts 17:23–28). For that potency to be
actuated means to become, as far as is possible within the limits of merely
created being, like Jesus Christ (1 Cor 15:49).

Being human has a meaning, and that meaning can be fulfilled by
nothing in this world (1 Cor 2:9). Humans cannot actuate this potency
themselves, for it must be made actual by a cause proportionate to the effect
produced (Eccl 3:10–11). Nothing in the universe of created being exists
in such an infinitely actual way (Job 38:1–7). Rather, God has prepared a
place for us in which we may dwell in him (John 14:1–3). This place is not
a simple geographical location, as if changing addresses could bring about
eternal life, but indicates and includes the active fulfillment of our being in
living a life given to us by Jesus Christ (John 14:12–14; 15:1–11).

God works through his plan of creation and salvation to bring us to
eternal life. As Irenaeus brings out in his economy of salvation, there is a
plan to the universe whose end is our salvation (Gen 12:1–3). The history
of this universe, and especially of human beings, tells a story whose beginning and end is Jesus Christ (Rev 1:17–18). This universe has its essential
unity and consistency because the Word active in its creation entered into
its history, recapitulating the human story, and making it fully his own (Eph
1:3–14).

---

112. Irenaeus, *Against Heresies*, 4.20.7.

113. Behr, *Irenaeus and Clement*, 56–57.

114. Irenaeus, *Against Heresies*, 3.19.1.

The divine pedagogy God undertakes in this economy works to transform every aspect of our being. As Kierkegaard brings out in his explanation of the stages, the way that we choose to orient our lives makes a profound difference for our ability to be our own true selves (Matt 16:26). By coming to live transparently in devotion to Jesus, we come to know—and become like—the truth who sets us free (John 8:32). As our lives become defined and changed by Christ, we come to recognize our ethical and aesthetic modes of existence for what they really are: pointers, through the dictates of conscience and the call of beauty, to the fullness of goodness, truth, and beauty that we are to become in Christ (Matt 6:33).

Fully actualized human existence, then, is human existence as sublated in a supernatural relationship with the Trinity. That such is the case does not deny the humanity of all who are still in development, who so far fall short of that goal; to be a developing human is still to be human, and we have need of exactly this completion precisely because we are human. Those of us in the life of this present world journey toward this fullness of life (1 Pet 1:13–20). We can also receive the abundant life, even here, in a partial, but real way through the gift of the Holy Spirit, who gives us the life of Christ (2 Cor 1:21–22).

Salvation, then, rather than being an add-on to an essentially natural human existence, is the revelation of true human existence in supernatural life. To fulfill the image of God, we material beings must participate in the blessedness God eternally knows and shares. Being human means to be created with this destiny, for only humanity fully revealed and transformed rightly participates in the glory of God (John 17:1–5).

3

The Darkest Night that Ever Fell

S I N

Human existence, radiant in good and destined for glory, stands contradicted by the darkness of evil and the stain of sin that mark our souls. If human life truly exists as part of the economy of God, and if God is enacting in us a cosmic destiny that unifies the universe and brings part of it into communion with himself, why does living in this world bring a suffering that breaks us and reduces us back to dust? Why are we, who are created for such good, so often and so intractably afflicted by evil and, not least, malefactors ourselves?

The Christian understanding of evil does not consider evil to be a competitor to the goodness of God, but rather something that God providentially allows and overcomes. Christian theology also maintains that the evil we suffer, as horrific as it may be, is not our deepest problem, for we are sinners who have set ourselves against the very source of our life and of everything good. Besides questions of evil and divine providence, then, we must carefully consider the evil we do and the untruth we have become.

We understand the way sin and evil afflict us only by understanding the cross. In Christ crucified, we see the declaration of the glory of God, and the revelation of the one true human being, juxtaposed with the full measure of human evil and sin. As enlightened by the cross, it is possible to discern the way that God's providence does not exclude but overcomes evil.

The revelation of Jesus Christ declares to us the mystery of our sinfulness, the inauthenticity by which we fail to be our own true selves. The human reality that we experience is fallen, and we must understand the meaning of that fallenness to see the full measure of the work that Christ has done. Lonergan's use of horizon and Aquinas' examination of human potency provide systematic distinctions that examine the way we miss the mark, known to us in Christ. These systematic distinctions enlighten the historical model provided by Irenaeus, as they explain the way that the cosmic order God has made includes the tragedy of our sinfulness and works to purge the ignorance and darkness within us. In Kierkegaard's examination of despair and in Lonergan's analysis of inauthenticity, absurdity, alienation, decline, and bias, we see the foul fruit of this sinfulness God's gracious order permits, but overcomes.

Differentiating Good and Evil

In Bernard Lonergan's analysis of the providential arrangement of this world, he used the analogy of a three-lane highway to differentiate the way that good and evil relate to the wisdom and will of God.[1] The highway itself represents the entirety of the created world; that which is off the edge of the highway does not exist at all, except for the God who made it. Within the highway's bounds are all the goods and evils that comprise this world.

The first lane of the highway represents what God directly wills, namely, every particular good and the overall good of order that relates the particular goods into a whole. For example, the cup of coffee I drink one morning is a particular good—an individual good thing—and as Raymond Chandler puts it, "The lifeblood of tired men."[2] Because coffee does not grow in central Illinois, and because I would not have the skill to cultivate and roast it if it did, the blessed morning cup of coffee requires an economic and trade arrangement—a good of order—to support it and guarantee its morning-after-morning repetition. The particular good of order that supports the repetition of this particular good is part of a world economy, which itself is one historical instance in the universal order wrought by God. To the extent that each of these particular goods and goods of order actually are good (and not participating in evil), Lonergan would affirm that God directly wills them according to his eternal wisdom.

The third lane of the highway represents what God does not will, but nevertheless permits. In this lane is sin, *malum culpae*, the choice of moral evil. God does not will sin, and it is impious to suppose he tempts anyone with it; rather God forbids sin (Jas 1:13–14). Nevertheless, creatures constituted freely by God in this universe have the ability to sin. Sin is exactly a

---

1. Lonergan, *Grace and Freedom*, 111–16; see also Stebbins, *Divine Initiative*, 279–80.

2. Raymond Chandler, *The Long Goodbye*, 319.

withdrawal from the wisdom of God, for in sin we fail to choose God's way by choosing our own.

By the second lane of the highway, in-between these two, Lonergan indicates the way actions have consequences.[3] As explained below, these consequences have to do with what one may term natural and penal evils. The essential point is that these consequences are often evil from a restricted point of view, whereas from an overall point of view they support an important aspect of the good. Being locked in a jail cell is evil, for example, from the point of view of the prisoner: freedom, an important good, has been restricted. Consider, however, what it would be like to live in a world in which justice had no meaning. Being caught under an avalanche is evil, from the point of view of those suffering this catastrophe: no sane person seeks out being crushed by snow, mud, and rocks. What would a universe be like, though, without any reality of order, in which natural causes have effects? Forest fires, reducing arboreal beauty to smoldering ashes, are evil; a good forester, however, will explain how restricted instances of forest fires serve to support the overall forest ecology.

Lonergan has two main points he wishes to draw from this analogy. The first is to clarify the relation of the will of God and evil. When free created beings choose evil, *malum culpae*, their choices have significance. The evil that results from those choices is always an evil for the person making the choice; often it also has grave consequences for other people (Matt 18:6–7).[4]

Aquinas' theology, which Lonergan drew on in crafting this analogy, terms the kind of evil that brings about suffering in rational creatures *malum poenae*. *Malum poenae* is a difficult phrase to translate; often it is translated "evil of punishment," but it is probably best to translate it "penal evil," or the evil from which we suffer, when considering Aquinas' theology. This aspect of evil includes both the direct and indirect results of sinful actions, as well as the way the natural world is often destructive to us. If created beings are going to live in a world ordered by the wisdom of God, yet withdraw from that wisdom, they will lose the ability to experience that order as always life-giving.[5] This indicates that human existence, in a universe that operates according to natural laws and understandable principles of human relations, can either intersect with the results of those laws and principles in a way that is consistently blessing, or not. That we experience the regularity and order

3. I thank Robert Doran for this insight.

4. See also Plato, *Gorgias*, 469a—79e; but this does not signify that it is inconsequential or good to suffer evil.

5. See Stebbins, *Divine Initiative*, 270–77.

of the world destructively is a sign to us that we are out of harmony with the will and wisdom of God. Penal evil does not always indicate that a person is either a malefactor or being punished by God. Rather, it indicates the way that the sinful choices of human will introduce violence and disorder into the world.[6]

Natural evil, *malum naturale*, results from God's establishing and upholding the order of the natural world. It indicates the way that created entities are subject to loss, corruption, and decay. Natural evil does not indicate that physics or chemistry began operating differently in the universe as a result of human sinfulness. Rather, it indicates the way that this universe, as naturally constituted, does not have the unity, stability, and perfection that would be characteristic of eternal life.

God wills the suffering and loss that result from penal and natural evil only insofar as he wills that there be order and justice in a world in which his creatures do not follow his wisdom. Note how different this is from God directly willing evil for a person. In that case, we would be speaking of a one-lane highway in which God ordains every good and evil circumstance and action equally.

God, though, never has an evil will and never wills evil to any being from an overall point of view. In the case of penal and natural evil, God permits suffering and loss (which are evil, from a restricted point of view) or sometimes causes them, because he wills—both in the world and for the persons involved—an overall good. Despite the horrors of human suffering, much of it of no fault of those who suffer, it is better to live in a world in which moral choices have significance, and justice and order have meaning. God wills for everyone these goods; indirectly, then, he wills some evils that adhere to them, but only insofar as he wills our continued participation in the overall good, given the consequences of evil.

Lonergan's second point is that neither our choice of evil, nor the terrible evils that result, nor the corruptible character of this universe, can escape from the range of the wisdom of God. God knows the evils we choose and those we experience, and they are accounted for in his providence. Even our very ability to withdraw from God's wisdom depends on the wise ordering and creative power of God. Evil does not annul or step outside of God's wisdom; rather, in all things—even the valley of the shadow of death—God works for the good (Ps 23:4; Rom 8:28).

That we participate in the order of nature and of society is a gift from God, and he fully understands the way that these orders can become destructive for us. God is not limited to dynamics of progress or decline

---

6. See Volk, *Historical Causality of Christ*, 64.

explainable in human terms, but he works powerfully to redeem. His redemption reaches even to our own malice, injustice, and un-wisdom; likewise it is not restricted by our place in the order of space and time. Rather, the whole order of this world, in which we so often choose darkness, is the preparation for the coming of the Christ and the gift to us of his new life.

To trust in this account, we will have to look to the cross. Aquinas followed Augustine in saying that,

> Since God, then, provides universally for all being, it belongs to His providence to permit certain defects in particular effects, that the perfect good of the universe may not be hindered, for if all evil were prevented, much good would be absent from the universe. A lion would cease to live, if there were no slaying of animals; and there would be no patience of martyrs if there were no tyrannical persecution. Thus Augustine says (*Enchiridion* 2): "Almighty God would in no wise permit evil to exist in His works, unless He were so almighty and so good as to produce good even from evil."[7]

In other words, God could have created a world in which there were no evil, but God thought it wiser to create this world, in which there is evil, and to overcome that evil through good.[8] The great sign and instance of the way that sacrificial love overcomes evil is the cross. It is by that great sign that we will trust and understand God's ordering of this world, or we will not understand it at all.[9]

The Ontology of Evil

One of Augustine's deepest insights is that evil is an absence of the good, or a failing to choose the good. In this way, the nature of evil is parasitic on the world of being, which, in and of itself, is entirely good. This argument is at the heart one of Augustine's earliest Christian works, *On Free Will*.[10] He also made it a central point in his magisterial *The City of God*.[11]

In the latter work, the form of his argument is interesting; instead of treating good and evil abstractly, he speaks of the way that war depends on peace. War itself, despite any goods that may be revealed or accomplished

7. *ST* I. 20.2 ad 2.

8. See Volk, *Historical Causality of Christ*, 84–88.

9. See Lonergan, *Understanding and Being*, 374–77, on suffering; see also Lonergan, *Method*, 117–18.

10. Augustine, *On Free Choice of Will*, 2.18.

11. Augustine, *City of God*, 19.12.

through it, is a destructive evil; yet, war cannot be conducted without the resources provided by our peaceful, constructive existence. Furthermore, war is conducted, if it is being undertaken justly, for the sake of peace. No one sane or honest declares a peace so that later we can have more war. One can see, here, the difference between a mere cease-fire and a true peace.

In this way, perhaps we can understand the nature of what Augustine means by his enigmatic declaration that evil does not exist. Wars certainly happen and exist. We give them names and mark their beginnings and endings with declarations and treaties. War, however, cannot be an original reality. It can only be derivative of peaceful existence, and the way it comes into existence can only be through reshaping the being that exists in peace into a being that exists in hostility.

Ontologically speaking, then, evil is a privation and misrelation. One may understand it through the analogy of a shadow or vacuum, something that "exists" and is knowable only by what it lacks. This is not to say, again, that evil actions and evil situations do not exist as present phenomena in the world. At a deeper level, though, what we are truly speaking of in these actions and situations is a lack of the good, a failure to choose or experience righteousness.[12]

An Ebola virus is not an evil if taken in isolation, or merely as an inhabitant in an environment. Neither is an avalanche in and of itself an evil; without any harm done by the event, it would be a spectacular show. Microbes and forces of nature become evil when they intersect with other created entities—especially living beings—in a way that is destructive. Natural evil, then, indicates the corruptible nature of created things; penal evil indicates the suffering consequent to a misrelation of things and forces that in and of themselves are good. These evils can be terrible, but they can only be parasitic on the world of being. Evil is not a force or entity that exists by itself and can introduce or create anything truly new.

With respect to moral evil, and another aspect of penal evil, consider what exactly makes a lie so destructive. It is good that humans have the ability to form meaningful communications, and that we have social and interpersonal frameworks that give significance to these communications. Likewise, it is good that one person is able to credit the good faith and truthfulness of another, perhaps relying on those qualities to a great extent. The destructive nature of a lie is not simply that one person communicates a false meaning to another, but that the ability we have to form meaningful speech has been used to harm the very network of personal relations it is supposed to reinforce and support. The same words, taken in isolation, or in

12. *ST* I 48.1, 2.

a different relation, would not necessarily be harmful; but speech becomes evil when the trustworthiness and truth it is supposed to communicate is subverted by malice or unconcern. Moral evil lies exactly in that malice or unconcern, motivating the lie. Here again, whether considering moral or penal evil, evil lies in the misrelation of things that in themselves are good and the corruption of the heart that leads to damage for a set of personal relations.

As created by God, according to the economy of his wisdom, omnipotence, and goodness, reality has an inherent meaning and value, a kind of vector moving it toward the consummation of God's plan.[13] When we speak of knowing evil, we are really speaking of how we can understand the way this good becomes distorted, that is, the way the good things God has made become misrelated to each other and to God himself.

Original Sin

Vladimir Lossky rightly declares that for us the question of evil cannot be treated in an abstract way, disconnected from our selves and the reality we bring about.[14] We confront not only the question of evil, but of evildoers; and, if we are honest in the face of God's revelation, we must acknowledge that we are evildoers ourselves. The Christian question of evil necessarily, then, includes the question of sin.

In the Western theological tradition, the sin we commit is commonly distinguished from the sinful nature we inherit; sin we commit may be termed "actual sin," whereas sinfulness we inherit bears the name "original sin." In this tradition, the doctrine of original sin has come to fulfill a number of momentous roles. It functions to declare that everyone needs salvation, to reinforce that salvation is by grace, and to clarify that even the faith by which we participate in grace is itself a result of grace. It serves to explain the universal human experiences of death, moral impotence, suffering, and the common feeling of the meaninglessness of this world; it also is brought into play to defend God's goodness, wisdom, and omnipotence in the face of these realities. We find evidence of a universal choice to sin and a brokenness present in all known human societies; original sin is used to explain this, too. Furthermore, it functions to explain the resistance shown by many individuals, and even whole cultures, to receiving the proclamation of the gospel; in fact, it provides a link between our ontological constitution and

13. This is the main point of Lonergan, "Finality, Love, Marriage;" see also Lonergan, *Insight*, 689–92, for comment on evil with respect to such a world order.

14. Lossky, *Orthodox Theology*, 79–80.

the deficient way that we behave. The doctrine of original sin also serves to set up the problem that the cross solves, as well as to orient our understandings of the present life and the gift of eternal life. Finally, it functions to vindicate God's justice concerning the fate of the reprobate and to declare the absoluteness of his mercy concerning those who are redeemed.

It would be foolish simply to discount a doctrine that plays so many significant roles, especially when that doctrine has been affirmed through sincere wrestling with Scripture.[15] It is no wonder that Aquinas considered it a tenet of the universal faith that Christians must affirm, and that modern authors sometimes equate questioning original sin with questioning the gospel itself.[16] Any responsible examination of original sin must address each of these identified functions.

However, it is arguable that by placing original sin so close to the heart of Christian theology, a significant and destructive inversion takes place. The revelation of sin, as well as that of salvation, comes to us in Jesus Christ. They depend on him, not the other way around.[17]

At the time when Jesus came, none of the Jewish parties thought that keeping the Law was impossible.[18] As far as they understood, they were all busy keeping it, whether that meant concentrating on the Temple sacrificial system, legal rectitude, philosophic probity, or ritual purity. Both historically and systematically, the doctrine of sin is derivative of the revelation of Christ and the Spirit, who show us the way to the Father. "This encounter with the Lord and the subsequent recognition that one is a sinner, but a forgiven sinner, is the basic movement for further theological reflection."[19] As with the rest of this world, radiantly good yet afflicted by darkness, we come to a right understanding of sin by understanding the cross.

Reflecting on the Christ and on God alive in them, the apostles and subsequent generations of Christians tried to understand and affirm what God has done and is doing. Some of those understandings included a teaching about original sin, while others did not; all of them did speak of sin in some way.[20] Jesus, however, did not need an existing understanding of original sin to validate his life and ministry, nor does the work of the Holy

15. Especially important are such Scriptures as Genesis 3, Psalm 51, and Romans 5.

16. *ST* I–II 81.1; see also Norman, "Human Sinfulness," 411.

17. One may see a preliminary revelation of sin in the Law of Moses, as Paul indicates in Rom 7:7, leading up to the revelation of Christ. The full state of our allegiance to the darkness, however, is only revealed by the coming of the true light; see John 3:19–20 and 15:24.

18. See Hurtado and Keith, *Jesus among Friends and Enemies*.

19. Behr, *Mystery of Christ*, 74.

20. See Fredricksen, *Sin*, and Beuteneff, *Beginnings*.

Spirit. If all our understandings of original sin (or of sin at all) came crashing to the ground, needing to be reformulated entirely, we would still stand amazed at the mystery of the Son of God, slain for us and resurrected, and the Spirit of God, living in us and in our midst.

Questions about original sin in the Western theological tradition are inextricably tied to questions about Adam and Eve. Partly because of this link with original sin, partly because of their place in Western cultural conflict over teachings of creation *versus* evolution, and partly because of their connection with concerns about the inerrancy of Scripture, discussions of Adam and Eve have aroused great emotion, and affirmations or denials about them have been tied to the very validity of the gospel.[21] Many Christians have defended the truth of Scripture and the gospel in a way that does not depend on a literal and historical Adam and Eve.[22] According to many other accounts, though, belief in the monogenesis of the human race from Adam and Eve is indispensable for the Christian faith.[23]

While Irenaeus, Maximus, Aquinas, and Kierkegaard believed in a literal Adam and Eve, it is clear that for these authors the importance of Adam and Eve depended on their *meanings* and the way that God teaches us through the Scriptural accounts. The questions we face about sin and humanity do not fundamentally have to do with Adam and Eve, but with *us*, as we come before our brokenness, and our destiny, known to us in Christ. As important as a correct understanding of Adam and Eve may be, the truth of the gospel depends not on them, but on Jesus Christ alone. Submitting to Scripture means coming to understand and obey its message through knowing and loving him. The variety of interpretations concerning Adam and Eve evidenced by the leading and most central teachers of the church's first centuries bears witness to this fact.[24]

The common Western model, rooted in the anti-Pelagian writings of Augustine, may, in fact, be the right one, although it is rejected by the other two major branches of Christianity (the Eastern Orthodox and Syrian traditions).[25] Truth is not determined by majority vote, and it is possible that the Western tradition contains an important truth that the Orthodox and Syrian traditions lack. According to the usual Western understanding,

21. See Noll, *Jesus Christ*, 108–24.

22. See Lewis, *The Problem of Pain*; Warfield, *Evolution*; Crysdale and Ormerod, *Creator God*; Cunningham, *Darwin's Pious Idea*; and Collins and Gibberson, *Language of Science and Faith*; and Enns, *Evolution of Adam*.

23. See Numbers, *Creationists*; Ashton, *In Six Days*; Brown, *In the Beginning*; Berkhoff, *Systematic Theology*, 150–77; Collins, *Adam and Eve*.

24. See Beuteneff, *Beginnings*, 55–168.

25. See Augustine, *On Predestination* and *Literal Meaning of Genesis*.

original sin is considered a defect in human nature, resulting in an irresistibly sinful nature, in guilt that makes all humans (except Christ) liable to damnation in hell, and in the certainty of death; this change from an original, complete, immortal and pure human nature is consequent upon Adam and Eve's disobedience in Eden, and passed down from them to all subsequent generations of humans. This is certainly a possible way to understand the message of Scripture. The purpose of this work, though, is to open up imaginative and intellectual space for better understandings of grace. By interacting with Irenaeus, Aquinas, and Kierkegaard, I hope that engagement with these contrasting viewpoints will foster the search for truth.

Inauthenticity and Horizon

This chapter's most basic argument concerning original sin is that the fullness of human life is found not in the account of Genesis, but only in Jesus Christ. In sin, we fail to be who we really are called to be, for true humanity is found in a complete way only in Jesus Christ. The inauthenticity—that is, the failure to be ourselves—by which we become untruth can be related to the horizon that constitutes our being. By living in a horizon not characterized by love, we therefore fail to actuate the potency of being human.[26]

Lonergan explained the state of sin as a "radical dimension of lovelessness."[27] He thereby emphasized that sin is not a mere moral failing, but a deeper kind of problem altogether. In moral failings, we do not live up to the requirements of the notion of value, the orienting principle that moves our being toward seeking what is truly choice-worthy.[28] In lovelessness, however, we close ourselves off from the world by a multitude of means, from *divertissement*, to a simmering hostility, to sheer unconcern.[29] The radicalism of this state indicates the way it penetrates our being, and our inability, therefore, to extract ourselves from it purely on our own terms.

Lonergan develops this insight partially through the modern anthropology of "horizon."[30] Taken literally, one's horizon is the limit of what one can see. As developed philosophically by Martin Heidegger and Hans Georg Gadamer, horizon functions to indicate the way that the world in which we live is shaped and characterized by the extent of our knowledge

26. See chapter 2.
27. Lonergan, *Method*, 242–43.
28. Ibid., 240–41.
29. See McLaughlin, *Knowledge*, 74–78; cf. Pascal, *Pensées*, 139.
30. Lonergan, *Method*, 220–24, 235–44.

and concern.[31] What we know about and care about is, in many ways, our world. What we neither know about nor find important does not enter, in a significant way, into the way we understand the real world.[32]

"Horizon" has both similarities with and differences from the familiar concept of "worldview." Worldviews have often been characterized as the set of glasses through which we see the world. The most recent discussions of worldview have also included the way that worldview is a multifaceted phenomenon that includes, not just understandings of the world, but also values.[33] What horizon brings to the fore is that the most basic understandings and concerns by which we know the world and live in it are not intellectual items that we can inspect, but rather the basic constitution of our selves that makes us able to think about things and care about them at all.

Horizon, thereby, functions at a deeper level than worldview. Worldviews indicate whether we identify ourselves and understand the world as Christian theists, Muslims, modern materialistic atheists, etc. These intentional choices of worldview, however, depend on and are shaped by deeper underlying concerns of what we truly care about, what we think is (most) worthwhile, what we think possible in the world, and how we understand ourselves—at a basic level—as knowing or not knowing truth.[34] Lonergan identifies the most fundamental of these as our basic stance toward truth (whether and how we can know reality), our basic stance toward morality (whether and how we will pursue what is actually choice-worthy), and whether and how we have been grasped by the love of God.[35] On the basis of these most fundamental questions, everything in our world becomes different for us. They do not determine in and of themselves what kind of worldview we will have or follow; rather, they set the ground-rules according to which our various worldviews will be able to exist and function.

Heidegger's insight, that Lonergan adapts, is that horizon is part of the ontological constitution of human beings—that is, an aspect of our being—because human being is fundamentally *historical*.[36] We do not live as abstract entities, disconnected from our times and the knowledge and concerns that animate us. We have being in time.

---

31. See Thiselton, *Two Horizons*, for an excellent discussion of "horizon" and its development.

32. See Cone, "Aquinas and Lonergan," and Snell and Cone, *Authentic Cosmopolitanism*, 44–65.

33. See, for example, Sire, *Naming the Elephant*.

34. See Lonergan, *Method*, 285–88.

35. Lonergan, "Self–Transcendence;" see also Cone, "Transforming Desire," 221–79, and Snell and Cone, *Authentic Cosmopolitanism*, 66–130.

36. See Cone, "Aquinas and Lonergan."

Horizon, therefore, also has an orientation, a direction and character-izing attitude (or mood) according to which we move through time.[37] As we are enmeshed in the contexts of the world in which we live, we are not neutral observers. We are living for something, and toward something. By becoming aware of the concerns that move us, we are able to see the shape of our lives.

Lonergan's point can be illuminated by what we have already discussed concerning Kierkegaard's understanding of the stages of human existence.[38] The lower stages (the aesthetic as related to the ethical and religious, the ethical as related to the religious, Religiousness A as related to Religiousness B) are radically incomplete from the viewpoint of the higher stages. The person in them is intending to operate according to a controlling concern, and perhaps even believes himself to be doing so, but the viewpoint of the higher stages reveals that the existence of the person who lives only in the lower stages in this way is failing to exactly live up to a commitment to ultimate concern.

A person who lives according to the ethical stage, for instance, intends to live with principles of conscience as the chief arbiter in life, making the most significant questions those of right and wrong. Kierkegaard points out the way that our reason and the voice of our conscience both function relative to the societies in which we are enmeshed. Because these societ-ies can be narcissistic, our consciences can come to function in a deeply distorted way.[39] To take an example from Mark Twain, when his character Huckleberry Finn experienced guilt over helping an escaped slave, Twain was showing how the societal institution of slavery distorts the oppressors just as surely as it enchains the oppressed.[40]

By making the ethical stage something it is not—the absolute and final voice in human affairs—a person in the merely ethical stage loses the neces-sary correction brought to our societies by the voice of God. She thereby becomes false with respect to the very purpose of the ethical stage: living with respect to right and wrong. From the standpoint of the higher stages, all of the lower stages function in this way. They all have a provisional kind of validity, and progress from one stage to another is real progress, but taken only in their own terms they become false to the very concerns that animate them.

37. See Lonergan, *Method*, 49–51, on orientation and conversion as aspects of hu-man ontology.

38. See chapter 2.

39. Lonergan deals with these issues in terms of group bias and major inauthentic-ity. See Lonergan, *Insight*, 247–50, and *Method*, 80, 240.

40. Twain, *Huckleberry Finn*; see also Bluefarb, *Escape Motif*, 12–24.

Each of the stages indicates the basic concern that constitutes the horizon of the person living in that stage. The aesthete who refuses the higher development of the ethical lives in a way that is characterized by an incessant search for new items of interest. For this person, each interesting new thing is an item in the inventory of a life lived toward this concern. As he actually exists—as his being occurs and he actuates or fails to actuate his human potential—the horizon in which he lives becomes limited by the shape of a life lived merely toward momentary pleasure. Because he is human, the reality of his life is intended to include items of interest, but to sublate concern for those items in higher horizons of concern. The stages, therefore, indicate not merely ways that we function in the world but the way in which we live up to or fail to be who we really are meant to be.[41]

Lonergan argues that the most fundamental determinant of horizon is love. We find authenticity in self-transcendence.[42] True self-transcendence is achieved only in love, for in love we have the openness to the world of being, the "universal antecedent willingness" to accept what is for what it is and to live in a way that gives the other its due.[43] Love, then, fulfills the requirements of our being, for when we love, we have and live out an insight into the reality that we are.

Just as our horizon, and thereby our being, can be characterized by love, it can also be characterized by a lack of love. This is what Lonergan means by sin's being a radical lovelessness, and not merely a moral failing. A person within the ethical stage may live fully according to that stage, but actually fail to be an ethical being, because the ethical stage itself is deficient without being sublated by receiving the voice of God and the gift of his love. Our ethical being has true and full validity, therefore, only as it is grounded by the gift of God's love.[44] In sin, we fail to live according to this grounding, becoming untruth, instead of actuating the potency of being made in the image of God.

The problem of sin, therefore, has an ontological character, inhering in our being-in-the-world. Radical lovelessness, as it comes to ground and characterize the horizon of our existence, affects not just what we do, but who we really are. The individual actions we undertake—that is, the sins we commit—reflect the grounding of this horizon. Even our very best efforts to live honestly and openly will reflect adherence to a broken standard, a

41. See the extended discussion of despair throughout Kierkegaard, *Sickness unto Death*.

42. Lonergan, *Method*, 104.

43. Lawrence, "The Human Good and Christian Conversion," 262.

44. See Cone, "Transforming Desire," 335–82.

horizon lacking in love; and without the motivation and openness of love, our very best efforts will be rarer and rarer. The light that is within us becomes darkness, and how great that darkness (Matt 6:23)!

The Inevitability of Sin

The historical nature of human existence is central to the understandings of sin in Irenaeus. As a second systematic distinction to assist this historical model, Thomas Aquinas offers an analysis of the inevitable nature of sin in those who do not live constantly as supported by God's grace. His argument has to do with the nature of rational beings that have a history, reflecting on the nature of potency as it indicates the way it is necessary for us to develop and grow.[45]

Taken at its most basic level, potency—or, as Aquinas would put it here, prime potency—indicates the ability material beings have to be individual and to change over time. That we are material beings, then, indicates not only that we are able to be unities, or individual human beings, but also that we grow and develop as we become our selves.[46] Prime potency of itself, though, has an indeterminate character; material beings can be of many different sorts, and change can happen or not in many respects. As we are formed as human beings, the potential that we have is actualized in concrete ways to include some of these options, and not everything that it is possible for material being to be.

The formed and completed nature of human being, therefore, has to do with the intelligible nature of human existence; our materiality is informed by a human nature. To the extent that this human nature comes fully into existence, the basically indeterminate character of material being becomes more and more definite, better defined, and more complete. Potency, then, stands in relation not just to act (the active completion of our being), but also to form (the intelligible nature of our being).[47] In and of itself, though, potency lacks both actuality and form, and has a thoroughgoing incompleteness. Prime potency itself—potency completely lacking both act and form—does not exist in a pure state; rather material beings exist who, to some extent, participate in both act and form.[48]

---

45. Aquinas, *Truth*, 24.11–12; see also Lonergan, *Grace and Freedom*, 44–58.

46. See chapter 2 of this work.

47. See Stump, *Aquinas*, 189–216.

48. See Kent, "Prime Matter," for a book-length discussion of prime matter in Aquinas.

As Maximus will forcefully argue, beings that come into existence are necessarily participating in change, for they express the most central change possible: beginning to exist.[49] Aquinas takes hold of human psychology to argue from this fact to the inevitability of sin in those who do not perfectly participate in God's grace. As material beings, we who are created are not completely actual and completely formed (as God is), but are coming to exist. This state of being has deep consequences for the way that we are capable of living and actually do live.

Aquinas (as Maximus, Irenaeus, Kierkegaard, and Lonergan) believed that it is necessary to consider human beings as free moral agents, capable of making significant choices for good and evil.[50] There are two ways for human beings to make consistently right choices in the situations of our lives. The first way is to deliberate, in which we seek an understanding of what is practically wise to do. Because we are beings who learn and who develop over time, we think and learn discursively, and we are capable of assessing situations through practical moral reasoning. However, we are not either required or able to deliberate concerning every situation we are in, but sometimes act spontaneously. The second way we can live righteously, then, is to act spontaneously in a way that is right.

Because we are not beings of infinite intelligence, though, we are not capable of deliberating what is right to do in every morally significant situation we find ourselves in. In any given situation, we are capable of slowing down, thinking things through, and making a moral choice. There is never, in Aquinas' estimation, an individual situation where we are constrained to act in an immoral manner. Moral action must be voluntary, not automatic or violently imposed from without; actions that cannot meet these criteria simply cannot be moral actions.[51] Because of the finite nature of our being, however, we will encounter situations in which we do not choose to deliberate, but choose to act spontaneously.

In this case, the material constitution of our being, in which we are partly formed and still developing as humans, affects the kind of choices we tend to make. Potency has an indeterminate character. Insofar as we have not been fully formed by habits of righteousness, the spontaneous way that we act will tend to have a randomness to it, and not an intelligent nature. Because there are many more ways to go wrong than there are to do right, when we act randomly in a situation, and not guided by deliberation or

49. Maximus, *Ambiguum 42*.

50. Aquinas did believe that human beings participate in original sin, as we will discuss later in this chapter. This argument from potency stands somewhat apart from that dogma and does not, it seems, necessarily depend on it.

51. *ST* I 83.1; see also Aristotle, *Nicomachean Ethics*, 3.

formed habits of righteousness, we will tend more often to do wrong and not right.

Beings who are being formed do not have perfectly formed habits of righteousness. Without formed habits of righteousness, eventually, we will not deliberate when we should, and we will choose to sin. We will thereby institute a psychological dynamic in which, in the future, it is easier for us and more likely for us to choose to sin, for there is a psychological continuity to our being that either reflects righteousness or its lack.

One could ask whether God, by making us exist in this way, is setting us up to have to sin. The answer to this is that habits of righteousness can come in two ways: they can be acquired over the course of a human history, or they can be infused in us by the grace of God. God also can and does supply actual graces supporting us and guiding us toward right decisions.[52] What the psychological inevitability of sin indicates is that humans were never designed to live apart from the supporting and forming grace of God.[53] To the extent that we do not live supported by this grace and in participation with it, the immaturity of our being will necessarily issue in sin.

Intermediate Conclusion on Original Sin

This chapter has offered, so far, a number of alternate explanations with respect to the litany of functions the Western theological tradition assigns to original sin. Some of these explanations are partial, and all of them need to be further developed by the declaration of Christ's work on the cross. It seems good to pause here and take stock before moving on to the historical model offered by Irenaeus.

The universal human need for salvation results partially from the material constitution of our being, for the potency with respect to which we are made provides a psychological inevitability to sin. This salvation must be by grace because the habits of righteousness that inform us and support both our spontaneous decisions and our deliberations must come by God's grace, either in some way that precedes our choice of sin or in a way that rescues us from the dynamics we instantiate by choosing sin. Thus, the universal finding of human moral impotence and the brokenness present in every known society testifies to the fact that true human being is actuated obedientially, for we cannot find the fulfillment of what it means to be human apart from having our being in-formed by God's grace.[54]

52. *ST* I–II 9.4, 6.; see also Lonergan, *Grace and Freedom*, 98–104.

53. See Snell and Cone, *Authentic Cosmopolitanism*, 87–104.

54. See chapter 2 on obediential potency.

The suffering that we experience does not, therefore, invalidate the wisdom, goodness, and omnipotence of God, but rather bears witness to the way that God continues to will our good despite our withdrawal from his wisdom. Our withdrawal from God's gracious wisdom has often-horrific consequences, both for us and for those we affect. The suffering we experience, though, is possible because God continues to will our participation in justice and order. In turning away from God's wisdom, furthermore, we experience this world as meaningless, for we have turned away from the only completely adequate source of meaning; additionally, we are subject to the choices of other people who also turn away. Natural and penal evil cannot be explained, however, simply as a withdrawal from God's wisdom, but indicate, even in the suffering, the will and wisdom of God, who gives to us the gifts of order and justice, and who works in all things to redeem and to save.

Human life, then, is a life lived toward eternal life, but it is not a life that can be lived on our own terms. Sin affects our very being. The horizons within which we live become characterized by a lack of love, and a lack of the fullness of being-in-love. By being-in-love, we experience actual human existence, living in a horizon characterized by the gift of God's love. Lacking that, the ethical and intellectual grounding of our being likewise becomes darkened and weakened, for we become both lacking in moral character and untrue to who we really are, by failing to love. By living in a way that denies God's gift, we live a life best characterized as living toward the ultimate horizon of death. The gift of eternal life, then, will require the establishment of us in a horizon in which our being is constituted by the universal openness of the gift of God's love.

The Historical Model of Irenaeus

Irenaeus presents an account of human origins and destiny that explains the history by which God brings us into existence and makes us fit for eternal life. His account also has a significant explanation of the way that sin comes to darken our existence and pull us away from the destiny created for us by God. In Irenaeus, the meaning of Adam and Eve functions in two contrasting ways in the economy of God, using meanings drawn from this original pair as they relate to Jesus Christ. Irenaeus understood them to be in relationship with Christ according to two somewhat contrasting analogies: immaturity and loss. It is according to these sets of meanings that Irenaeus tries to understand the way God is working to heal and perfect the human race.

The Analogy of Immaturity

According to the analogy of immaturity, Adam and Eve show the beginning stage of human development, pointing to the maturity of Christ. Irenaeus pictured Adam and Eve as "infants" (*napioi*); argument exists as to whether Irenaeus considered them literally and physically to have been infants (or at least, youths), or whether the designation is metaphorical.[55] The fundamental shape of the economy, as indicated by this analogy, is pedagogical; that is, the world order God providentially establishes is one designed to educate human beings and promote our advance. Human beings, made in God's image, are destined to grow into the maturity of the life of the Trinity; this mature human life becomes present in the world in the incarnation of the Christ and reaches its consummation at his return.[56]

The purpose of Eden was to provide a fitting environment for Adam and Eve's education.[57] The Son of God walked with Adam and Eve in the Garden, prefiguring the maturity of human life he would affect.[58] By thus describing the life of Eden, Irenaeus therefore sets the stage for the recapitulation analogy of salvation that he understood Christ to fulfill, in which the meaning of human history is transformed by being gathered together and summed up in Christ.[59]

Adam and Eve committed apostasy against God because they were young and inexperienced, and thus easily deceived by the devil.[60] On the basis of this disobedience, they were cast out of Eden into the present world, losing the ability to be incorruptible and live eternally. According to this analogy, then, the meaning of the apostasy has to do with ignorance and immaturity, which again point to the fullness of wisdom and human life declared and found in Christ.

Irenaeus, however, considered Eden to have been a place fundamentally different from this world, not a life existing in continuity with the world we know.[61] Rather than seeing Eden as a prehistory of the human race, Irenaeus likely understood Adam and Eve's being "cast out" of Eden to

55. Irenaeus, *Against Heresies*, 3.22.4, 3.23.5, 4.38.1–2; *Demonstration*, 12, 14; see Steenberg, *Irenaeus*, 142–45.

56. Steenberg, *Irenaeus*, 145; see also Osborn, *Irenaeus*, 215–16.

57. Irenaeus, *Against Heresies*, 5.5.1; *Demonstration*, 12; see Behr, *Irenaeus and Clement*, 42–43.

58. Steenberg, *Irenaeus*, 140.

59. See chapter 5 in this work.

60. Steenberg, *Irenaeus*, 157–76.

61. Irenaeus, *Demonstration*, 12.

be equivalent with their creation itself.[62] The account of Eden, then, would explain the meaning of human life according to God's intention, providing an account that would help us understand our life here and the way that God works to create and save us.[63]

Irenaeus, in fact, considered the whole account of Eden to reveal aspects of God's creation of humans. The prohibition to eat from the Tree of the Knowledge of Good and Evil, for example, is not something subsequently given to an already-formed human creature; rather receiving this prohibition is a part of God's creation of the human beings (Gen 2:16–17).[64] The commandment itself is part of the formative work of the creating God, for humans do not exist as humans without being in a relationship with God of moral responsibility, receiving God's command and instruction.[65]

Whether he is correct in this conception or not, there are important things to learn from his rationale, not the least with respect to the questions it raises for modern readers. This understanding of Eden, for example, occasions the question of whether Irenaeus is envisioning Adam and Eve to have been created as fallen. After all, if Eden is an explanatory account of human creation and not something that took place historically, when Adam and Eve were created, they were created as "cast out" of Eden subsequent to their apostasy. Such an understanding seems to raise questions concerning the perfection of God's creation and about God's fairness, and thereby about the goodness, omnipotence, and wisdom of God.

Irenaeus, however, did not read Genesis to communicate that human beings started out complete and perfect and then experienced a fall.

> What is of importance to the present consideration is that, in his eschatologically-oriented reading of creation, which affixes the image of perfected humanity to the *telos* rather than the commencement of the divine economy, Irenaeus interprets the scriptural material wholly in conformity to this Christological orientation. As "adulthood"—that is, human perfection—is that toward which the race is striving and which the incarnation makes attainable to the human person in the eschaton, the protology of human existence cannot start from such a point of perfected adulthood. It must begin with the other terminus of human growth, that of the babe, the infant, who needs to be suckled on milk before it can graduate to firmer food, which Irenaeus calls the "bread of immortality—the Spirit of the

62. Steenberg, *Irenaeus*, 140–41n130.

63. See Behr, *Irenaeus and Clement*, 49n50; see also Beuteneff, *Beginnings*, 84.

64. Irenaeus, *Declaration*, 15.

65. Steenberg, *Irenaeus*, 154.

Father." As such, Irenaeus finds in Genesis 1–3 not a story of perfection/fall leading to redemption, but of imperfection, growing, and maturing into fullness of life, which is ultimately the life of Christ.[66]

Full and complete humanity is found only, then, in Jesus Christ, and in those he will bring to perfection in the life of the new heavens and new earth (Rev 21).[67] Because Adam and Eve did not have this complete and mature humanity, they did not have the qualities that attend it.[68] God did not create them in a state of disobedience; their purpose and calling, however, was to grow—to be educated and formed—into immortal life.[69] Human creation, to be completed by salvation, is not just an initiatory event but is still in progress as we mature toward the whole fullness of Christ.[70]

The question of a fall, and fallenness, does not only include the question of whether humans are sinful. Irenaeus clearly believed we are sinful; and salvation is only in Jesus. What is in question is whether some kind of ontological loss happened in human nature, based on Adam and Eve's sin, such that all of their descendants do not have the ability to live a life that is right before God. Because Irenaeus considered Adam and Eve to have been infants, and not already- or almost-perfected beings, the change he saw was not one that stripped away an already perfect and mature human nature. Adam and Eve succumbed to deceit and became apostate, losing the likeness to God (as discussed below, in the analogy of loss).

The opponents of Irenaeus' view, however, questioned why God would create humans in such a vulnerable state, easy prey for the devil.[71] Irenaeus begins his answer with stating the omnipotence of God, affirming that God could have created Adam and Eve as perfectly mature and in union with him.[72] Yet, in light of this omnipotence, Irenaeus asks the question not just of what God can do, but also what the being he creates is capable of receiving.

Making a created being that is equal with God is a contradiction in terms, and the perfection that God communicates to created being is therefore something less than his eternal and infinite being. Moreover, because

66. Ibid., 143.

67. See Irenaeus, *Against Heresies*, 5.18.1–2.

68. For an instance of how this creation-consummation logic developed in the Christian tradition, see Leithart, *Athanasius*, 108–16.

69. Behr, *Irenaeus and Clement*, 49.

70. Davis, *Encountering Evil*, 40–42.

71. Irenaeus, *Against Heresies*, 4.37.6.

72. Ibid., 4.38; Behr, *Irenaeus and Clement*, 46–47.

God is free, wise, and completely good, being made in his image and entering into complete communion with him requires exercise of an intelligent free will. Being made as a free and rational creature, destined for union with God, then, necessitates exercise of wisdom and a good will in order to actually live out what it means to be in communion with him. To be creatures who come into existence with a need to exercise wisdom and intelligence necessarily implies in those created beings a need for growth.[73]

This analogy of immaturity also raises questions concerning the connection of sin and death. Is death really the wages of sin according to this account, as well as something that rightly applies to every member of the human race (Rom 5:12–23; 6:23)? Irenaeus clearly connected death with the transgression of Adam and Eve, but he did so in terms of the mercy of God given the fact of their disobedience, and not in terms of revenge or a punishment for that disobedience.[74] Death keeps Adam and Eve (and us, their fellow-humans) from living an eternal existence characterized by the results of disobedience and alienation from the ways of God.[75] An existence apart from obedient relationship with God is exactly equivalent with hell. By death, God chastises us and corrects us, with an end not to our destruction but to the way that in Christ he will give us new life. Death is the wages of sin; but, as understood through the analogy of immaturity, these wages are God's mercy and goodness to us in our apostate state.[76]

Irenaeus furthermore points to the way the humans described in Genesis 1–3 were neither truly immortal nor yet mortal, but an admixture of both.[77] Immortality and incorruption were offered to them as gifts, yet it was possible for them to be corrupted and die. In their immaturity, they turned away from God's wisdom, and therefore from these precious gifts. Until we are completed in Christ, therefore, human reality un-graced by salvation likewise turns away from eternal life and is subject to death.[78]

Finally, if the whole Eden account is a true explanation of God's creation of human beings, does that indicate that the devil has a part in human creation? The serpent, with his temptation, is part of Genesis 3. Irenaeus,

---

73. Irenaeus, *Against Heresies*, 4.8.

74. Ibid., 3.23.6.

75. Bouteneff, *Beginnings*, 88.

76. Irenaeus, *Against Heresies*, 3.20.2.

77. Irenaeus, *Demonstration*, 15.

78. Irenaeus' view agrees with that of his contemporary, Clement of Alexandria. As Clement affirms, Adam was created perfect, and therefore immortal, meaning that nothing essential was lacking for him, but this perfection was not completely actual in him and required him to grow. See Clement, *Stromata*, 4.13.19.1 and 6.12.96; see also Bouteneff, *Beginnings*, 87n79.

however, would certainly deny any role of the enemy in human creation. The cosmic economy of which humans are a part does include the angelic and demonic beings. The role of creator, though, belongs to God alone. In this case, the meaning of the serpent's temptation would be that humans are intrinsically formed in such a way as to be able to be tempted, either to succumb or to resist. Our place in the universe and the freedom we have is not the final stability of those redeemed by God. The freedom of human beings, as created, has an element of fragility, susceptible to temptation, but also capable of moral resolve and growth.[79]

One thing that should not be in question, though, is whether Irenaeus considered the Genesis account to be true. His works mainly concern the right interpretation of Scripture, whose truth he defends against the heretics. Genesis, as with the rest of Scripture, must be read according to the correct hypothesis in order to be interpreted correctly, and that hypothesis is the economy of salvation in Jesus Christ.

Whether or not Irenaeus is right about Eden as God's conception of true humanity, he stands in consonance with many other patristic authors in denying a radical change in human nature as a result of Adam and Eve's disobedience. In the ancient Syrian tradition of Christianity, for example, Aprahat argued that Adam's sin could not affect humanity as a whole.[80] Ephrem the Syrian agreed with this assessment and argued that the darkening of human nature present in Adam's descendants is not from any kind of original sin but from personally committed sin, for sin is a matter of freedom whose roots must be in a free will. Theodore of Mopsuestia reinforced Ephrem's view, affirming the essential integrity of human nature and the continuance of free will in us subsequent to Adam's sin. All of these teachers—the most influential in the Syrian stream of Christianity—also affirmed the presence of inordinate and disordered degrees of desire in Adam prior to his choice to sin, rather than a mature and disciplined will that only tends toward good. The Syrian tradition also affirmed that Adam and Eve were created able to die, with the chance to become immortal but not the secure gift of eternal life. The human existence Adam and Eve had was, then, a task, not a secure achievement, as they were called to grow in moral and spiritual perfection.

Maximus also agrees with Irenaeus that created beings enter the world not in a state of accomplished perfection, but as those in need of completion by eternal life. One way in which he argues for this point is through

79. This understanding of human freedom and original sin is parallel to Kierkegaard's account of anxiety in *Concept of Anxiety*.

80. The following analysis draws on Vööbus, "Theological Reflections on Human Nature in Ancient Syrian Traditions," 31–50.

the progression he outlines from mere "being," to "well-being," which itself needs to be competed by "eternal being."[81] Created being, Maximus argues, is necessarily in motion, for it experiences the most fundamental motion of coming to exist. It is therefore impossible for created being to begin at a state of final rest. The motion of created being can either be according to the *logoi* by which it is made—participating therefore in the being of the *Logos*—or not.[82] By bringing us into existence, God gives us being, but the being we have must come to express the life of Christ, the Word. The end goal of creation, though, is not a cycle of endless motion but the Sabbath rest of God (Gen 2:1–3). In eternal being, the gift of being that we have by creation is confirmed and strengthened to live in true communion with God. We thereby live with a purpose, as walking with Christ and enduring with him leads us also to reign with him (Rev 2–3).

The Analogy of Loss

This relation of human sin and death with our immaturity accords well with Aquinas' analysis of the psychological inevitability of sin according to our material nature. Just as this analysis is not the only understanding of sin in Aquinas, so also Irenaeus presents a powerfully different analysis of the meaning of Adam and Eve according to the analogy of loss. One can meaningfully connect Irenaeus' second analogy with the further aspects of Aquinas' analysis of original sin.

According to the analogy of immaturity alone, one could perhaps take the apostasy of Adam and Eve as trivial, a mere youthful dalliance. Irenaeus, however, sees it as a catastrophe; it is a great tragedy, the very destruction of human beings, and their bondage to the devil and to death.[83] The analogy of loss is not separate from the analogy of immaturity in terms of contradicting it or being disengaged from it.[84] There is only one overall divine economy. Loss, however, does indicate the grievous character of apostate human life—that is, an existence that is disobedient to God, rejecting his commands, and falling away from his offer of life—in a way that the analogy of immaturity does not.

Taken literally, a "loss" indicates that something that used to be in one's possession is no longer there. As a metaphor, Irenaeus uses the analogy of loss to indicate the great separation between what humans were created to

81. Maximus, *Ambiguum* 42.

82. See chapter 1.

83. Irenaeus, *Against Heresies*, 3.18.2 and 5.21.3.

84. See Behr, *Irenaeus and Clement*, 52.

be and what we actually attain, short of union with Christ. In particular, he speaks of the loss of the likeness of God by the humans made in God's image (Gen 1:26–27).[85]

Numerous modern authors have complained about the way that Irenaeus (and other authors, such as Origen) distinguishes image and likeness in Genesis, claiming that Irenaeus misses the functioning of Hebrew parallelism, and that the terms should be used interchangeably, not contrasted.[86] Hebrew parallelism, however, often uses different terms for the same reality precisely because the terms themselves are not purely interchangeable; they each bring out something true concerning the multifaceted reality.[87] By distinguishing image and likeness, Irenaeus is not functioning purely exegetically, but is trying to understand, on the basis of Scripture, what changes and what stays the same with respect to the glory God has created us as and for, with respect to human history as it gloriously and tragically unfolds.[88]

That humans are made in the image of God, and in particular the image of the Son of God, is at the heart of Irenaeus' theology.[89] The image of God, according to Irenaeus, indicates the work of God, through the work of the Son and the Spirit, to fashion humans in relationship with God's own life.[90] Irenaeus does not here indicate a mere symbolic likeness, but the most formative and foundational aspect of human being. According to Irenaeus, the Son of God is the specific referent according to which we are made in God's image. Therefore, to be made in the image of God means to be the kind of creature capable of receiving the life of Jesus, a life that has an immortal and incorruptible relationship with the Father and the Spirit characterized by endless wisdom and love.[91]

Irenaeus understands the "likeness" of God to indicate the way the ontological constitution of human beings—the basic constitution we have as humans—finds fulfillment in history.[92] Being made in the image of God, then, indicates the potency humans have toward deification; possessing the likeness of God means to actuate that salvation. The reference point, chief instance, and giver of this life is Jesus, and having the likeness of God means, as far as is possible for a merely created being, to be just like him. To lose the image of God, then, would mean ceasing to be human; insofar as humans

---

85. Irenaeus, *Against Heresies*, 3.23.5, 4.4.3, 5.6.1, and 5.16.2.

86. See Grenz, *Theology*, 169–70.

87. See Kugel, *Biblical Poetry*, 8.

88. See Steenberg, *God and Man*, 29–30.

89. Ibid., 29–34.

90. Ibid., 32.

91. See Behr, *Irenaeus and Clement*, 42–43.

92. Steenberg, *God and Man*, 37–38.

live out a disobedient existence, they have lost the likeness of God. Adam and Eve, having both the image and likeness of God in God's intention for the human race, lost the likeness by choosing apostasy.

With respect to Irenaeus' two analogies for Adam, the immaturity analogy relates best to sin as a penal evil, but the loss analogy relates best to sin as a moral evil. Penal evil indicates our experience of suffering due to not participating perfectly in God's wise ordering of the world. Moral evil has to do with the kind of disorder in which a free choice is directly made for evil. Many analogies for original sin and fallenness have compared them to penal evil, similar to a disease or birth defect transmitted to us by our human parents. Aquinas' explanation of the universality of sin according to our material nature partially functions in this way. His understanding of original sin, however, compared original sin to moral evil: we do not just participate in it as a result of being in the wrong place at the wrong time, or by having the wrong parents, but rather there is some kind of deficiency or fault expressed that participates in a brokenness of will, withdrawing the human will from the will of God.[93]

These terms—penal and moral evil—are both analogies. Especially, original sin as analogous to a moral evil indicates a deficiency inherent in our matter, which Aquinas took to be connected to our relation to Adam's fall and to include the guilt of his will.[94] However, original sin could equally well, perhaps, indicate the way that the disorder of our being is intractable to correction without supernatural grace. The analogy of immaturity could indicate a mere need for gradual growth into eternal life. The analogy of loss, however, indicates a need for transformation—conversion—to a different basis of life: God's life given to us, actuating the potency of our being.

The analogy of loss, and its connection with a fault or defect in our wills, also gives rationale as to why ascetic struggle, and other spiritual disciplines, are so important.[95] We must discipline our matter, not just in terms of performing the athletics of the spirit, but also in terms of taking up our cross daily. It is in the emptying of ourselves—surrendering our broken selves and receiving our true selves in Christ—that we find the fullness of eternal life; one can understand this according to both the immaturity and the loss analogies, but on different terms.

The great difference affected by connecting Aquinas' theology of original sin with the analogies of loss and immaturity in Irenaeus is that the analogous character of moral evil would not in this case indicate an inherent

93. *ST* I–II 81.1; 85.1.

94. See te Velde, "Evil, Sin, and Death."

95. See the place of ascetic struggle in the great redemptive vision of Maximus, *Ambiguum 7*.

and inherited guilt that includes necessary damnation to hell for those born human.[96] It would, rather, indicate an inherent liability of death and need for transformation in order to live the life of heaven. We are disordered and cannot be immortal on our own terms, not just because we are immature but because our very existence cries out against it, until it has been conformed and transformed into the image of Christ.

The analogy of loss would, then, indicate the nature of a world at whose heart stands a cross and whose culmination is the victor of an empty tomb, joined by many brothers and sisters, a world in which God overcomes evil by good through sacrificial love. In this way, it is clear that no great chain of being connects natural and supernatural reality.[97] The reality of this present world resists the work of the kingdom of God and must be overcome, for the gift of a rational will leads to its own downfall, not just prolonged adolescence, if union with supernatural life does not complete it. To return to Kierkegaard's model, in the terms of the lower stages of life themselves we do not choose the higher sublation in God's love, but we must be given it freely by grace; yet without that completion by grace the life of the lower stages eventually collapses into an ultimate meaninglessness.

The pagan creation stories knew the conflict of the gods winning order from chaos.[98] The Old Testament showed the revelation of two parallel accounts of God bringing order to chaos in majestic procession and overcoming the primeval sea-monster and dragon (Gen 1:1—2:4; Ps 74:14, 104:26; Job 9:13; 26:12). The only reconciliation of these accounts is in the Word made flesh, enthroned on Golgotha, in whose death we find the declaration of the glory of God and the one true man, the completion of this world as God enters it to heal and save. For, it is here that we find the image and likeness of God, the full declaration and achievement of God's original purpose in creating, the one by whose long-ordained death the gates of hell are dashed to pieces and the sons and daughters of God are revealed (John 1:29, 19:30; Rev 12:11; 13:8; 14:1; 17:4; 22:3).

Irenaeus speaks of this holy mystery in terms of the sign of Jonah.

> [S]o also, from the beginning, did God permit man to be swallowed up by the great whale, who was the author of transgression, not that he should perish altogether when so engulphed; but, arranging and preparing the plan of salvation, which was

96. See the progression noted by Sullivan, "Infants Who Die Unbaptized," 3–8.

97. For an exposition of a supposed great chain of being, linking the natural and supernatural orders, see Lovejoy, *Great Chain of Being*.

98. See, for example, the account of Ouranos and Gaia in Hesiod, *Works and Days*, and the account of Marduk and Tiamat in the *Enûma Eliš*.

accomplished by the Word, through the sign of Jonah, for those who held the same opinion as Jonah regarding the Lord, and who confessed, and said, "I am a servant of the Lord, and I worship the Lord God of heaven, who hath made the sea and the dry land." [This was done] that man, receiving an unhoped-for salvation from God, might rise from the dead, and glorify God, and repeat that word which was uttered in prophecy by Jonah: "I cried by reason of mine affliction to the Lord my God, and He heard me out of the belly of hell"; and that he might always continue glorifying God, and giving thanks without ceasing, for that salvation which he has derived from Him, "that no flesh should glory in the Lord's presence"; and that man should never adopt an opposite opinion with regard to God, supposing that the incorruptibility which belongs to him is his own naturally, and by thus not holding the truth, should boast with empty superciliousness, as if he were naturally like to God. For he (Satan) thus rendered him (man) more ungrateful towards his Creator, obscured the love which God had towards man, and blinded his mind not to perceive what is worthy of God, comparing himself with, and judging himself equal to, God.[99]

Of ourselves and apart from receiving the likeness of God, then, we would suppose that immortality should be ours by right, and that God is someone we can relate to in the arrogant disobedience evinced by Jonah. Through our pride we are subject to the great devouring beast, the devil, who swallows us as we become subject to the reign of death. God allowed this because of his longsuffering, that, calling out to him in contrition, we would be "cast out" of the beast and given the fulfillment of our creation in the likeness of God.[100]

Two pointed questions arise according to this explanation for modern readers. First, does it indicate an ontology of original violence instead of an ontology of peace?[101] Second, does it indicate a defect in the created nature assumed by Christ, where Christ would necessarily be subject to original sin?

An ontology of peace is one in which the sinfulness and violence of this present world is understood to be a historical accident and not something inherent in human nature or the constitution of the universe as such. By "historical accident," what is meant is that evil and violence have a factual character as situations that came to be the case in time, but that they do not

---

99. Irenaeus, *Against Heresies*, 3.20.1.

100. See Behr, *Irenaeus and Clement*, 48–50.

101. See Hart's extended discussion in *Beauty of the Infinite*.

have a rationally necessary character as what *must* be because of the way the universe or human nature have being. Ontologies of violence see alienation and separation as intrinsic to human reality and to the universe itself; we are strangers, and at enmity, with God, each other, and even ourselves, because of the fundamental constitution of who and what we are. If the reality of this world resists the work of the kingdom, would not an ontology of violence, not an ontology of peace, be true?

According to Irenaeus' analogy of loss, there is no final unity and completion of the universe short of Jesus Christ. This does not indicate an ontology of violence because the intention of creation, the meaningful nature inherent in who and what we are, is that this incompleteness and disunity points to and is overcome in Jesus Christ. Jesus Christ is not extrinsic to the nature of the universe, because the universe exists for him and according to him (the *Logos*). He is its basis, fulfillment, and goal, and it would be fundamentally wrong to envision a universe that could have peace without him. The foundation of this world, its essential ontology, is one of peace because he is real, and because he is the one Scripture proclaims him to be.

Additionally, this interpretation of the analogy of loss coheres with an ontology of peace because it treats the basic and obstinate state of human sinfulness as a fact, not as a necessary conclusion of our ontological state. It is not ontologically necessary that we should be disunited with Christ; in fact, the entire drama of the universe is purposed to bring about that union. The factual character of human existence, as we experience it and know it by faith, however, is one in which we, apart from Christ's work of redemption, have not yet received that completion and are unable to live a life that is in harmony with God.[102]

The analogy of loss, therefore, does not indicate a defect that would inhere in the created nature of the Christ. That which is disunited and unruly apart from Christ becomes unified and tractable to God's will and ways precisely in him. Conceived by the Holy Spirit of the Virgin Mary, Jesus constitutes in his person this universe's ultimate perfection and peace. Both the image of God and God's perfect likeness are fully present in him (2 Cor 4:4; 1 Cor 15:49).

Second Intermediate Conclusion on Original Sin

The biblical logic of "perfect creation–fall–redemption" has a risk of always looking backward, wishing to get back to the place where, once, we belonged

---

102. See te Velde, "Evil, Sin, and Death," 150–53, on original sin as a factual claim concerning humanity, based on the light of faith.

and had a home. There is something right about this way of understanding the universe, for God's intention in creating us includes everything we are to become, and the sinful reality we experience does not measure up to that. What Irenaeus' biblical logic insists on is always looking *forward* to the second coming, walking on the way of the cross according to God's plan.

Irenaeus did not believe that humans are or ever were created fallen, but he did believe we are created with a task. This task is seen in a preliminary way in the language of Eden, and fully only in Jesus of Nazareth. In being conformed to him, we find the meaning of human life and the purpose of this created world.

Augustine's prayer can succinctly express his contrasting logic of grace, "Give what you command, and then command what you will."[103] Again, there is something right about this logic. We must depend on the graciousness of God in everything, for apart from the grace of Christ, we can do nothing; God is not a harsh taskmaster who demands of his children the impossible (John 15:5; Matt 12:20). The difficulty with this view is that grace is pictured only as a finished product that must be initially delivered before anything can commence, a reservoir of resources upon which we must draw, but not a stream of blessing flowing down to make us grow.

Augustine certainly did believe that already-graced Christians need more grace; one of his complaints against the Pelagians was that they did not (according to him) adequately believe in the need for asking for grace by praying the Lord's Prayer.[104] What he seems to desire—*contra* the Pelagians—is to make sure that a person cannot claim merit for good works (or for choosing God) in which that person exercises a will and capability that go beyond what God has supplied. Augustine thereby views grace as something that must be given to a person entire, and not something that could inherently allow a person to grow.

Irenaeus offers a different analogy of grace. The entire economy of the world is gracious, and God has arranged every part of it according to his plan. We have been created in his image, as beings who have the potency to achieve and receive union with him. The function of grace is to bring us to Jesus by the power of the Spirit. The fullness of that grace comes only at the end, when we know as we are fully known (1 Cor 13:12). God gives us enough light for each step of the way, which we sometimes accept and sometimes do not, but the fullness of light is only Jesus Christ, who is coming into the world (Ps 119:105; John 1:9; Rev 21:23).

---

103. Augustine, *Confessions*, 10.45.

104. See Augustine, *Against Two Letters of the Pelagians*, 4.27.

Every human being, without exception, needs salvation because no created being can start out with the fullness of participation in the life of God. We also all need salvation because the being we have all-too-willingly follows the darkness, becoming engulfed by the whale of rebellion, destruction, and death (Ps 51:5). Every aspect of our salvation participates in and depends on grace, including the faith by which we believe in Christ, because the free response by which we choose God is one we must grow into, both chastised and supported by God's grace, and the culmination of union with God is completely disproportionate to life on our own terms. Every step of the economy in which we move toward God is a step of growth, made in union with God's grace, and ending only in the fullness of the maturity of Jesus Christ (Eph 4:13).

The typical Western theology of original sin has often seemed to function with an aim of making sure that there are no "gaps" in Paul's proclamation that "all have sinned and fallen short of the glory of God" (Rom 3:23, NRSV). Original sin functions as the theological fallback plan that makes sure that everyone, everywhere, falls subject to this dictum. If our sinful state depended only on actual sin, and if actual sin requires developing a mature rational nature in which we can make reasoned choices for good and evil, it might be possible for some person to achieve that level of maturity and then make a right choice, without having first made a wrong choice. In that moment, that person would not be sinful, and therefore, the common logic goes, Paul's statement would be incorrect, and this person would not need the cross.

Irenaeus, again, offers a different explanation. Every person, except those already glorified in heaven, falls short of the glory of God revealed on the cross (John 12:20–33). The cross does not, then, have a purely negative function, for it not only affects the forgiveness of sins but also brings about and makes available the fullness of human life. God, also, has providentially allowed us to be swallowed by the whale, declaring that, as those who so easily follow the deceiver, we are not just immature but ready rebels; all humans are subject to both of these realities. The death we universally experience has, in one respect, a corrective and merciful function to limit the evil we would do and the evil we are subject to. The reality of death, in another aspect, though, reigns over us, holding us in its dominion apart from salvation by him who now holds the keys of death and hell (Matt 20:28; Mark 10:45; 1 Pet 1:18–19; Heb 2:14–15; Rev 1:18–19).

It is natural for us to ask why God would set up a world that functions this way, in which exactly the part of the universe he created for union with him is subject to evil and resists his work of salvation. It is possible for us to know *that* this world order is better, for we can know God's existence and goodness, rightly affirming the limitless nature of his wisdom and power. The question of *why* it is better is in many ways the question of Gethsemane, and the answer given is only the reality of our weakness—not even watching and praying for one hour with our Lord—and the glory of God enthroned on the cross. Just as Job's piercing cry received its answer only by the presence of God himself, so also the answer given to us is that this economy of God satisfied Jesus Christ, and in him God has come to live in us today.[105]

The work of Christ will therefore reshape human reality, correcting it and bringing it to completion, satisfying the intention of the Father, and thereby exposing and conquering the lies that hold us captive to death. Irenaeus powerfully declares Christ's work, therefore, according to the analogies of ransom and recapitulation.[106] As those made in the image of God but lacking his likeness, our selves and our societies are thereby healed and perfected according to God's plan, through the work of Christ and the Holy Spirit.

Actual Sin

The sin we commit includes both individual actions and an entire way of life.[107] The individual actions turn away from the wisdom and love of God in manifold ways. The life comprised of these actions, lacking the redemption of Christ, bears witness to the way that we do not live in a horizon grounded by and characterized by the gift of God's love.

Bernard Lonergan offers a multifaceted analysis of the way we fall short of the glory of God. The heart of this analysis is that through sin we fail to be who we are truly called to be. Lonergan specifies the dynamics of life by which we live out this inauthenticity in terms of absurdity, alienation, bias, and decline.

Absurdity indicates that the lies we live out in our inauthenticity come more and more to characterize our existence until they become a defining aspect of who we are.[108] Absurdity connotes a lack of intelligibility; perhaps its most pernicious aspect is that those who are truly deceived do not know they are deceived. Although progress remains possible for us, for we have not lost the image of God, the distortion of our lives wrought by sin means

105. I thank Jeremy Wilkins for his probing examination of Christology, assisting me to see this point.

106. See chapter 5.

107. For a much more extensive treatment of these aspects of sin, see Snell and Cone, *Authentic Cosmopolitanism*, 87–104, and Cone, "Transforming Desire," 188–220.

108. Lonergan, "The Subject," 86.

that what seems reasonable to us comes to include an aspect of unreason-ableness. We no longer know the truth, and when it comes to us, we do not recognize it for what it is.

Alienation is also a necessary accompaniment to inauthenticity. In inauthenticity, we are false—strangers—to who we really are.[109] At the heart of this alienation is we have become estranged from God, the source of truth, goodness, and all life. Because we no longer really know who we are, and because so much of our being is distasteful to us, being dark, we no longer have the ability to live lives of truth and love with each other. Violence comes to characterize our relationships, supplanting dynamics of community and love.

Bias tells the story of how sin comes to corrupt the way we think, choose, and love.[110] Far from being a sanctuary of righteousness, our intel-lectual and volitional nature comes to turn away from the truth. Lonergan analyzed bias in four parts: individual, group, general, and dramatic biases.

Individual bias is personal egoism, the death-knell of self-love.[111] Lo-nergan would agree with Aristotle (and the gospel) that self-love is legiti-mate. However, when our regard for our personal good and ourselves turns us away from the legitimate concerns and value of others, self-love becomes distorted. How easy it is for us to see the right of a system that benefits us; how easy to overlook the situations that call for self-sacrifice. In individual bias, we refuse to take into account and give credit to insights that would conflict with our personal good in favor of the overall good.

Group bias is individual bias written in the fabric of our societies.[112] Its most visible forms—such as racial prejudice and ethnocentrism—show the privileging of one's own group at the expense of another defined as dif-ferent. Again, it is not wrong to have groups that form a cohesive society by promoting common sets of understandings and values; in fact, it is neces-sary, and human life could not function absent the life of community. When the story of our group, however, leads us to discount the validity of another group, we have gone astray. This does not mean, in either individual or group bias, a weak acceptance or tolerance of anything that comes. It rather indicates the radical openness of love that tests all things by the standard, not of what is good only for us, but what is most choice-worthy given every legitimate concern.

---

109. Lonergan, *Method*, 55 and 357.

110. Lonergan, *Insight*, 242–43.

111. Ibid., 244–47.

112. Ibid., 246–47.

While individual and group biases indicate distortions in our social being, general bias indicates a distortion present in our relation to time.[113] We live in the present; it is therefore much easier for us to pay attention to solutions to problems that are of immediate practical utility. However, what is most wise often requires sacrifice in the present in favor of a long-term solution. Just as individual and group biases are the death-knell of forms of self-love, so general bias is the self-imposed destruction of practical wisdom. Analyzing a system in terms of overall function and long-term consequences requires development of a theoretical point of view. Theoretical points of view are exactly not practical: they are concerned with what is true overall, not with what is of immediate utility. No person and no culture can live without paying attention to what is of immediate utility. Practical wisdom, however, tends toward imperialism, to seeing the whole world in its own terms and, thereby, discounting the legitimate need for and contributions of theoretical study. Many of the solutions a society needs, however, are only operative with a long-term point of view. By privileging what is immediately practical, our use of practical wisdom imprisons us in time, robbing us of our ability to discover and implement those long-term solutions that ensure and improve overall societal health.

While individual, group, and general bias have to do with distortions in our relation with the world, dramatic bias has to do with distortions present in ourselves, as ourselves.[114] Dramatic bias has to do with our noetic relation with the performance of our lives. We know, and are deeply disturbed, that we do not live up to who we are supposed to be. Our very unconscious motivations, then, and the penumbra of feelings that accompany our focal consciousness, conspire to hide from our conscious knowledge the darker aspects of our being.[115] Lonergan connects this bias, in later work, with the radical moral impotence that faith must overcome: the way in which we turn away from the light and love the darkness because we know our deeds are evil.[116] Shame, taboo, and feelings of guilt come to characterize our lives

---

113. Lonergan, *Method*, 54, and Lonergan, *Insight*, 247–50.

114. Lonergan, *Insight*, 214–31; Lonergan, "Moral Theology and the Human Sciences," 305 and 309.

115. Lonergan's early explanation of this bias dealt primarily with the insights of depth psychology in terms of legitimate and illegitimate defense mechanisms present in the operation of our psyche. For a significant development of this position, and its amendment, see Robert Doran's analysis of psychic conversion. Doran, *Theology and the Dialectics of History*, 233–35.

116. Lonergan, "Moral Theology and the Human Sciences," 309; John 3:17–21; in this respect, Lonergan's examination of sin would also apply to aspects of original sin.

as an undertow to our consciousness, instead of the love and openness that should be there.

The results of absurdity, alienation, and bias are cumulative. Both individually and societally, therefore, we come to see decline.[117] Because we have incorporated lies, violence, and oversight of the truth into our very existence, we no longer recognize the truth when it is presented to us, and sometimes hate it even when it is recognized for what it is. The progress of which we are capable comes to exist in dialectic with decline, for aspects of our absurdity come to be incorporated into everything we are and do. Our solutions create new problems, and in the end, even our repentance needs to be repented of, for we do not know and love the truth.

Lonergan's analysis accords well with Kierkegaard's explanation of despair in *The Sickness unto Death*. At the heart of our problem is inauthenticity: by misrelating to ourselves and to God, we lose the ability to be who we really are. Inauthenticity is despair, present in all its dark and varied aspects, the deepest form of which lives blissfully unaware of its own tragic state. We have become untruth, unable to be taught correctly, for we can no longer remember the truth.[118] Truly, we need a savior, to enlighten our darkness and, by giving his life to us, bring us to our own true selves.

Conclusion

If Irenaeus' account has merit, as interpreted in concert with Aquinas, Maximus, Kierkegaard, and Lonergan, the claim that sin came into the world through (*dia*) one human being would mean that the reality of humanity seen in our creation is one that looks to and radically needs completion and salvation by Jesus Christ (Rom 5:12). That death came through sin would indicate, first, the mercy of God in limiting the destructive potential of our fallen state, and second, the patience of God in overcoming our enemy and the rebellious state of our lost existence. The first stage of this pedagogy and conquest was the giving of the Law (Rom 5:13). Both the Law given through Moses, and the state of life and death inherent in immature and rebellious human existence, anticipate the healing and conquering fullness of human being present in Jesus Christ (Rom 5:14). By summing up and redefining human reality in himself, thereby offering us completion, and by

117. Lonergan, "*Existenz* and *Aggiornamento*," 227–28; Lonergan, *Method*, 53–55; Lawrence, "Hermeneutic Revolution," 349.

118. See Kierkegaard's extended analysis of human existence as untruth in *Philosophical Fragments*. Kierkegaard's pseudonym Anti-Climacus, to whom *Sickness unto Death* is ascribed, completes the perspectives presented by the earlier pseudonym, Johannes Climacus, author of *Philosophical Fragments*, from a Christian perspective.

persuading and overcoming the evil in the devil, the world, and ourselves, Jesus Christ will give abundant life and fulfillment to us, who on the terms of our immature and apostate human existence find only death, as Adam did (Rom 5:15–17).

The choice of sin, exemplified by Adam, stands in stark contrast to the justifying sacrifice of Jesus Christ; insofar as we participate in apostasy against God, we find death, but insofar as we participate in Christ's sacrifice, we find abundant life (Rom 5:18–19). The gift of the Law, given through Moses, intensifies this contrast, for it both taught the people of Israel clearly about God and his ways and showed the way that humans are unable to live up to those ways on our own terms. The purpose of the Law, however, was not human condemnation but rather a pedagogy leading us to Christ and a stark assessment of our fallen and lost state relative to the true humanity revealed in him. Christ educates us, declaring to us the Father and true life in God, and Christ overcomes the dominion of sin over us and in us; by the abundant grace of our Lord, we who are subject to and lost in death receive the gift of forgiveness and eternal life (Rom 5:18–21).

By being baptized in him, united with the fullness of life revealed by his death, we ourselves receive resurrection: the gift of a life like his that is real now and that prefigures the complete life of the world to come (Rom 6:1–4). We thereby come to know and experience a life in which the suffering of this present world need not destroy us, because God gives us a life, brought into existence by union with his Spirit, in which we are reshaped through the suffering to conform to the character of Christ; this life has ultimate meaning, that nothing in this present world can discredit and destroy, because God's great and precious promises are being fulfilled in us. Trusting in God, and in his work through the incarnation of Christ, we are transformed by the gift of God's love to live in a way and have a mode of being that conforms to right relationship with him (Rom 5:1–5).

It is by participating in Christ's work and love, then, that we who are human—made in God's image—reach the fulfillment of that humanity by being made like God. As far as is possible for a creature, we become by grace like Jesus Christ. Being set right with God requires not just that an account against us is wiped clean, but that the being we have been given comes to exist in conformity with God's justice and order. Christ, through his incarnation, death, and resurrection, makes available for us and real in us this reconciliation with God (Rom 5:6–11).[119]

---

119. I will discuss salvation and the gift of new life in more detail in chapter 6.

4

That God May Be All in All

FREEDOM AND GRACE

Any Christian understanding of salvation must affirm God, and God alone, as its cause. And God is himself completely uncaused. Yet, God is capable of relating himself both intimately and intelligently with his creation. God, and his wisdom, will, and actions, are not within the created nexus of contingency and necessity but are its source and ground. Thomas Aquinas argues, therefore, that the action of God's providence may act to bring about certain effects through either necessary or contingent causes. Rather than appeal to a compatibilist notion of grace and freedom, or a Pelagian declaration that libertarian human freedom suffices for salvation, Thomas argues that the absolutely dependent, but still chosen, character of election is analogous to a conditional necessity—something that does not have to be but in fact is.

Human freedom, therefore, has a role within the compass of divine election, and the freedom we have as those created by grace has a real relation to our being in the image of God. Participatory ontologies, such as "the distinction," help explain how freedom intrinsically relates us to God and shows the character of true human life. Human freedom operates, as well, within a horizon; we are free in natural terms, as we are created, but we find the fullness of freedom in the gift of supernatural life. Human freedom, furthermore, is a necessary condition for either blessedness or damnation, for both righteousness and sin presuppose an individual who is created and remains free.

Predestination, then, speaks of God's choice of individuals for salvation. God's providence includes every individual aspect of creation, in addition to the good of order; likewise, freedom and sin, also, are operative at an individual level as well as in societies and histories. Because we are incorporated into the life of God as free individuals, and as members of a community, God's choice must indicate an individual, not merely a group or a plan. The basis of God's gift of grace is his unmerited love for us.

Questions of grace and predestination quite naturally raise the question of hell. Because hell is a penal evil, it cannot, strictly speaking, be a question of predestination, nor can it literally indicate a state of separation from God. Being separated from God, as illuminated by a participatory ontology, is simply non-being; hell is God's giving significance to our choices, and to us, even in the incomprehensible choice of refusing him and his love. As is clear from Scripture, there is no salvation apart from Jesus, and there is immense importance in choosing him.

Human Freedom

Bernard Lonergan argues that human freedom is a condition obtained when four conditions are met.[1] First, humans must exist in such a way and under such conditions that more than one course of action is objectively possible for them. Second, humans must possess the kind and capacity of intelligence that can work out more than one course of action. Third, humans must not be automatically determined to accept or choose the first course of action that their intelligence delineates. Fourth, the human will must move itself.

In other words, for humans to be free they must first of all have morally and intellectually differentiable options available to them. If only one candidate is ever allowed to run for office, even if elections are held, they are not free elections. Freedom requires the possibility of real and significant choices. However, the objective existence of these choices is not enough; the existence of multiple options is immaterial unless humans are able to realize these options exist and can make reasonable assessments of them. Freedom requires the ability, then, to deliberate concerning morally and intellectually diverse choices. With these two conditions in place, however, we could still be subject to determinism of time. Because humans reason discursively, and learn by experience, in order to be free we must be able to wait, and to assess multiple possibly valid options instead of simply choosing whatever our intelligence comes up with first.

Lonergan's final point is that the will must move itself. This account of human freedom occurs early in Lonergan's authorship and reflects the terminology and thought-framework of Aquinas. Lonergan's point has to

---

1. Lonergan, *Grace and Freedom*, 96; see also Stebbins, *Divine Initiative*, 84–87.

do with the essential spontaneity of human choice that must not be effaced, either by reasons internal to us or by factors external to us. In the terms of his later theological method, one would say that questions for deliberation in which we judge values and choose courses of action are never completely settled by judgments we come to as fact.[2] Nor can a free decision completely be imposed upon one from an external force or agent. Once one has assessed the state of affairs in a given situation, one must still exercise—and be able to exercise—wisdom and creativity to figure out what is good and evil and what is best to do. In order for human freedom to be a reality, then, we must be able to make creative decisions on the basis of our assessment of reality, and not be determined toward a certain course of action once that assessment of reality has taken place.

In this *schema*, Lonergan (following Aquinas) does not rule out God's moving the human will.[3] In fact, Lonergan argues for a permeability of the human will and divine action in which the will's ability to make free choices depends on God's causality. But, the way God affects the will does not abrogate but rather makes human freedom possible and real. God's work is to create and save us, establishing us as the kind of beings who live in a universe in which the conditions of freedom obtain, and working in us to support and enhance this freedom.

Human freedom, in fact, exists as a participation in the unlimited freedom of God. That humans exist as beings able to choose among multiple options echoes the omnipotence of God. That we can deliberate intelligently among these choices imitates God's omniscience. Our ability to be patient, rather than being determined by the temporal sequence, emanates from the eternity of God. The spontaneity of our decisions includes our ability to be generous, to forgive, and to go beyond what is necessary in a given situation; such is a reflection of the ultimate freedom of God's love. God did not have to create, but created in the freedom of love. By imitating the loving, long-suffering, and wise power of our Creator, we show what it means to be made in God's image, and we gain the likeness of God.[4]

2. Lonergan, *Method*, 34–41.

3. See Stebbins, *Divine Initiative*, 84–92.

4. See Irenaeus' distinction of the image *versus* the likeness of God, discussed in chapter 3.

The Supernatural Order

Lonergan considered of central importance for theology Aquinas' distinction between the natural and supernatural orders.[5] An "order" is a set of relations according to which something has the kind of existence it has. For example, in the natural political order, I am a resident of the State of Illinois and a citizen of the United States of America; in the natural familial order, I am a part of the Cone family of Illinois; and, in the natural temporal order I am a child of the late 1960s, who came to maturity in the 1980s and 1990s, and who now lives on into the twenty-first century. All of these sets of relations remain true and valid when considering the supernatural order, for the supernatural order sublates the natural order and does not annul it. With respect to the supernatural order, if I am truly saved, I also participate—in a supervening, sublating, or suspending way—in the kingdom of heaven and of God's dear Son; having received adoption into the family of God, I live, even now, the very beginnings of eternal life (Luke 9:27; 17:21; Rom 8:15, 23; Col 1:13; Eph 1:5; John 3:16; 11:25–27).

Both the natural and supernatural orders indicate real relations human have with God, for created human reality is made to participate in grace. In this light, Aquinas delineated a natural love for God in which, according to the terms in which we are created, we strive for God and seek him (Acts 17:26–28).[6] The natural order indicates the kinds of relations proportionate to us—that is, possible and appropriate for us—according to the way we are created by God. The supernatural order indicates the sets of relations proportionate to us only by God's gift of saving grace; it is in this order that we receive the special friendship with God indicated by charity, the certainty of a future beyond the grave that comes with hope, and the revelation of who God is and of his trustworthiness received in faith.[7] The natural order does not include—but naturally seeks—supernatural fulfillment, for the meaning of who we are as humans is that we are those who are created to receive divinization by the grace of God.

Human freedom operates in both the natural and supernatural orders, but we are not capable of achieving the supernatural order in natural terms (1 Cor 15:50).[8] Created by grace as members of the natural order, we must receive entry into the supernatural order by a different kind of grace. Intrinsic to both orders is a *telos*, or end, according to which they are known and in terms of which they have meaning. The *telos* of the natural order

5. Lonergan, *Grace and Freedom*, 14–20.

6. *ST* I 62.1.

7. *ST* I 26.3; II–II 4.1; 17.1, 2; 23.1.

8. *ST* I 12.1.

is a natural beatitude—a life of natural wisdom, intelligence, knowledge, prudence, justice, temperance, and fortitude—by which our created being can be assessed, and has meaning, as it seeks the ultimate fulfillment of eternal life. The supernatural order sublates this natural beatitude—in all its perfection and imperfection—as we are healed and elevated by the gift of saving grace; the virtues of the natural life find their true meaning through the gifts of faith, hope, and love. The *telos* of the supernatural order is nothing less than being like God, whom we will know as he really is (1 John 3:2).[9]

Strictly speaking, human freedom has to do with the choice of means, and proximate ends, but not ultimate ends.[10] Lonergan's four conditions of freedom have to do with the way that we are able to deliberate and make choices that fulfill the call to love. Deliberation, though, has to do with practical possibilities, that is, with means to an end, not with the ultimate ends themselves. For example, one can deliberate about whether to exercise and diet in order to increase one's physical fitness, and one can deliberate what kind of exercise, which diet, to choose; these are means to the end of becoming physically fit. But, no one can simply choose to lose twenty pounds of weight and lower one's resting heartrate by ten beats per minute; we must choose means that are ordered to these ends. In relative terms, we are able to choose among proximate ends, such as whether to pursue becoming more physically fit or becoming more intelligent. But, in absolute terms, we choose each of those proximate ends because we are ordered toward the overall good, and this ordering comes from God. It is the framework of good that allows us to assess options and make responsible choices. We make choices because we think, in some way, that they will be good; short of insanity, we are not capable truly of willing something in which we see no aspect of good.[11]

The question is, though, what is the kind of good toward which we are ordered?[12] As we are created, we are ordered within a horizon bounded by natural beatitude, the penultimate kind of blessedness that can be achieved in human terms; this life of natural beatitude is not apart from grace, but the end it seeks, through what graces are received, is a life of blessedness in natural terms. Saving grace reorders us, placing us in a horizon ordered toward a supernatural end, in which the good we seek—and begin to participate in—is eternal life with God. This reordering must be by the free gift of God; it is the actuation of an obediential potency, according to which the

9. *ST* I 12.2, 4; Aquinas, *Summa contra Gentiles*, 3.51.

10. See Stebbins, *Divine Initiative*, 87, and 324n102.

11. *ST* I 83.1 ad 5.

12. See Cone, "Transforming Desire," 128–32.

meaning of human existence can be achieved. Such a gift does not violate human freedom because human freedom applies to matters of possible deliberation and does not pertain to the choice of our ultimate end; human freedom is possible because God places us in a horizon ordered toward an ultimate end.[13]

Predestination

To deal with salvation only in these terms, however, does not answer all of the relevant questions. In particular, it does not answer the question as to whether human freedom, although not able to choose a supernatural end, has any role to play in our salvation. We cannot will ends, and cannot will any aspect of supernatural life in the natural terms of created human existence; such is only possible by the gift of saving grace. That does not necessarily mean, however, that the choices we are capable of making are of no account with respect to God's free gift to us of salvation.

The Question of Operative Grace

Grace, according to Aquinas, can be understood in three main ways.[14] First, one might refer to God's love toward us, which we do not merit on our own terms, as the dispositional aspect of grace. This is the most central sense of grace in Aquinas, for the other senses depend on it, making Aquinas' understanding of grace essentially relational. Thomas argues that we can also understand grace as the way God works in us, apart from any contribution on our part. Operative grace, therefore, is "in us, but not of us," for it refers to the production in us of an effect by the work of God alone. Finally, by grace we may indicate our response to God's work. Cooperative grace, then, shows the way God's grace allows us to participate in his work. This sense of grace is both "in us, and of us," for in cooperation we speak of the work of two or more parties combining to produce an effect.[15]

God's disposition of love toward us depends on his eternal being and character, not on anything in the created world. It is clearly not a reflection of human freedom but is rather the very ground of our being. Cooperative grace, conversely, necessarily involves human freedom; the grace that is "of us" is not separate from God's work—it is still a grace—but it also

---

13. To see the way that this insight functions within Lonergan's mature theology, see Cone, "Transforming Desire," 153–59.

14. *ST* I–II 110.1.

15. Lonergan, *Grace and Freedom*, 303–5.

by definition must involve our free response. Saving grace (*gratia gratum faciens*), however, is an operative grace; it is in us, but not of us, and it must be so because it pertains, among other things, to a fundamental choice of ends we are unable to make.[16] The relation of human freedom and salvation hinges on the right way to understand human freedom relative to this operative grace.

Operative grace is not necessarily apart from any role of human freedom because God is capable of relating himself intelligently to the creation he brings into existence, and because the eternal mode of God's being transcends the limitations of temporal, finite being. Our salvation depends on God alone, and God is dependent on nothing. It is possible, and should be affirmed, though, that God causes our salvation not apart from the free action of our will but with it.

Thomas on Providence and Predestination

Aquinas' understanding of predestination provides an extremely helpful historical and systematic model for understanding this point. Predestination, for Thomas, is a specific aspect of providence.[17] Whereas providence has to do with every aspect of God's wise ordering of all of reality, predestination concerns God's ordering of specific individuals to salvation based on his gracious love.[18]

As Thomas unfolds the doctrine of predestination, quite a problem emerges with respect to the importance of human freedom in salvation, which he also consistently affirmed.[19] Predestination has to do with God's gracious election of specific individuals, and it operates infallibly and irresistibly, because it is based on the determinate choice of God, whom none can hinder, whose knowledge and wisdom are complete, and who does not change.[20] God, furthermore, is completely uncaused; the choices of his will, therefore, are not the result of something's influencing him, nor are they the result of his inspecting created reality—by foreknowledge or other means—and coming to a decision based on it.[21]

The complex nature of this problem has a rich history, especially with respect to the Western theological tradition. Augustine's contemporary,

---

16. *ST* I–II 111.1.

17. *ST* I 23.1.

18. *ST* I 23.4.

19. See Goris, "Divine Foreknowledge," 99–100.

20. See Wawrkow, "Grace," 200–201.

21. Aquinas, *ST*, I 23.5, 6.

John Cassian, for example, in one of his *Conferences*, lays out over one hundred Scriptures that teach about grace and salvation. Taken in their most natural senses, half of these Scriptures teach that God alone accomplishes salvation, and the other half teach that human freedom plays an important part.[22] Thomas' intention, then, is to be faithful to the entire biblical witness, maintaining both the absolute priority of God and also the faithfulness of God with respect to the significance of the creatures he has made.

Harm Goris very helpfully clarifies that, in Thomas, there are two related but distinct aspects to this problem.[23] First, temporal fatalism seems to result from God's foreknowledge of events, which is total; second, causal determinism seems to result from God's causation of events, which is irresistible. With respect to both of these aspects it is necessary to clarify in what way God's knowledge and causation, respectively, are compatible with genuine contingency in created reality. It is also, then, necessary to show how the human freedom this contingency indicates can be significant with respect to God's choice of election and the gift of saving grace.

Thomas' solution rests on his bedrock theological position that we cannot know God as he is in his essence within the bounds of this life.[24] In other words, his answer fundamentally will be in terms of negative theology, in which we can deny of God that which is inappropriate of God and offer analogies that explain what God is like. The point of the negative solution with respect to this problem, besides maintaining the appropriate humility before God, is to place the paradox we are bound to encounter in the right place.

In other words, when considering human freedom and divine omniscience and omnipotence, one will run into a series of paradoxes (or antinomies). The nature of these paradoxes, though, should be able to be reduced to our inability to understand the exact mode of God's being, and not either to conclusions that impugn God's character or to relations within the created world. Conclusions that would impugn God's character are those that would suggest God is unwise or evil. Relations within the created world are those in which we are able to understand the operating factors univocally; in that case one is likely not speaking of a paradox but of a contradiction.

"Contingent," according to Thomas, has three meanings. It can refer to a creature (including, in some cases, an emphasis on that creature's corruptibility), to the *per accidens* (that which has only a factual, and not a logically

22. Cassian, *Conferences*, 13. Robert Rea's dissertation on Cassian remains a seminal work for studying the differing solutions of Cassian and Augustine with respect to the theology of grace (Rea, *John Cassian*).

23. Goris, "Divine Foreknowledge," 105–6.

24. *ST* I 13.5.

necessary, relation to a given set of causes, effects, or circumstances), and to a free act of will.[25] Contingency seems militated against by necessity. God, not any creature, is the necessary being, and he cannot be corrupted; the *per accidens*, by definition, must exclude logical necessity; and, a free act of will is exactly one that is not restricted by the iron rails of any determinism.

Even in this restricted discussion, however, one may see several senses of the word, "necessary."[26] We may speak of logical, moral, and legal necessity, as well as of a number of other senses. Aquinas, in fact, argues that God's knowledge of all of reality is necessary in a different way than is his causation of reality, and this difference is significant for the relation of human freedom and predestination. With respect to knowledge, the necessity of God's knowledge is transcendent, for it is included in his own eternal being. With respect to God's causation of salvation, however, the necessity is what Aquinas terms hypothetical (see below).

Temporal Fatalism and the "Standing Now"

When speaking of past, present, and future, it is possible to speak of static sets of relations in which the events that have taken place, are now taking place, and will take place are equally determinate in character. Whatever has been, has been, whatever will be, will be, and what happens now is simply another coordinate on an already determinate line. Future events, by this understanding, have a real and determinate character according to which true or false statements may be made about them.

Conversely, it is possible to consider that the designations "past," "present," and "future," indicate real differences in the determinate nature of the realities designated by them. That which is past is determinate, for it happened. That which is present is determinate; given that something happens, it necessarily happens. But, that which is future, by this understanding, is open, and not determinate. In this case, there can be no future facts: "the future lacks the factual and temporal necessity and determinateness of the past and present."[27] While some have argued that Thomas' views on God's omniscience are most compatible with the former view (in which past,

---

25. See Lonergan, *Grace and Freedom*, 110n80 and 336n41, concerning these senses of "*contingens*" and "*possibile*."

26. The discussion of several senses of necessity goes back at least to Aristotle. See Acar, *God and Creation*, 163n73.

27. Goris, "Divine Foreknowledge," 105.

present, and future events are determinate and equally necessary), it is clear that Thomas explicitly subscribed to the latter, more open, understanding.[28]

In other words, Thomas thought of the future as a realm of genuine possibility. It is not "somewhere out there," just waiting to appear or be actuated. While some aspects of the future may be set by current conditions (such as the ballistic flight path of a baseball coming off of a bat), much of the future is open to different—contingent—actualizations of possibility. If that is the case, it is not possible, from a human point of view, to make either true or false statements about contingent future events. So, one should not say it is a fact that one will travel to Chicago tomorrow, and make such-and-such determinate purchases (Jas 4:13–15). At present, this situation is not absolutely determined, and can neither be true nor false. Rather, we can state the fact of our plans (which are a present reality, and thus determinate), study the probabilities of achieving those, and realize both that we can change our mind and that many factors are out of our control.

In this case, Thomas' understandings of divine omniscience and creaturely freedom seem imperiled. Thomas believed that God knows all of reality exhaustively, including every aspect of the past, present, and future; furthermore, he believed that God knows the future (and the rest of created reality) not in terms of idea, potential, or possibility, but concretely, in all its individuality, and determinately.[29] But, if future realities do not exist in a determinate way, can they serve as the object of knowledge, even for God? Conversely, if God knows them completely, is it right to consider any of them to be contingent? God's knowledge is infallible, and the future must become what he knows it to be.[30]

The heart of Thomas' answer is that things are known according to the mode of being of the knower, not according to the mode of being they have in themselves.[31] For example, we know the reality of frogs not according to the mental capacities of a frog, but according to the realities of human cognition. Conversely, we would expect a frog's knowledge of us to be, for want of a better term, "froggy." Thomas applies this principle powerfully with respect to our use of theological language. God in himself is absolutely simple, but we are complex. Therefore, when we know God, we do not know him according to his essence, the existence he has in himself, but according to the composite mode of our being. Therefore, that which is absolutely the

28. Craig, *Divine Foreknowledge*; Aquinas, *Truth* 2.12 ad 7; *ST* I 14.13 ad 2; see Goris, "Divine Foreknowledge," 100–109.

29. *ST* II–II 95.1.

30. *ST* I 22.4.

31. *ST* I 12.4.

same and unified in God—for example, his being, character, knowledge, and will—is known by us in manifold ways.

Augustine convincingly argued, in his *The Trinity*, that God's attributes are part of his essence. That is to say, when we say God is wise, good, or powerful, or when we attribute to God any of his other eternal attributes, it is not really different from saying that God is God. To speak of a God who is not wise, for example, is really to embrace atheism, for there is nothing that is not all-knowing (omniscient) that deserves the appellation, "God." To speak of a God who depends on anything or who changes with respect to his attributes, such as knowledge, love, eternity, or the like, would mean defining a God who depends on something or who changes with respect to being God.[32] Hence Aquinas defends God's simplicity, which indicates both God's transcendence and the infinity of his being, which exceeds every category and cannot be limited in any way.[33] This situation does not prevent us from having real knowledge of God; God reveals himself to us, and we do know him. It does mean that we cannot know him according to his essence—on the terms of his own being—in this life, for we always now know him according to the human terms and conditions of this life.

God is able to know the future determinately because he knows it according to the mode of his being, which is eternal.[34] Future events, according to the mode of their own being, are contingent and undetermined, but according to the mode of God's being there is no distinction of past, present, and future. Furthermore, God does not know the universe by inspecting it, and he therefore does not know the future as "future." His knowledge is part of his being, and no aspect of his being is contingent or in any way determined. Whether or not God creates a universe, for any of it to exist, his knowledge is the same; his knowledge of the universe and himself is absolutely, transcendently, necessary—for he is a necessary being. Future events, in themselves, then, can be contingent and undetermined, and this does not affect the state of God's knowledge concerning them, for God's knowledge of them has not to do with them, essentially, but with himself.

God does not know this world by having to wait and see what will occur. If this were so, then any relation of human free choice to salvation would necessarily be cooperative, not operative; God would either have to

32. Augustine, *The Trinity*, 5.

33. *ST* I 3.

34. Goris, "Divine Foreknowledge," 111–12. Gregory of Nazianzus says of God, "God always was and always is, and always will be; or rather, God always Is. For Was and Will Be are fragments of our time, and of changeable nature. But He is Eternal Being; and this is the Name He gives Himself when giving the Oracles to Moses in the Mount." Gregory of Nazianzus, "Oration 45," 3.

wait and see, or somehow foreknow, what we would choose and do. Human freedom could then only result from operative grace and not have a real relation to God's giving of it. More adequately imagined, however, we may glimpse the kind of knowledge God has of this world by analogy with the kind of knowledge a craftsman has of the artifact he has made; this analogy stresses God's intimate involvement with creation and its absolute dependence on him.[35]

The question that remains is what God's mode of being is like, so that he can know determinately, according to his eternal mode of being, things that are indeterminate according to their own temporal mode of being. The paradox lies exactly here, and it is where we should expect it to be: we cannot know or understand God as he is in his essence. When we discuss eternity, we use analogies, and those analogies are simultaneously helpful and fall short of their ultimate mark.

One analogy that Aquinas drew from the late-Roman philosopher and theologian Boethius is to compare eternity to a "standing now" (*nunc stanus*).[36] A "standing now" indicates some sense of eternal presence or present. The two words in this analogy, however, remind us that applying this concept to God requires stripping away connotations appropriate only for the created world. As Goris puts it, "standing," reminds us "not to think of God's existence as a static, frozen, isolated instant, or as an evanescent instant which elapses as soon as it occurs, or as the atemporality of abstract entities like numbers or universals;" "now," indicates that we must not "conceptualize God's existence as tenseless extension or as tensed succession."[37] God's being is not static, for he is the most moving of all, moving everything else. Nor is God's being dynamic, for he does not change. "Static" and "dynamic" are both aspects of the created order; the fixed or indeterminate nature of things in this universe is not a determinate of the being or knowledge of God, for whom all of our times are present.

Causal Determinism and Hypothetical Necessity

God's knowledge does not, strictly speaking, cause events to take place; otherwise God's knowledge of evil events would make God the cause of

35. *ST* I 14.16.

36. *ST* I 10.1, 2; Boethius, *God Is One God*, 4; *Consolation of Philosophy*, 5.6; see Goris, "Divine Foreknowledge," 109–10.

37. Goris, "Divine Foreknowledge," 110. See also Lonergan, *Grace and Freedom*, 105n63.

evil.[38] To speak of God's knowledge as causal requires adding to the concept of knowledge the concourse of the divine will; but if this is the case, then God's knowledge of things, which is absolute, does not necessarily indicate an absolutely necessary character to the things themselves.[39] God can cause the things he has knowledge of to happen or come about through absolutely necessary temporal causes. However, this is not the only relation possible between created reality and the divine will.

Used as a pair of terms, necessary and contingent, just as static and dynamic, indicate aspects of the created world. "Necessary," of course, in its strongest and most proper sense, does indicate the being of God, for God cannot not exist. However, God has no opposite; therefore, the necessity he has does not indicate a strict pairing or contrast with possibility or non-being, but simply, "I Am Who Am" (Exod 3:14).[40] The pairing of necessary and contingent exists only as an aspect of the world that depends on the God Who Is.

Created beings presuppose something upon which to operate and a causal framework within which to operate, but God can create without pre-suppositions, out of nothing. Within the created causal order, creatures have a proper, causal role, but rather than being separate from God's causation, this causation depends on God's causation. *Esse*, the most particular and most intimate actuality of things, comes from God. But, the created causes and the divine cause operate at different levels, and so do not compete with each other. God's causation operates at the transcendent level of the gift of being, the created causes operate within the created causal nexus.[41]

In one respect, to speak of God's will is to speak of his eternal being, for God's purposes and plans are not contingent upon any other; yet, in another respect, God's will indicates a causal relation God establishes with the created world, and such relations are temporal.[42] God's work of causation does not take place within the created nexus of necessary *versus* contingent causation; rather it makes this nexus possible, operating on a different order of reality than is available within it. Goris summarizes Aquinas' theology this way:

> God causes necessary created causes to bring forth necessary effects and contingent causes to produce forth contingent effects. Elsewhere, Aquinas states that God's will is beyond the

38. Aquinas, I *Sent.* D.38 q.1 art.5.

39. Goris, "Divine Foreknowledge," 106–12.

40. See Maximus, *Chapters on Love*, 3.28.

41. Goris, "Divine Foreknowledge," 114.

42. Ibid., 101.

order of contingency and necessity, for it is the very cause of being as such and, hence, of the modal order. We may use different models, derived from our created reality, to illustrate the relation between divine and created causation: the Aristotelian models of first and secondary causes, remote and proximate causes, and principal and instrumental causes, or the Platonic idea of participation. But none of these captures adequately or expresses univocally the transcendence of the divine cause.[43]

In other words, while what God wills to take place necessarily does take place, it is possible for God to bring about these effects (such as salvation) through either necessary causes (such as some form of determinism) or contingent causes (such as the operation of a free will).

Again, this understanding of grace expresses a paradox, and again it is located precisely where we should expect it to be. We do not understand what it would mean to be the kind of transcendent cause that, establishing the created order of necessity and contingence, can bring about certain effects through contingent means. But, again, this is just to say that we do not know God according to his essence in this life, and cannot understand the kinds of causality that can create being out of nothing.

To say that God must bring about necessary effects in a necessary way would reduce God to being like the most effective cause in the created order of things.[44] Furthermore, to say that God causing our salvation in an absolutely necessary way is compatible with human free will is a contradiction in terms; we understand univocally both the meaning of the absolute necessity that operates in this world and the nature of human free will, and the two simply are not compatible. Human free will is a contingent, not an absolutely necessary, factor; if we are going to speak of any necessity that occasions it, we must do so in terms of the necessity of an absolutely transcendent cause, which brings both hypothetically and absolutely necessary causes into being.

While we cannot know God as he is in himself, we can know what he is not and what he is like. Thomas, again, offers an analogy that helps us understand the nature of divine causation of free actions, that of hypothetical necessity. Something that has hypothetical necessity is necessary, given the satisfaction of certain conditions. For example, if A exists, then it is necessary that A exists; if B is a car, then it is necessarily true that B is a car. Something that is absolutely necessary, though, has no conditions to

43. Ibid., 114. Goris refers to Aquinas, *On Interpretation*. I, 14, 197; *Metaphysics*, VI, 3, 1222; and *De Potentia*, q.3 a.7.

44. Wawrykow, "Grace," 202–3.

fulfill. It simply is, or is the case, and must be so, irrespective of any other action or reality. Furthermore, hypothetical necessity can be subdivided into that whose conditions are fulfilled necessarily and that whose conditions are fulfilled in a contingent way.[45]

In his discussion of predestination, Aquinas specified that the analogy according to which we should understand God causing our salvation is that of a hypothetical necessity whose conditions are fulfilled in a contingent way.[46] While Aquinas' statements of this teaching are mostly negative, dealing with objections, it is possible to restate them positively, as Lonergan does.

> Such a positive statement is the affirmation that God knows with equal infallibility, he wills with equal irresistibility, he effects with equal efficacy, both the necessary and the contingent. For, however infallible the knowledge, however irresistible the will, however efficacious the action, what is known, willed, effected is no more than hypothetically necessary. And what is hypothetically necessary, absolutely may be necessary or contingent.[47]

If Aquinas is correct in this assessment, the operative grace of the gift of salvation must involve human free will as a significant factor, because it is with our free choices, and not against them or irrespective of them, that God has chosen to save. It is the prerogative of the Creator to relate himself to his creation in such a way that the creation's being, character, and free choices are significant, although the gift of saving grace remains the work and choice of God alone.

Perhaps it is helpful to compare Thomas' teaching on predestination with his teaching on the efficacy of petitionary prayer.[48] In considering whether it is befitting for humans to pray, Aquinas first laid out three errors found in non-Christian or sub-Christian understandings of prayer. The first error is to hold that human affairs are not governed by divine providence; the second is that human affairs happen of necessity, either as a result of the changelessness of the divine providence or by other deterministic factors; the third is that the disposition of the divine providence is changeable, able to be influenced by prayers or rituals. God's providence, however, governs not just human affairs but also the entire universe. It is not mutable, for it is an aspect of the wisdom of God, which is not different from his being. Yet

45. Lonergan, *Grace and Freedom*, 106; Aquinas, *On Interpretation*, I, 14, 196; *ST* I 14.13 ad 2.

46. *ST* I 23.6, 8.

47. Lonergan, *Grace and Freedom*, 109; see *ST* III 46.2.

48. *ST* II–II 83.2.

Christian theology affirms both human freedom and that God hears our prayers in a way that is significant for what happens in history.

Thomas answered this conundrum in the following way.

> In order to throw light on this question we must consider that Divine providence disposes not only what effects shall take place, but also from what causes and in what order these effects shall proceed. Now among other causes human acts are the causes of certain effects. Wherefore it must be that men do certain actions, not that thereby they may change the Divine disposition, but that by those actions they may achieve certain effects according to the order of the Divine disposition: and the same is to be said of natural causes. And so is it with regard to prayer. For we pray not that we may change the Divine disposition, but that we may impetrate that which God has disposed to be fulfilled by our prayers in other words "that by asking, men may deserve to receive what Almighty God from eternity has disposed to give," as Gregory says (Dial. i, 8).[49]

Human prayers have a secondary kind of causality of the events for which we pray in that, through them, God has given us the gift of acting in concert with the divine causation of the universe. In prayer, we do not alter the divine intention for the world. But, God's intention for this world includes the operation of created free beings, that certain effects would be brought about with them and through them, and not without.

Because humans have a secondary, imperfect kind of causality for the events for which we pray, prayer is a cooperative grace.[50] Saving grace is operative, and it therefore does not include even imperfect human causation. Yet, if God's predestination of certain individuals to receive saving grace may be understood according to the analogy of a hypothetical necessity whose conditions are fulfilled by contingent means, this operative grace can be illuminated by the intelligibility of prayer. For, in this case, the necessity by which God causes our salvation is not necessary in transcendent terms, such as would apply to the procession of the Son from the Father in the transcendent necessity of God's being, nor is it necessary in created terms by absolute necessity, such as the necessity that attends purely physical processes in which human choice has no role. Rather, the choices of free beings are intrinsically included in the way that God chooses to elect.

49. Ibid.

50. *ST* II–II 83.1. Our causation of events prayed for is considered imperfect because our prayers are not in themselves sufficient to bring about the effects for which we pray, but we must depend on God.

According to this understanding of election, it is impossible for a human to lose the saving grace God bestows according to predestination; rather God gives the gift of perseverance to those he elects.[51] However, we must recall that God gives election not against human free choice, but *with it*. The choices thus indicated are not necessarily those of any one moment, but can indicate the shape of an entire life lived for or against God. For us within the temporal order, it remains a question as to whether God elects us or not.[52] Short of some specific revelation of one's salvific state, in this life we may answer this question only by faith, as we live out a life marked by the gift of charity, in hope of an eternal reward (Phil 3:7–16). In Christ, we may have great confidence that his faithfulness forgives and covers over what our broken human choices are able or unable to do, but we should not believe that the operation of his grace makes any choice we are able to make irrelevant with respect to salvation (2 Tim 2:8–13).

If the later Augustine could ask Thomas a question concerning this answer, perhaps it would be how any human choice could be a part of God's gift of saving grace; the good will by which we make any kind of meritorious choice is itself a result of God's grace, and not anything that could be a condition for receiving it. Thomas could answer this question in two ways. First, saving grace is an operative grace and dependent upon nothing except God's will. Human choices do not condition God's gift of saving grace, but rather God freely chooses to work through them. Second, the natural being we have is itself deeply graced, with the grace of rationality and free choice, given us by creation and not totally effaced by sin. Although entry into the supernatural order of being cannot be achieved through natural knowledge and choices, it is not the case that our natural knowledge and choices must be of *no* importance with respect to the supernatural order, nor is it the case that they must *all* be completely disordered and at enmity with God.

Maximus' understanding of "the eighth day of creation" coheres well with this explanation of Aquinas' views of election. According to Maximus' theology, the eighth day of creation symbolized final deification, in which we enter into the new life given to us by God after bodily resurrection. Deification, the defining characteristic and gift of the eighth day, is completely the work of grace. Just as the initial gift of being is not dependent on any merit in the created, so also those who are saved do not earn the gift of deification. Yet, God chooses to bestow this free grace upon those who have become adapted to choosing good and loving wisdom during "the seventh day of creation," which symbolizes the life of the present world. The gift of

---

51. *ST* I 23.6.

52. See Calvin, *Institutes*, 3.21.2; 4.1.2–3, 8; 4.12.9.

salvation is free and unconditioned, yet there is a relation between the free choices of the present age and the way God chooses to bestow that free gift.[53]

The Question of Hell

Thomas, in concert with the great majority of church tradition, maintained that while God predestines individuals for salvation, he does not predestine individuals for damnation.[54] In saying this, Aquinas affirmed that reprobation (the state of a person's being condemned to hell) is subject to God's knowledge, but that it is not the effect of God's causation. God does know who will be saved and who will be damned, but the cause of reprobation is the individual's own sins, not the eternal will of God.

Thomas' teaching on this subject is perhaps clearest in his commentary on Romans 9. Paul here clearly teaches that there is a priority of God with respect to both election and reprobation (Rom 9:11–16). Aquinas argues that with respect to reprobation, the priority has to do with God's knowledge of who will be damned, but that it cannot have to do with God's causing this damnation.[55] Sin, strictly speaking, is unintelligible, and has no cause.[56] It is a withdrawal from God's wisdom and a failure to choose what is good. There can be no sufficient reason for it; there is never a reason for sin that is good enough. But, God's (and any other kind) of causation has to do with sets of intelligible relations. God's reprobation, then, amounts not to God causing a person to sin, or to exist in a state of sin, but rather in God permitting that person to sin.

Thomas fleshes out this insistence by examining the case, raised by the Apostle, of Pharaoh, judged by God in the exodus. Paul, again, uses Pharaoh to exemplify the way that God moves human beings with respect to good and evil (Rom 9:17–18).

> However, He stirs them to good and to evil in different ways: for he inclines men's wills to good directly as the author of these good deeds; but he is said to incline or stir up men to evil as an occasional cause, namely, inasmuch as God puts before a person, either in him or outside of him something which of itself is conducive to good but which through his own malice he uses

---

53. Maximus, *Chapters on Knowledge*, 1.55.

54. *ST* I 23.3 ad 2; see, for example, *Second Council of Orange*; see Wawrykow, "Grace," 201–3.

55. Aquinas, *Romans*, c. 9, lect. 2 (sect. 764); c. 9, lect. 3 (sect. 781); see Lonergan, *Grace and Freedom*, 344.

56. See the discussion of *malum culpae* and of the ontology of evil in chapter 3.

for evil: "Do you not know that God's kindness is meant to lead you to repentance? But by your hard and impenitent heart you are storing up wrath for yourself on the day of wrath" (Rom 2:4–5) and "God gave his place for penance: and he abused it unto pride" (Jb 24:23).

Similarly, as far as in him lies, God enlightens a man inwardly to good, say a king to defend the rights of his kingdom or to punish rebels. But he abuses this good impulse according to the malice of his heart. This is plain in Is (10:6) where it is said of Assyria: "Against a godless nation I send him and against the people of my wrath I command him to take spoil and seize plunder . . ." and further on: "But he does not so intend, and his mind does not so think, but it is in his mind to destroy." That is the way it happened with Pharaoh, who, when he was prompted by God to defend his kingdom, abused this suggestion and practiced cruelty.[57]

With respect to the reprobate, the only thing God does toward them is that he lets them do what they want. What he provides for them is a situation, according to the divine intention, in which they may exercise free choice of the good. The choice of the reprobate, however, is against God's will, and God permits this evil choice.[58]

The judgment of the reprobate by God, in condemning them to hell, is then—paradoxically, but really—the gift to them of as much good as they are willing to receive.[59] Turning against the will and wisdom of God, the reprobate deserve nothing good in this world; God, however, continues to will for them the continued good of justice. In reprobation, he exercises retributive justice toward them on account of their sins (Rev 19:15).[60]

Thomas' teaching on hell raises a number of questions for the interpreter. First, if God knows those who will be condemned to hell, why does he bring any of them into existence? Second, because the Christian understanding of our final end includes only two options—either heaven or hell—does God's predestining of the elect effectively then include his predestining of the reprobate? Finally, given that what it means to be human is to be destined for union with God, does God's creation of an individual

57. Aquinas, *Romans*, c. 9, lect. 3 ad fin (sect. 781).

58. See lane three of the three-lane highway discussed in chapter 3, in which God permits, although he forbids, the choice of moral evil.

59. See Potts, "Aquinas, Hell," 341–50; see also the discussion of *malum poenae* in chapter 2.

60. Aquinas, *Romans*, c. 9, lect. 4 (sect. 793).

necessitate that he elect that person to salvation; in other words, will there, in fact, be any reprobate, or will every created human be saved?

With respect to the first question, it is the height of presumption to consider any person's existence and say that it is not worthwhile. How easily we play at being God in this case, and snuff people not just out of heaven, but also out of even the possibility of existence. Second, there is a goodness of God shown even to the reprobate that is beyond their deserts. For, to be a rational being, to have existence at all, and to experience justice, are all goods. They are all objectively infinitely superior to nothingness, whatever the subjective state that attends them. That the reprobate continue to have persistence of being, and an exalted kind of being at that, shows God's generosity.

With respect to the second question, if God's reprobation is not causal, and if his election is according to a hypothetical necessity that operates through free will, those who are created human are always created with an opportunity to live eternally with him. Both election and reprobation have a relation to our choices and deeds, although a different relation. That God creates us is a gift of an opportunity to live eternally, and that God knows the reprobate indicates that he gives this grace abundantly and freely, even to those he knows will choose to hold onto their sins instead of receiving eternal life from him.

The final question deals with universalism, but it is strange that it attends to an understanding of heaven and hell that speaks so highly of the importance of the individual's free will. For, universalism seems to insist on an assured result that no human choice could contravene. Even the later writings of Origen, who wrote so confidently of God's restoration of all created beings to himself, contains an awareness that there may be a limit to God's patience with evildoers.[61] The gift of rational being is the gift of the ability to make a choice. God's judgment in reprobation is the final affirmation of that gift, requiring the choices of rational beings to have significance.[62]

In this way, the question of salvation and damnation is reckoned, not according to the necessity of being, but according to the dynamics of personal love. Love requires a choice, and the choice can be for or against. God creates us with the intention of our having eternal relation with him, and his intention will be realized. What our choices affect, however, is the character of that relation.[63] We are offered relation to a divine lover, but we are also

61. See Heine, *Origen*, 239–40.

62. See VanArragon, "Freely Reject God," 29–43, for one consideration of what it might mean for a person freely and forever to reject God.

63. See Volk, *Historical Causality of Christ*, 83–84.

given the ability to refuse that. In that case, the reprobate do not lose relation with God absolutely, for that would mean to lose even the gift of being
itself.[64] Yet the character of being that they experience is that of those who
have refused the goal and ground of their being.

Such an understanding coheres with Kierkegaard's exposition of the
eternal state of despair in *Sickness Unto Death*.

> This is the state of despair. No matter how much the despairing
> person avoids it, no matter how successfully he has completely
> lost himself . . . eternity nevertheless will make it manifest that
> his condition was despair and will nail him to himself so that his
> torment will still be that he cannot rid himself of his self, and
> it will become obvious that he was just imagining that he had
> succeeded in doing so. Eternity is obliged to do this, because to
> have a self, to be a self, is the greatest concession, an infinite con-
> cession, given to man, but it is also eternity's claim upon him.[65]

Perdition means eternally receiving exactly the result of one's own choices,
and God's judgment upon the damned consists exactly of requiring those
choices to have meaning.[66]

One could continue to press this point by asking whether there is not
a wideness in God's mercy that would contravene his punishing even those
who reject him, for it is exactly mercy on those who reject him that we see in
the cross. Hans Urs von Balthazar strongly argues that the essence of Christianity is to hope all may be saved.[67] The New Testament states explicitly,
twice, that it is God's will everyone be saved (1 Tim 2:4; 2 Pet 3:9).[68]

Any Christian theologian must take with utmost seriousness the explicit scriptural statement of God's will. It is our Christian duty to align our
wills with the will of God, hoping that his mercy is very wide, indeed. One
must also maintain that there is no limit to God's ability to forgive sin.[69]
God expects us to forgive, without hesitation or reservation, and it would
be absurd to maintain that God holds humans to a moral standard he is
unable or unwilling to meet himself (Jer 31:34; Matt 6:12–15; 18:21–35; Eph
4:32; Col 3:13). Christ's work on the cross, furthermore, shows that God

---

64. See Stump, "The Problem of Evil," 397–405.

65. Kierkegaard, *Sickness unto Death*, 21.

66. See Simpson, *Truth Is the Way*, 123–24.

67. Von Balthazar, *Dare We Hope?*

68. See also John 3:15–16, as well as the many Old Testament passages pointing to
the universal intention of God's saving work (such as Gen 12:1–3).

69. *ST* III 46 2 re 3.

is not essentially wrathful, and that his justice and his forgiveness are not contradictory, but rather reinforce each other.[70]

If hell were only a question of punishment for those whose earthly lives warrant it, condemnation to hell could simply be replaced and resolved by the boundless mercy and forgiveness of God. But, if hell is a question of accepting or refusing a love relationship, such is not necessarily the case.[71] The offer of love by one party does not and cannot necessitate that the other party requite that love. In fact, the very offer of love by one party can even spur the other party on to greater hatred and rejection.

God does have the ability to change our hearts, replacing our hearts of stone with hearts of flesh, responsive to his will (Ezek 11:19; 36:26).[72] The result of that change, though, is to make the question of God a question that requires our decision.[73] In the work of his grace, God moves decisively to offer us relationship with him of supernatural love. This very move of grace, though, does not contravene our ability to make free choices, but rather empowers that freedom in a fuller and elevated way. The very meaning of the call of God, in which God offers himself to us and enlivens our hearts, is that we have to choose.

The Economy of Grace and Faith

This understanding of predestination and human freedom also raises the question of the relation of saving grace and faith. One of Augustine's essential insights is that our act of faith itself has an intimate relation to grace.[74] Aquinas' understanding of the nature of faith, and its place in the divine economy, helps shed light on this truth.

Aquinas follows Augustine in distinguishing three interconnected meanings of faith: believing God, believing in a God, and believing in God (*credere Deo, credere Deum et credere in Deum*).[75] In each of them, faith is an act of the intellect, but it is the kind of act in which the whole rational and volitional being of the one believing is involved.[76] Believing God (*credere Deo*) indicates assent to articles of the faith because one understands them to speak the truth about God. This aspect of faith includes the propositions

70. See the discussion of satisfaction in chapter 5.
71. See Lamont, "The Justice and Goodness of Hell."
72. See the discussion of religious conversion in chapter 6.
73. Lonergan, *Method*, 116.
74. See Levering, *Augustine*, 74–75.
75. *ST* II–II 2.2.
76. *ST* II–II 2.1; see Marshall, "*Quod Scit*," 13–14.

expressed in creeds and other formal expressions of faith, presented to us to believe. Believing in a God (the usual translation of *credere Deum*) means to believe in something for the sake of God, believing something about God, because one believes that the authority of God supports the truths presented for belief. This aspect of faith includes trust and commitment of the will; faith is not the kind of knowledge generated by the intellect alone, but we must commit ourselves to something of which we cannot have immanently generated certainly. Believing in God (*credere in Deum*) indicates the relationship a saved person has with the God she believes in. This aspect of faith is relational, indicating the way that we who believe rest in God, as both our present good and the source of our ultimate good in eternal life.

Believing in God (*credere in Deum*) constitutes saving faith, for it is only by the relationship of salvation that we truly abide in God; believing in God is therefore the essential ground of the other two senses. Just as in the three senses of grace, then, Aquinas' examination is holistic, considering the multifaceted way that God works in this world, but it is also essentially and unmistakably relational.[77] Both grace and faith ultimately indicate the dependence we have on the bountiful and free love of the God who finds us and takes us home.

Saving faith, just as saving grace, is the free gift of God (Eph 2:8–10). In Lonergan's theological transposition of Thomas' distinctions, God places us in the horizon of faith as a result of the gift of his love to us.[78] There is no cause within the created world that is proportionate to create this relationship, and the supernatural life that begins by this gift brings about the reorientation of our entire being, in relationship with God.[79] Just as with saving grace, the correct analogy to understand God's gift of saving faith is that of a hypothetical necessity that operates through contingency.

In considering the relation between grace and faith, though, it is helpful to distinguish between a metaphysical law and a norm. A metaphysical law is a principle or set of understandings that admit no exceptions or variation.[80] A norm, on the other hand, is a standard that gives meaning to the variegated nature that occurs.

In Christian theology, for example, creation out of nothing is a metaphysical law. There are no exceptions to creation out of nothing; if one could

77. See the discussion of dispositional, operative, and cooperative grace in chapter 3.

78. Lonergan, *Method*, 115–16.

79. See Cone, "Transforming Desire," 153–87; for an explanation of the relation of Thomas' and Lonergan's uses of "faith," see Cone, "Aquinas' Sanctifying Grace and Lonergan's Religious Conversion."

80. Lonergan, "The Supernatural Order," 251.

find even one thing that is neither created by God, nor God himself (who is uncreated), then one would have disproved the doctrine of creation out of nothing. Even one exception would indicate that the principle itself is invalid and needs to be reformulated to account for the data.

Norms operate on different terms. Norms are standards that help us understand the variation we encounter. The metric measure of a liter is a norm. It has a precisely defined intelligibility: the amount of fluid contained by one thousand cubic centimeters. This meaning is intrinsic to its existence and does not vary. But the purpose of the defined intelligibility is to allow one to meaningfully assess varying volumes of fluid.

In the economy of grace and faith, grace operates with the necessity appropriate for a metaphysical law. If we are not saved by the grace of Jesus, we will not be saved at all (Acts 4:12). There are no exceptions to this; even to posit one would be to discount the sufficiency and necessity of Christ's work of redemption.

It may be better, however, to see faith as operating according to the necessity of a norm, not that of a metaphysical law. There is a necessity to faith (Heb 11:6). This is to say, whenever God saves someone by grace, he always does so by bringing that person into a relationship with himself. This relationship also must have some kind of intellectual content, for faith cannot be entirely implicit.[81] Normatively, that content begins with trusting in Jesus alone for salvation and in affirming the central truths of the Christian faith, based on the authority of the God who reveals.[82] This is what it means to come alive in Christ, and the life of Christ is exactly a life that lives out these truths, always and forever relying on and permeated by God's grace.[83] Eternal life, in fact, has already begun in the one who truly believes (John 11:25–27).[84]

Yet, if faith has necessity as a norm, the meaning of this standard of faith—lived out by the heroes of the faith and ultimately referred to the human nature of Christ himself—is to allow one to understand and assess in a reasonable way the different forms God might choose and work through in bringing a person into saving relationship with himself. If faith operates as a norm, a lack of or defect in faith would not necessarily condemn to hell someone like an infant who dies during childbirth. In fact, one could see a

---

81. Lonergan, "Analysis of Faith," 457–59.

82. Such as set forth by the Nicene Creed or the Apostles Creed, themselves crystallizations of the message of Scripture.

83. Note the great variety of life-forms and explicit commitments exhibited by those praised by the author of Hebrews 11 for their faith.

84. See ST II–II 4.1.

reasonable account of why faith was impossible or hindered for such a one, and great reason to hope in God's grace.

This distinction may also shed light on the question of inclusivism. Inclusivists ask whether we may hope that Christ's saving grace (for there is no other kind) will be applied to at least some adherents of non-Christian religions, or whether all members of the world religions are inevitably damned. Inclusivism has often been seen as reducing the importance of Christ's cross, looking for salvation based on some other means than faith in him, and blunting the evangelistic fervor of the church. The New Testament clearly teaches against any of these effects (John 3:15–21; 1 Cor 1:18–23; Matt 28:18–20).

If faith operates as a norm, however, in the economy grounded by the metaphysical law of God's grace, then it may be that God would have some way of assessing those without explicit Christian commitment. If this assessment is made according to the norm of faith, it would not mean that God is "getting around" faith to save someone, but that some response to God's mercy, offered in a person's life, coheres in some way known to God with the meaning of faith.

An imperfect example of this coherence may perhaps be seen in the Old Testament saints. Hebrews 11 tells us of their great faith, yet 1 Pet 1:12 tells us that they did not know the full intelligibility of Christ. These individuals lived before Christ's coming, and it is strongly argued by Augustine that they participated in the grace of Christ, given in a preparatory, incomplete, but real way.[85] In other words, those were heroes of faith who responded to what God offered them with what they had, in the terms they could know, leading up to Christ. If the inclusivist hope has a truly Christian form, it will exactly be that truth given to adherents of other faiths and responses they give to God's work will connect them—in a way made effective by God's mercy—with the fullness of truth and salvation in Christ.

It is by no means certain that God's mercy will be offered in this way. It is abundantly clear from the New Testament that there is great importance in knowing Jesus, and that coming to trust in him explicitly is nothing less than moving from death to life (John 20:31; Acts 16:31; Rom 8:10, 10:9; 2 Tim 1:10; 1 John 3:14). Yet, as God wills the salvation of all, again, it is a Christian attitude to expect those among whom we minister to be ones in whom the Holy Spirit has been at work, preparing them and pointing them to Christ, and to hope that God's mercy to them extends beyond human understanding, even to eternal life, found in Christ (1 Tim 2:4; 2 Pet 3:9; Acts 17:27–28). Such an understanding of inclusivism would not, then,

---

85. Augustine, *Against Two Letters of the Pelagians*, 1.12, 3.13.

blunt evangelistic fervor, for those doing the work of evangelism would have confidence that they are doing the work of the God who has gone before them, and that in the explicit offer of Christ there is the fullness and certainty of hope that can come in no other way.

If this analysis of grace and faith is correct, then it seems that in Eph 2:8–10, the Apostle Paul offers accounts of two different economies: one of grace and faith, one of works and boasting. He declares the latter to be a bankrupt economy, for no created being can claim (boast) that God is obliged to save her. Yet, the economy of grace and faith is abundant and rich in true life. To live out faith is to bring into existence a life of good works, which God has prepared beforehand for us to walk in. This life of good works is itself cooperation with God's grace, founded on his free and abundant gift to us, due to his great love for us.

Conclusion

God alone, then, is the cause of salvation, from first to last (Eph 2:8–9). The economy of grace by which God calls us includes the choices of good that we make, and does not exist apart from those choices (Eph 2:10). God alone regenerates our hearts, making us pleasing to him (Rom 5:5). This regeneration is given in concert with, and not without, our perseverance and the development of our character into the character of Christ (Rom 5:1–4).

Because God has eternal being, and because creation, in its every detail, depends on him, God knows intimately and absolutely those who will be saved (John 2:24–25; 10:23). This knowledge does not mean that the events and outcomes of our lives are set, and that we move deterministically toward them (Deut 30:15–20). We are called to exercise genuine and significant moral choice (Josh 24:15; John 5:24). But, because of God's eternal mode of being, that which is future and indeterminate in its own terms is present and known to him (Isa 46:10).

God's knowledge has a causal relation with this world, however, only in concourse with the divine will (Isa 46:11). God exercises the sovereignty of his will over creation in order to predestine and save (Rom 8:29). The good works we do and the good choices we make are not a cause of God's predestination or election (Rom 5:6). But, God sovereignly chooses to elect along with the motion of our free will, and not without or against it, working through the economy of grace and faith (Rom 9:32–33).

Reprobation does not result from the will of God but from the will of the sinner (Acts 13:46). Predestination and election, then, apply only to the gift of eternal life (Acts 13:48). Although Christian theology must resolutely conform itself to God's universal salvific will, it is necessary to acknowledge that this very gift of God requires of us a choice (2 Pet 3:8–13). The reprobation of the damned, then, is the gift of justice to those who have rejected the source of every good gift (Rom 2:12–15).

5

The Power and Wisdom of God

THE CROSS

Jesus Christ crucified is the heart of Christian understanding and hope. The proclamation that the very Lord was crucified formed the climax of the church's first sermon and the foundational conviction of the greatest apostle (Acts 2:36; 1 Cor 1:22–24). It is on this basis that we have peace with God, the forgiveness of sins, and entry into eternal life.

In the cross, we find the center of the meaning of the world, that in which all the divine economies are drawn together, and that by which they are all propelled toward their culmination. Because, as Irenaeus argued, there are many particular economies composing the one great economy of God, we find in the cross a great wealth of meanings by which we may approach this cardinal work of God. None of them will exhaust the work by which Christ saves us, and all of our approximations of them will in some measure fall short.

I will explore the meaning of the cross using five analogies: satisfaction, sacrifice, moral communication, ransom, and recapitulation. By offering satisfaction for sins, Christ vicariously achieved what we could not and averted the punishment that was due us. By sacrificing himself for us, Christ overturns the dark logic of this world and covers over our sins, mediating between God and us. By communicating to us God's love and our own true human nature, Christ transforms our moral being in concert with the work of the Holy Spirit. By offering himself as our ransom, Christ fulfills the law of the Father, and by persuasion and conquest, overcomes the evil in us and in our enemy. By recapitulating human existence in himself, Christ redefines and completes the human story, passing through death to resurrection.

A Meaning that Changes History

If Christ crucified is the wisdom of God, we should not expect any single human understanding to capture the totality of this meaning. But, we should expect, in the cross, to find a meaning. And, if Christ crucified is the power of God, we should expect to find in it the way God's wisdom transforms history. For, by his might God brings to pass on the earth what his heavenly council has long decreed. Bernard Lonergan captures this two-sided coin by speaking of the intelligibility of the cross and of the way that, by the cross, Christ works redemption in human history.

One of the more controversial questions about the cross is the degree and kind of necessity that attends it. If in the cross we have the central meaning of history, is the cross something God chose by necessity, given the nature and composition of this world? Lonergan here agrees with Augustine and Aquinas in stating that there were many ways that, given his decision to create this world, God could have chosen to save.[1] Aquinas' analysis is especially interesting on this point, arguing that given God ordained Christ would suffer, Christ necessarily went to the cross. This is, however, a hypothetical necessity operating through contingent causes, dependent on this supposition of God's free choice. So, the Lamb was slain from before the foundation of the world, but the necessity of his sacrifice does not come from any kind of requirement inherent in this world or in God, but only from the free and wise choice of God's love. God could have saved in many ways, but thought it best—most wise and fitting—to save by a cross.[2] In the cross, then, we have an intelligibility, but one that expresses God's wisdom, not a necessity.

Lonergan, furthermore, argues that the meaning we find in the cross is dynamic.[3] By this he means we will in this regard approach it best not by analogy with logical syllogisms, in which input closely correlates with output, but by seeing its dialectical character: namely, its ability to envision and bring about the reversal of roles. In the cross, death brings forth life, as evil is swallowed up in victory (1 Cor 15:54–57). The meaning of the cross, then, is a transformative one that overturns, by God's seeming foolishness and weakness, the so-called strength and wisdom of this world (1 Cor 1:18–25).

In his later great work, *Method in Theology*, Lonergan explains the meanings present in human existence by a number of interlocking "realms"

---

1. Lonergan, *The Divine Redeemer*, 148–50; "On Redemption," 3; Augustine, *The Trinity*, 8.10; *ST* III 46.2.

2. Whether this analysis truly departs from Anselm's argument in *Cur Deus Homo* will be examined below.

3. Lonergan, "On Redemption," 4.

of meaning.[4] The greatest and most-encompassing of these is incarnate meaning, which speaks of the meaning of a person, not in any particular word or aspect, but in his entire life.[5] In the cross, we assuredly find an incarnate meaning.[6] "Christ crucified is a symbol of endless meaning, and it is not only a symbol but also a real death."[7] The meaning of the cross, then, includes not just Christ's soul or spirit but also his very flesh, along with all the complex relations among the different aspects of his personal reality.

The meaning we find in the cross, although springing ultimately from the wisdom of God, also includes the (un-)reality of sin.[8] Because sin is simply unintelligible—there never is a reason good enough for it—the meaning of the cross will be what Lonergan terms "complex." His intention in using this word is to make an analogy with the way mathematicians create "complex numbers" by combining real numbers and imaginary numbers (such as the square root of -1). What Lonergan intends to communicate with this analogy is that because redemption involves sin, the meaning of the cross will not consist of "a simple intelligibility but of the transcendent intelligibility of God meeting the unintelligibility of sin."[9] God's wisdom can encompass the relation of intelligible causes and the strict privation of meaning we find in true evil; that fact does not render evil itself intelligible, and the meaning of the cross will include that complex relationship.

One of the results of this complex intelligibility, and also of the superabundant nature of God's wisdom, is that no single analogy or explanation for the cross will succeed in totally communicating its meaning.[10] Hence, the meaning of the cross will be a multiple one.[11] That is, we will be able to communicate different aspects of the meaning of the cross through different analogies, but we will not be able to form a grand unified theory of the cross, the one master analogy that includes or subjugates all the others. It should be possible to show that the meanings of the different analogies do not contradict each other, but not one of them will be able to totally subsume the others.

We should not, therefore, expect each of the analogies to be equally useful in explaining all the different aspects of the cross. Each of them has

4. Lonergan, *Method*, 81–85.

5. Ibid., 85.

6. Lonergan, "On Redemption," 10–11.

7. Ibid., 10.

8. Ibid., 12.

9. Ibid.

10. See also Baker, "How the Cross Saves," 45–46, and Lossky, *Orthodox Theology*, 110–12.

11. Lonergan, "On Redemption," 13.

questions or insights on which it centers, and each of them will not provide equally satisfactory answers for the kinds of questions it is not centrally considering. Again, the intelligibility of the cross is not like that of a logical deduction, in which all the parts have necessity in a chain of premises and conclusions, but it is the intelligibility of a factual event, the choice of God's wisdom, given for the salvation of the world.

The meaning of the cross is something operative in and transformative of human history. Lonergan's analysis of history deals especially with what was "going forward."[12] That is, beyond the forces of personal and cultural inertia, what are the ways that human freedom, operative in the presence or absence of intelligence and love, is changing the world? But in the cross, we paradoxically see the greatest freedom combined with the fruit of a wisdom and a love that are greater than this world (John 10:17–18). Lonergan saw this victory that overcomes the world to be especially encapsulated by what he calls the Law of the Cross, and we will examine what he means by that both in this chapter's discussion of the moral analogy and in chapter 6's discussion of salvation. Put briefly, the Law of the Cross is the way the mission of the incarnate Word introduces hope and new life into the world.

Satisfaction for Sins

In his theological masterpiece, *Cur Deus Homo*, Anselm of Canterbury explored the question of "for what cause or necessity, in sooth, God became man, and by his own death, as we believe and affirm, restored life to the world; when he might have done this, by means of some other being, angelic or human, or merely by his will."[13] The meaning of "cause or necessity" in this question is by no means easy to parse.[14] Anselm had no disciples who were theologians to comment on his work, and he did not produce commentaries on his own work.

If we read Anselm's account carefully, the basis or mechanism of the "necessity" of which he speaks is time and again referred at its most crucial points to the divine love and compassion, and to what is fitting for this wise, just, and compassionate God.[15] It would be a strikingly different analysis if the logic of love were removed—in fact, one that bears no resemblance to

12. Lonergan, *Method*, 178.

13. Anselm, *Cur Deus Homo*, 1.1.

14. Lonergan, "On Redemption," 8.

15. See, for example, Anselm, *Cur Deus Homo*, 1.12; 1.15; 1.21; 1.23; 1.25; 2.16; 2.20; see also Johnson, "A Fuller Account," 304–5n7, on fittingness in Anselm *versus* in Aquinas.

what Anselm did in fact argue. He knew very well and expressed explicitly that God is not subject to any kind of compulsion. Therefore, instead of looking at Anselm's logic of the incarnation, and the atonement theology that attends it, as the way God adhered to a required standard, internal or external, it is better to see it as the way divine rationality and love receive ultimate expression in the world.

Satisfying God's Justice

Anselm explained the "necessity" of the incarnation in relation to our salvation. In the beginning, God created humans in a state of original righteousness (justice), with the goal of bringing humanity into an even greater state of eternal blessedness and communion with himself. Both the original righteousness and the intended eternal blessedness were contingent on our being obedient to God. Everything, however, did not go well. Through disobedience, humans introduced disorder and un-wisdom into the universe.[16]

To explain our problem, and the wonderful nature of God's solution, Anselm used an analogy with the world he knew, that of medieval European society. His analogy revolved around "honor," which was the basis of the feudal bonds that held together his civilization. According to his analogy, human sin is an offense against the honor of God, whom he pictures as an infinitely great king.

Honor, in Anselm's society, had to do with a person's right to exist in the capacity in which they held. Offending the honor of a king, for instance, was to act as if and thereby claim that the king had no right to be king, that the king should not exist in that society as king. To offend against the honor of God is to say that we, not God, will be God.

But, God's place in the order of creature and Creator is, in actuality, absolutely secure. While the "currency" of Anselm's analysis is the divine honor, he is also explicit that God's own honor can neither increase nor decrease due to any factor whatsoever.[17] Human disobedience does not damage God's honor, because it cannot be damaged. What it damages is us disobedient ones. That we give God right honor means that we exist in the universe as rightly related to him, and we cannot exist in justice with God while ourselves being unjust. But existing in right relation with God is intrinsic to and constitutive of eternal blessedness, for which gift we are created. God's eternal plans (making us for blessedness and communion

---

16. Anselm, *Cur Deus* Homo, 1.15.
17. Ibid.

with God), therefore, seemed frustrated by the factual character of his creation—an untenable situation.

The power of Anselm's analogy comes to the fore when he explores the question of how God's wisdom can overcome this dire situation. He sets up two questions dealing with the relation of human sin and God's justice: first, could God not just forgive humans, thereby solving the problem; second, if it is not fitting for God just to forgive us, is there any other solution to the problem than a retributive justice that eternally punishes us? Notice that neither of these questions inherently opposes God's justice and his gracious nature. What is questioned is whether either simple forgiveness or the punishment that attends retributive justice are appropriate (fitting) answers to the human situation and the wisdom of the just and loving God.

Anselm argues that it is not fitting for God simply to forgive sinners out of compassion because that would be contrary to his honor; however, if read carefully, Anselm's point is that if God were merely to forgive us, without the incarnation, it would not be for our ultimate good. Restoring us without satisfaction made by the God-man would be a false compassion.[18] There would be no real change in the status of any member of the human race with respect to the conditions of eternal blessedness, a state that requires not only an absence of punishment but also the reestablishment of a right relationship of humans with God.[19]

With respect to punishment, Anselm argues that there is a greater justice of God, established and declared by the incarnation, than the punishment that attends retributive justice. Within Anselm's feudal society—the basis of the analogy he is explaining—an unjust offense against a person's honor could be dealt with in more than one way. It would be possible, and just, for the offended party to demand retributive justice that would punish the offender for her crime. However, it would also be just, instead of demanding punishment, for the offended party to accept an offer of satisfaction.[20]

For an offender to make satisfaction for an offense is to offer the offended party something of greater worth—something more pleasing to the offended party—compared to the gravity of the offense. Herein lies a problem, however: all of creation pales in significance compared to the honor of God offended by sin. Humans have nothing to offer God in satisfaction that is adequate.[21] Because God is an infinitely great king, the least aspect of his will is of greater value than all of creation. Sin, therefore, deserves an infinitely great punishment (given in retributive justice). A life of suffering, and

18. Ibid., 1.24.
19. Ibid., 1.20–21.
20. Ibid., 1.15.
21. Ibid., 1.20.

physical death followed by eternal damnation in hell does not completely reach up to the gravity of offending the honor of God. Of ourselves, we can only await this punishment, for we have no satisfaction to offer.

The good offered for satisfaction, in this case, must be of infinite worth. God, of course, has himself the ability to make this satisfaction—his worth is infinite, as are his resources. However, it is not right for God, in his own terms alone, to make the satisfaction; he is not the one who committed the offense.[22] Anselm's famous solution is that if God took on human nature, the God-man would have the resources to make satisfaction (being God) and would have the right to make satisfaction (being human).[23]

However, there is a further difficulty, even if Christ, the God-man, should come to exist. As human, Christ owed to God perfect obedience (just as every other human). Everything he could ever do in life was already owed to God (if you know to do good, and do it not, that is sin—Jas 4:17). What, then, could even Christ offer to make the satisfaction?

Because Christ was human, he owed God everything in his life. But, because he was sinless, he therefore did not owe God a death, for death is the wages of sin (Rom 6:23). So, if Christ would willingly accept death on behalf of a helpless humankind, that would be something he could offer to God to make satisfaction. And, in fact, it would be something of infinite worth—the life of the incarnate God.[24]

By this analysis, it is quite important for Anselm that Christ's death on the cross was not a mere act of obedience.[25] Being a monk, bishop, and theologian, he knew very well the New Testament scriptures describing Christ's death exactly as an act of obedience (Heb 5:8; Phil 2:8). His point, however, is that Christ's death must be something he freely chose, not merely something he was compelled to do, of obligation, by the Father. Otherwise, it would fall under the rubric of "what is owed God," on the basis of which no satisfaction may be offered. The way Anselm pictured Christ's obedience unto death, therefore, was not as someone who receives an order that he is under compulsion to follow, but as someone who follows—by free will and out of love—an agreed-upon plan he is given to complete.[26]

The rationale of Anselm's analogy strongly opposes the punishment of retributive justice to the satisfaction made by Christ; according to the justice of Anselm's society, one could choose satisfaction *or* punishment in response to an offense, and could not justly choose both. According to Anselm, the

22. Ibid., 2.6.

23. Ibid.

24. Ibid., 2.10.

25. Ibid.

26. Anselm, *Cur Deus Homo* 1.9–10; 2.17; see also *ST* III 47 2 re 1.

cross is *not* a punishment, but rather it is the good by which Christ offers satisfaction to God for our sins.[27] This does not mean that retributive justice has no place in the cross. It is not the retribution of punishment, however, but rather that of reward. Retribution pays back what is owed, and Christ's work on our behalf—a great good that went beyond anything he was required to do—deserves a payment of great merit. Being perfect, Christ did not need the reward of his good work for himself. Therefore, out of love, he asked that it be credited to our account, as satisfaction for our sins.[28]

That Christ satisfies the honor of God means he fully acknowledges and credits God with being God. In so doing, he stands as a member of the human race, so right relationship with God may be reintroduced into the human race. Because temptation was not able to win over Christ, human nature was not entirely conquered and abolished by our choice of disobedience and our consequent injustice. To enter into an eternal blessedness while being in fact a miserable and unjust creature is a contradiction in terms, and that is exactly the state humans would have been in had God merely forgiven and not made satisfaction through the incarnation. But because of the work of Christ, the real status of humans can change. The "debt" we owe to God in Anselm's analogy is a stand-in concept for the obedience of secure right relationship with God. Because of the death of Christ, the universe is different, and we are different, that we may be effective in giving this obedience, in being in this right relationship, that leads to eternal life.

The counterpart of retributive justice is distributive justice.[29] Distributive justice has to do with the right arrangement of a society, or by analogy, of whatever whole is being contemplated. Distributive justice is more fundamental than retributive justice, for it is only in the context of a society that the rights and wrongs accounted for by retribution may be given their appropriate measure. In his *Cur Deus Homo*, Anselm shows that the grace of God and his justice are friends. Rather than measure out punishment to us for our sins, God fulfills the requirements of retributive justice (by accepting satisfaction and awarding merit) in a way that shows the wisdom of his providence, declaring in the cross a distributive justice that gives life by overcoming evil and sin.

This is the justice of God that Anselm extols, the expression of the divine wisdom that justifies sinners, giving his own righteousness to them by joining to them in Christ, that they may become joined to him in eternal fellowship; God's relentless pursuit of this justice does not stop until we are

27. Anselm, *Cur Deus Homo* 1.15.

28. Ibid. 2.19–20.

29. Aristotle, *Nicomachean Ethics*, 5.2; *ST* II–II 61.1.

fully and truly restored.[30] The cross does not result from a legal necessity balancing God's justice against his desire to forgive. Rather, the cross is the declaration of the Father's justice—the right arrangement of the universe—in which his love is made manifest as the righteous God-man's performing for us what we could not do; giving to the Father what we owe, rightly because he is one of us, and perfectly because he is himself God.

God and Violence: First Reflection

Anselm's analogy raises a number of questions that he did not deal with completely in his work. First, how could a violent murder satisfy God? Second, how could someone else's actions have moral worth for us? Finally, is it right to exclude the notion of punishment completely from our account of the cross?

Peter Abelard strongly protested against Anselm's satisfaction analogy, arguing that Christ's violent death was the worst crime ever committed, and that such an offense, rather than satisfying God, was repugnant to God.[31] A number of modern scholars, particularly Anabaptist and feminist theologians, have also argued that Anselm's solution seems to conceive God as a wrathful being who loves violence.[32] It is the case that, in the logic of Anselm's analogy, that which is offered to God must be something pleasing—in fact, infinitely pleasing—to him, else no satisfaction may be made. How, though, could a violent and unjust death serve to please God?

In his multifaceted analysis of the atonement, Aquinas offers an insight that helps solve this quandary. The murder of Christ was an offense against God and did not please God. However, Christ's perfect willingness to sacrifice himself on our behalf was pleasing to God, and that made the satisfaction.[33]

This willingness of Christ was his willingness to say, "Yes," in the actual deliberation of accepting the death of the cross. It was not a hypothetical consideration. His being willing to make satisfaction intrinsically included the actuality of his death: not just Gethsemane, but also Golgotha, for the "Yes" was not complete until he gave up his spirit into the Father's hands. The murder of Christ was an evil, and neither injustice nor violence pleases God. Yet, Christ's great love for us, the attitude by which he cared more

30. Anselm, *Cur Deus Homo*, 1.24.

31. Abelard, *Romans*, 2.2.

32. See, for example, Weaver, "Violence in Christian Theology," 155–59, and Ruether, *Introducing Redemption*, 97–100.

33. *ST* III 48.2.

for our good than for his own situation, and in which he was willing to surrender his life, is cherished by God and rewarded by him as the greatest possible human good (John 15:13; Phil 2:5–11).

Lonergan's analysis of the goods and evils in the cross also helps to bring precision to our understanding of how, exactly, God was pleased by the cross.

> God in no way wills the moral evil, but merely lets it be done; therefore neither directly nor indirectly did God will the formal element of the formal sin of those who hated and killed Christ. God does will the evil of natural defects and the evil of punishment, not directly, of course, since the object of the will is good, but indirectly inasmuch as he intends and cares for the good of universal order. The evils inflicted upon Christ, therefore, insofar as they were the consequences of sin, were only indirectly willed by God. On the other hand, God does directly will a good and holy will, and so God directly willed the acceptance of suffering and death on the part of the obedient Christ. Moreover, actions that are in accordance with the precepts of the Gospels are virtuous. Now the Gospel rejects the law of retaliation, *lex talionis*, commands love of one's enemies (Matthew 5.38–48), and praises the suffering of evil for the sake of justice (Matthew 5.10–12); hence St Peter proposes the sufferings and death of Christ as examples for us to follow (1 Peter 2.19–24). The whole of Christ's passion and death, therefore, inasmuch as it proceeded from the gentle and humble Christ, was directly willed by God.[34]

The evil wills of those who betrayed, deserted, falsely tried, and killed Christ, then, and their evil deeds consequent upon that bad will, were instances of moral evil. God never wills moral evil (*malum culpae*, analogous to the third lane of the highway discussed in chapter 3), but does not entirely stop it from occurring. The suffering of Christ, a *malum poenae* (the evil from which we suffer, analogous to the second lane of the highway), was willed by God only insofar as he willed Christ's participation in a greater good, even in the face of moral evil. The good will by which Christ accepted suffering and death, however, was both a particular good and also the very foundation of this whole universe's good of order—the heart of the divine economy. Analogous to the first lane of the highway, this great good was directly willed by God and made satisfaction for sins.[35]

34. Lonergan, *The Divine Redeemer*, 105–6.
35. See Miller, "Why the Passion?" 214–17.

By this analysis, one may note the great difference between the wholeness of personhood by which Christ voluntarily proceeded to the cross and the loss of personhood implied by cycles of abuse. What was pleasing to God was Christ's perfect will, in which his human will perfectly cohered with his divine will. A good will is a reflection of the ultimate rightness of being in a person, for we find the completion and fullness of freedom by being rightly in relation to God. A situation in which a person, due to violence, loses rightness of being is not analogous to Christ's satisfaction but is one of the evils Christ died to save us from. It is not violence that pleases God, but a heart that is both free and upright.

Aristotle categorized violent motion as that kind of change that takes place against something's nature.[36] While his analysis of physics has been superseded, it is helpful for understanding something of the way that violence is destructive relative to human nature and existence. Humans have a natural motion, a vector given them to change into the likeness of God. This vector involves our growth as attentive, intelligent, reasonable, responsible, and loving beings. Violence works to impose limits on that growth, or to contradict it. By choosing moral evil, we do great violence to ourselves by turning away from right relationship with God. By being subject to penal evil—the evil from which we suffer—we are given a choice either to transcend that suffering or to accept its wrongness as an aspect of our being. The evil of violence is imposing on another person, or on ourselves, such a propulsive force away from the fulfillment of our being.

Even in his exercise of retributive justice on evildoers, though, God is demanding of them that they participate in some aspect of the good for which they are made. Rather than turning them away from their true natures—they have made that choice themselves, by choosing moral evil, and we all to some extent do the same—God insists that they participate in the good of his divine ordering of the universe; this is the good according to which our natures exist and toward which they naturally tend.

The violence in God's judgment of evil, then, is performed by the evildoers themselves, upon themselves, not by God. Turning to evil means to turn away from our own natures, for we are created good and for good. What God gives to evildoers is participation in the good, in which he demands participation in the gift of having a self and a God-given nature, either by receiving the punishment of retributive justice or by receiving redemption that restores us to ourselves and to God. The function of God's wrath, then, is to bring us to account for the gift of creation if we will not accept his redemption (Matt 25:14–30), not to turn us away from our true

36. Aristotle, *Physics*, 5.6.

selves (Luke 8:16–18). God does not model violence for us, then, but rather calls us to self-transcendence in love (Rom 5:1–5).

Moral Good from a Friend

The second question Anselm's analogy must face is how Christ's action can solve a moral problem we have with God. Can one person truly act in a way that has moral significance for another? As Western individualists, recovering from the Enlightenment, this question gives us great difficulty. Immanuel Kant flatly denied that it is possible.[37] We see our true selves as closed in on ourselves and isolated: me—myself—alone.

The ancient world, to the contrary, saw people as fundamentally connected. Who we are is really and essentially bound up with other people, with whom we share life. Lonergan is again worth quoting at length on this matter.

> So it is that a friend is said to be one's alter ego;[38] and Augustine in the *Confessions* exclaims, "Well has someone said of his friend that he is 'half of his soul.'"[39] As to the greatness and excellence of Christ's love for us, he himself has given ample testimony by his deeds and also in his words: "There is no greater love than this, to lay down one's life for one's friends" (John 15.13). . . .
>
> Now if between husband and wife and between friends "all mine is yours and all yours is mine" (see John 17.10), how could it be otherwise than that Christ should make our cross his own? So thoroughly did he do so, in fact, that we forget it is our cross and usually refer simply to "the cross of Christ." But in point of fact it is through the mystery of the cross that sinners are to come into friendship with God. Christ, however, was sinless (1 Peter 2.22) and a stranger to sin (2 Corinthians 5.21), tempted in every way as we are, though without sin (Hebrews 4.15); he was a holy priest, innocent, unsullied, set apart from sinful men and, while not needing to offer sacrifice for his own sins (Hebrews 7.26–27), offered himself to God as a pure and spotless lamb (1 Peter 1.19). Thus did he make his own a cross that was not his. He knew well that we are taught more effectively by example than by precept. And this also he knew, that "if I am lifted up from the earth, I will draw all people to myself" (John 12.32). In this way, then, he not only assimilated and united himself to

---

37. Kant, *Religion within the Limits of Reason Alone*, 48–49.

38. Aristotle, *Nicomachean Ethics*, 9.4.

39. Augustine, *Confessions*, 4.6; see *ST* I–II 28.1.

us, but in a most compelling manner invited us into assimilation
and union with him.[40]

Therefore, we who were enemies of God are brought into peace with God
through the actions of one who came to be our closest and truest friend,
who laid down his life for us. We are saved not as isolated selves—for that is
not who we are—but in communion with the Friend of Sinners, our Savior.

Satisfaction or Punishment

The final question Anselm's analogy must face is whether it is right to exclude
the notion of punishment entirely from our understanding of the cross.
While *Cur Deus Homo* addresses a great number of issues and Scriptures
in its treatment of the atonement, there is no discussion or explanation of
Isaiah 53. While some later Western theologians did follow Anslem in arguing that the cross is not a punishment, most others followed the traditional
language and logic that included punishment. However, in Anselm's logic,
Christ's vicarious satisfaction, made for us, absolutely excludes punishment;
to accept satisfaction and give punishment, too, would be unjust, for exactly
in accepting the satisfaction a just judge is laying aside punishment.

In this question itself, there are three significant points to consider.
First, what, specifically, is intended by "punishment"? Second, is God essentially wrathful such that he has to punish sin? Finally, is there any relation of
punishment with the cross?

Christ's death was certainly a *malum poenae*, an example of the evil
from which we suffer as a consequence of some sin.[41] But, not every *malum
poenae*, or penal evil, is an example of a person's being punished by God.
Some is just the result of being in the wrong place at the wrong time, and
much other penal evil indicates suffering the result of another person's sin.
However, much Christian tradition does understand the cross to be a punishment of Christ *by God*.

Just punishment normally indicates having suffering imposed upon
a person for two possible reasons: either as a wrongdoer receiving punishment as retributive justice, or as someone otherwise in need of amendment,
for whom the punishment is therapeutic of one's character.[42] The former
instance refers to a specific wrong action that deserves punishment, while
the second refers to discipline for the improvement of one's soul. Christ,

40. Lonergan, *The Divine Redeemer*, 155–56.

41. See the "three-lane highway" discussion of chapter 3.

42. Lonergan, *The Divine Redeemer*, 166–67.

however, was not a wrongdoer, nor did his character need improvement. It remains to be seen, however, whether there is any third sense of punishment that rightly applies to Christ, or any way that one of the first two senses can somehow be applied to him.

Punishment has connection with the wrath of God (Num 16:46; Deut 9:8; Ps 38:1; Isa 13:9; Rom 2:5; Eph 5:6). Wrath, however, cannot be an eternal—that is, essential—aspect of the character of God. God's character is not different from his being, and there is no eternal reality except God himself. For wrath to be an eternal aspect of the character of God, there would need to be an appropriate expression of wrath among the immanent Trinitarian persons. That means there would need to be some right and appropriate use of wrath from the Father to the Son or Spirit, from the Spirit to the Father or Son, from the Son to the Father or Spirit, or for all of the above, just as there is a mutual interpenetration of wisdom and love. This wrathful expression would need to attend eternal, not temporal reality. Because wrath only rightly attends to some situation or aspect of wrong, to affirm wrath as an aspect of God's eternal character would therefore be to deny the goodness of God, either by saying that there is wrong in one (or more) of the persons of God to which wrath can rightly attach, or by saying that God is inappropriately wrathful.

God's wrath, then, is an external (*ad extra*) relation. It reflects God's eternal character, but it is not part of it. Aquinas saw it as reflecting God's justice with respect to those who are disobedient.[43] It is important to note, however, that God is simple, not divided against himself, and it would be inappropriate to suggest that wrath reflects God's justice in a way that is opposed to, exclusive of, or lacking with respect to his love. Justice and love cannot compete in God because there is no real distinction between them. They are both ways that we complex and developing beings understand the one, eternal, and simple substance of God.

God's love and his wrath function quite differently, therefore. God's love is true and present, even to the worst of sinners, for it is an aspect of the being that God is. Wrath, however, is a temporal relation given in response to a sinful act or situation. If the reason for the wrath were gone, then, no wrath would remain, for God is not angry without reason. To the extent that Christ's vicarious work for us effectively satisfies for sin (or to use a different metaphor, discussed below, to the extent that his sacrifice expiates our sin), there remains no basis for wrath. But, it would be great impiety to suggest that the effectiveness of Christ's satisfying work is not complete, as if the

---

43. *ST* I–II 47.1 ad. 1.

life he had to offer to the Father were of less than infinite worth, or as if the intention by which he offered it was incomplete or impure.

Perhaps, though, the requirements of justice, not his wrath, lead God to punish Jesus in our place on the cross. Justice is an eternal characteristic of God. Although God expects us to forgive sin without punishment, would it actually be good for the one who governs on a cosmic scale to do the same?

Aquinas, conversely, argues that it is precisely because of God's transcendent and preeminent nature that he, alone, is truly able to simply forgive sins without violating justice.

> Even this justice depends on the Divine will, requiring satisfaction for sin from the human race. But if He had willed to free man from sin without any satisfaction, He would not have acted against justice. For a judge, while preserving justice, cannot pardon fault without penalty, if he must visit fault committed against another—for instance, against another man, or against the State, or any Prince in higher authority. But God has no one higher than Himself, for He is the sovereign and common good of the whole universe. Consequently, if He forgive sin, which has the formality of fault in that it is committed against Himself, He wrongs no one: just as anyone else, overlooking a personal trespass, without satisfaction, acts mercifully and not unjustly. And so David exclaimed when he sought mercy: "To Thee only have I sinned" (Psalm 50:6), as if to say: "Thou canst pardon me without injustice."[44]

To say that God is *required* to punish due to the demands of justice would either be to say that there is an external standard God must live up to (which is absurd), or that the magnanimity God gives to us—indeed, commands of us in imitation of him—is something he cannot rightly have in himself. But, in that case, freely forgiving our enemies from our heart would not be an imitation of the life of God; it, therefore, could not rightly be part of the Christ-life God creates in us. In reality, however, it is so central to that deification that Christ strictly warned us that we cannot participate in his kingdom without it (Matt 6:14–15).

God will avenge (Deut 32:35; Rom 12:19; Heb 10:30), but this assurance does not indicate that God's moral operations are such that actions that are evil by any other consideration are good when done by him. We know what evil is because we learn about good from the character and actions of God. In Rom 9:19–24, for example, Paul applies the standards of human

---

44. *ST* III 46 2 re 3.

ethics as having explanatory power for the moral decisions of God; that Paul can do so indicates there is not such a radical rupture between human and divine ethics that evil for us is good for God. In Matt 5:48, Jesus explains imitating God as the very basis of the ethics of the kingdom of God. If God, precisely by being God, is vindictive, then the ethics Jesus commanded in Matthew 5–7 simply have no relation to the perfection of God; or rather, it has a contrary relation, and to follow Jesus we must learn that imitating God means only to do what he says and not what he does. But this is exactly the hypocrisy for which Jesus condemned the Jewish leaders (Matt 23:2–3), and not the method by which we should try to obey God.

C. S. Lewis pointedly reflects concerning this viewpoint,

> The word *good*, applied to [God], becomes meaningless: like abracadabra. We have no motive for obeying Him. Not even fear. It is true that we have threats and promises. But why should we believe them? If cruelty is from His point of view "good," telling lies may be "good" too. Even if they are true, what then? If His ideas of good are so very different from ours, what He calls "Heaven" might well be what we should call Hell, and vice-versa. . . . This knot comes undone when you try to pull it tight.[45]

Saying that God's standard of ethics is different from ours in this respect does not honor God's transcendence; it inadequately understands our absolute dependence on him.[46] God's goodness is assuredly something very strange to us and beyond our understanding, but that is because God himself perfectly and completely exists as the infinite perfection to which we are finitely ordered.

If God's judgment reflects the character of Jesus, then it indicates that God gives to evildoers participation in retributive justice when they will accept no other good. Jesus did not oppose the corrupt Jewish leaders with parables, rather than fire from heaven, because he was limited in the scope of his power. He taught them in parables because he is the infinite and omnipotent God, whose fullness dwells in human form (John 11:22). In the face of corruption, Jesus offered education, healing, and a call to repentance; he also sternly warns of the horrible consequences of refusing this participation in the good (Matt 24:45–51). God exercises power only according to his will, and his will is *always* good.

Perhaps, though, the factual nature of the cross leads us to determine it is a punishment. Christ died on it, and death seems to be a punishment.[47]

45. Lewis, *A Grief Observed*, 45.

46. See "the distinction," in chapter 1.

47. Lonergan, *The Divine Redeemer*, 173.

Christ, also, died hanging on a tree, and Scripture points especially to this death as being under God's curse (Deut 21:23).

As discussed in chapter 3, death relates to human reality, and our sin, in more than one sense. Considered one way, it is a gracious limiting of the human capacity for evil, and not in itself a punishment. We are restrained from living eternally on our own terms, apart from communion with God, and from practicing and receiving the destruction that would attend that eternal state. Lossky states,

> The curse of death has never been a judgment of God. It was the punishment of a loving father, not the obtuse anger of a tyrant. Its character was educative and restorative. It prevented the perpetuation of an estranged life, the apathetic induction into an anti-natural condition. It not only put a limit on the decomposition of our nature, but, by the anguish of finitude, helped man to become alive to his condition and turn to God.[48]

Although Lossky here uses language of "curse" and "punishment," his statements clearly rule out connotations of retributive justice. In this sense, death is the wound given by a faithful friend (Prov 27:6).

It is impossible, however, for this understanding of death to explain the death of Christ. Christ never practiced evil, and he resisted every temptation. This is the way that death is the wages of sin, for it results from God's compassion on a sinful humanity that needs to be restrained. Christ, however, did not need to be restrained, but lived in the way the first Adam could not, always and only for the good.

The second sense of death, discussed in chapter 3, is the way that we are swallowed by the whale, subject to the forces of evil and the evil of our own being. This understanding of death—the sign of Jonah—explicitly does apply to the death of Christ, but we must examine carefully in what way (Matt 12:39–41; Luke 11:29–32). Christ was not subject to any evil of his own being, whether resulting from any sense of actual or original sin (Heb 4:15). The darkness tried to claim him, but it could not, because it did not understand him and had no place in him (John 1:5; 14:30). Christ submitted himself to be swallowed by the whale, so that death itself might be swallowed up by his victory (1 Cor 15:54–57). Rather than a punishment, then, Christ's dereliction and suffering indicate the great battle by which he overcomes the evil of the world, the flesh, and the devil. This understanding of Christ's death will be treated more fully in the ransom analogy, below.

With respect to the curse of hanging on a tree, we must remember that the intelligibility of the cross is dynamic, not purely syllogistic. According

48. Lossky, *Orthodox Theology*, 113.

to a straightforward syllogism, if God curses those who hang on a tree, and Christ hung on a tree, then Christ must be accursed. But the logic of the cross is a great inversion. It transforms, stepping outside and reversing the way things normally come to be. Rather than himself being cursed by God, it was by hanging on the cross that Christ overcame our curse. Again, then, we see here not Christ's punishment, but his victory.

Perhaps, though, we must fall back onto the language of Scripture and submit to Isaiah's dictum that, in the cross, God laid on Christ the punishment for us all (Isa 53:5). While there is a complex history of the interpretation of the Fourth Song of the Suffering Servant (Isa 52:13—53:12) as read by Jewish interpreters leading up to the time of Christ, there is no doubt about the way the early Christians came to understand this passage of Scripture as speaking centrally and definitively about Jesus and his work on the cross. This connection is witnessed to abundantly in the New Testament and in the literature that survives from the era of the apologists and the patristic writers.[49] The authorization to interpret the Scripture this way comes from Jesus' own words, such as when he tells his disciples, preparing them for his passion, "For I tell you, this scripture must be fulfilled in me, 'And he was counted among the lawless'; and indeed what is written about me is being fulfilled" (Luke 22:37, NRSV).[50] To be "counted among the lawless" indicates Christ's expectation that he will die a transgressors' death, and Isa 53:5 specifically labels this death a "punishment" (NRSV).

It is important to remember that the readers of Scripture leading up to Christ's coming did not understand Isaiah 53 to refer to God's dying on a cross. As much as the earliest Christian communities, including the authors of the New Testament, used Isaiah 53 to help them understand what happened on Calvary, the fundamental interpretive principle and fact was the death and resurrection of Christ itself. That is to say, it is important to see exactly how the New Testament—both remembering the words of Christ and interpreting his meaning—uses Isaiah 53, and not simply to apply what we think to be the in-built meanings of the Scripture to him.[51] The reality of Jesus lets us know what Isaiah 53 means, and from it we can come back, enlightened, to him; but the fundamental principle and test of all understanding remains him.

---

49. See Smith, *Isaiah*, 464–73.

50. Jesus here refers to Isa 53:12. For just a few of the more substantial direct references in the New Testament to Isaiah 53, see also Matt 8:17; John 12:38; Acts 8:32–33; Rom 10:16; 1 Pet 2:22–24.

51. See Smith, *Isaiah*, 472n454 and 472n455, for a bibliography on New Testament use of Isaiah 53.

The New Testament's application of Isaiah 53 to Jesus follows a number of rationales. Matthew 8:17 dynamically connects Christ's taking on our infirmities (Isa 53:4) with his ministry of divine healing and exorcism. John 12:38 connects Isa 53:1 with the moral impotence and refusal of the covenant people to believe in Christ and receive the light. Acts 8:32–33 proclaims that Jesus incarnates the meaning of the Song itself, especially in his suffering and death. Romans 10:16 connects Isa 53:1 with the need of the unevangelized to hear the gospel and come to faith. And, 1 Pet 2:22–24 encourages those who are themselves "servants" or "slaves" in the present order of the world to look to the way that Christ, through his innocence in the face of suffering, overcame evil by good (referring to Isa 53:9).

It is by no means certain, then, that Jesus' words in Luke 22:37 were intended to be read according to a syllogistic logic that would apply punishment for transgression to Christ. Rather, it is at least as likely that the logic Christ intends is dynamic, indicating the way that by dying a criminal's death he would redeem us from our crimes. Luke's Gospel, in fact, states and restates that Christ was innocent, and that the injustice was on the part of his accusers and condemners (Luke 23:4, 13–16, 22–24, 40–41, 47). Rather than by receiving the application of just punishment, in retributive justice, it is by a deprivation of (human) justice that Christ overcomes and brings new life.

Despite its extensive use of Isaiah 53, the New Testament nowhere clearly connects divine punishment with the death of Christ. Perhaps the closest referent is Heb 12:6, which states, "for the Lord disciplines those whom he loves, / and chastises every child whom he accepts" (NRSV). The word here translated, "disciplines," is *paideuei,* and it has the same root as the word the Septuagint uses for "punishment" in Isa 53:5 (*paideia*). This is, of course, the ordinary Greek word for education and child rearing, but it can have the sense of "chastisement."[52] That this passage would apply to the cross could be indicated by its close proximity to mention of Christ's crucifixion (Heb 12:2), and the importance Hebrews places on Christ's being the Son (see, for example, Heb 5:8).

There are two items to note concerning this usage. First, the reference to the crucifixion specifically indicates that Christ was "despising its shame" (Heb 12:2 NRSV). Now, Christ despised nothing that came from God. Therefore, as applied to what Christ received from God, the verb "discipline" (*paideuō*) cannot indicate anything that brings shame; yet, it is exactly the condemnation that attends retributive justice that rightfully brings shame.

52. See Liddell, *Greek-English Lexicon,* "*paideia.*"

Second, Heb 5:8–9 indicates of Christ, "Although he was a Son, he learned obedience through what he suffered; and having been made perfect, he became the source of eternal salvation for all who obey him, having been designated by God a high priest according to the order of Melchizedek." Learning obedience by what he suffered does seem to refer to the cross, and learning (from *manthanō*) does seem to be the desired result of educating (*paideuō*).

Hebrews, furthermore, emphasizes that Jesus, our high priest, is able to sympathize with us in our weakness, having been tested in every way while remaining without sin (Heb 4:15). While it is a challenge to parse out exactly how faith, the beatific vision, and suffering function in the human consciousness of the Christ, it is clearly indicated by Scripture that Jesus learned.[53] To remain consonant with the message of Hebrews, though, the education and learning of Christ must take place, not by having a share of sin, but by the fact of his being apart from it. Perhaps, then, the "discipline" Hebrews 12 speaks of refers to the education, by suffering, of the human nature of the Christ, without any sense of condemnation from God on Christ, but with complete sympathy with God's condemnation of sin.

Perhaps, though, the Christian tradition of redemptive suffering, expressed especially in the genuine sorrow of repentance, leads us to believe that although Christ makes satisfaction for sins, some punishment in the cross must remain. Many Christian understandings of Christ's death have connected it with the sacramental functioning of penance.[54] Even those who would reject a sacramental penance system may look to the Christian experience of freedom from sin, based on confession and repentance, testified to by each generation and each strand of Christian tradition.

In this case, it matters greatly to which understanding and experience of repentance one appeals. In the Catholic sacrament of penance, although the guilt of sin is absolved, some temporal punishment for sin remains and is applied to the penitent ones as an act of contrition. By analogy with this penitential system, one might expect the redemptive suffering of Christ on the cross to include a punishment, even if he is not afflicted by guilt.

The Orthodox sacrament of repentance and confession, however, differs from the Catholic understanding at exactly this point.[55] Repentance, in Orthodox understanding, always brings healing, not punishment. If there is an act of contrition required by the priest receiving the confession, its intention is always therapeutic, not punitive. While Orthodoxy has a strong

53. In addition to this passage from Hebrews, see Luke 2:40, 52. See *ST* III 9.
54. Lonergan, *The Divine Redeemer*, 189–90.
55. Greek Orthodox Archdiocese of America, "Repentance and Confession."

understanding of redemptive suffering, it is not a punishment from God but rather an aspect of our deification.

It goes without saying that the Protestant understanding of confession and repentance accords better with the experience of the Orthodox Church than with the explanation given by Roman Catholicism. Exactly by proclaiming indulgences and the (late-medieval Catholic) penitential system to be travesties of the gospel, Luther was declaring a justice from God that justifies sinners freely, without the fear of temporal punishment.[56] Repentance brings freedom and reconciliation, not further punishment.

Luther, however, would have insisted that our freedom from punishment results from God's punishing Christ for our sins, having imputed them to him.[57] The imputation of sin and righteousness, however, are difficult concepts to account for both biblically and theologically. As the various authors connected with the New Perspective on Paul convincingly argue, imputation is a concept that has a dubious-at-best pedigree in the Jewish context of the New Testament.[58] Few of these authors would doubt that we are redeemed by Christ and that our sins are paid for by him, but what they show is that the horizon of the New Testament has no real place for this to happen according to the logic of imputed sin and imputed righteousness.

With respect to a theological account of our sins being imputed to Christ, again, Lonergan's comments are instructive. His first complaint is that an imputed sinfulness does not reconcile with the real status of Christ's suffering and death.

> Our first objection, then, against this opinion imputing guilt to an innocent Christ is its inconsistency, in that it mixes fact and fiction. The passion and death of Christ were not fictions, nor were his innocence and his sinlessness, indeed his impeccability. But if to these very true and real facts you add an imputation of guilt, you only confuse your own mind rather than attain in whatever way you can the truth of the matter. You maintain that Christ was condemned by a just judge for sins that were not his but were simply imputed to him; but at the same time you know that this just judge was aware that Christ was totally innocent, and therefore that in reality God the Father did not condemn his Son. Because this imputation of sins is a fiction, so also is his condemnation. You hold that Christ received punishment in the strict sense, and yet you know that he was innocent and was not really condemned but simply satisfied vicariously for

56. See Luther, *95 Theses*, in *Selected Works of Martin Luther*.

57. See Luther's commentary on Galatians in *Luther's Works*, 26:279; 26:277; 26:288.

58. See, for example, Wright, *Justification*.

the sins of others. Therefore, just as the imputation of guilt and his condemnation were fictitious, so also was this punishment that is said to be punishment in the strict sense. You say that the anger of God towards sinners was through imputation redirected towards Christ, yet you know that Christ was innocent and the beloved Son of God the Father; so on top of fictitious imputation and fictitious condemnation and fictitious punishment you add the fictitious anger of God. But the passion of Christ was real, and so was his death. You seem to be playing games, trying to explain realities by means of fictions. No, let us rather "in all things show that we are God's servants . . . by a love free of pretense, by a word of truth" (2 Corinthians 6.4, 6–7). For sincere love can only diminish when we depart from the word of truth.[59]

If Christ dealt with our sins—and he did—he did so according to reality. Both as a biblical and as a theological concept, imputation seems to introduce confusion. It therefore does not serve as a clear basis for affirming that, in the cross, God punished Christ.

Perhaps, in the end, we will simply judge that Anselm's analogy is inadequate, tied too closely to medieval European society, and not of sufficient explanatory power to lead away from the traditional notion of the cross as a punishment. However, the problem with Anselm's analogy is that it cannot give enough credit to the work of Christ, who is a divine person; it is assuredly not the case that Christ's work falls short of Anselm's explanation. Nor does Christian tradition speak with one voice on this issue; the Eastern Orthodox tradition, mirroring many patristic voices, has never accepted that the cross was a punishment from God visited on Christ.[60]

The strongest indication that the cross was not a punishment by God, visited on Christ, is that Christ is the exact revelation of the Father (John 1:18). But, on the cross, Jesus was not condemnatory. Rather, his every word and action was—especially with respect to those who deserved punishment—to forgive (Luke 23:24). If the cross was a condemnation of Christ by God, then Christ did not reveal the Father on the cross. The seven sayings of the cross contain the dereliction of Christ's suffering, but have no word of wrath (Matt 27:46; Mark 15:34; Luke 23:34, 43, 46; John 19:26, 27, 28, 30). To picture the Father as pouring out punishment on the Son, while the Son

---

59. Lonergan, *The Divine Redeemer*, 186; on page 187, Lonergan goes on to add four further significant arguments against the teaching that, on the cross, God imputed sin to Christ.

60. Lossky, *Orthodox Theology*, 113.

meekly submits and offers forgiveness, would be to propose a bifurcation in the character of God in exactly this most revelatory moment.

Maximus the Confessor does have an intriguing understanding of punishment and the cross. According to Maximus, Christ "suffered, and converted the use of death so that in him it would be a condemnation not of our nature but manifestly only of sin itself."[61] Christ's mortal body, and his suffering, serve as the fulcrum by which God condemns and punishes the destructiveness of our sinful nature and of our enemy.[62] The cross, then, is a divine punishment, but not of Christ; rather it is that by which God visits divine retribution on sin, the powers of darkness, and the logic of this fallen world (Rom 8:3–4; 1 Cor 1:27–28; Col 1:15–23).[63] Christ's complete satisfaction opened the way for God to condemn them without condemning us, too.

The Perfect Sacrifice

Arguably, the strongest context for Christ's atoning death in the New Testament is that of sacrifice.[64] Christ is our Passover Lamb, sacrificed for us (John 1:29; 1 Cor 5:7). His death occurred during Passover Week, and the great sign of his death that he left us—Holy Communion—was given as part of a Passover meal (Mark 14:12–16, 22–25).

The purpose of a sacrifice is to mediate between humans and God.[65] The sacrificial victim becomes the representative of the sacrificer, whose destruction or complete devotion to God brings reconciliation. Thus, in the Old Testament we see atonement offerings, guilt offerings, fellowship offerings, peace offerings, sin offerings, in addition to spontaneous, or free-will offerings.[66]

God and Violence: Second Reflection

If an ancient Jew or Greek, Roman or Egyptian came and observed the worship services in modern America or Europe, perhaps what might most strike her is the lack of blood. Animal sacrifice permeated ancient worship.

61. Maximus, *Ad Thallassium 61*.

62. I thank Christopher Ben Simpson for this insight, and the language of "fulcrum."

63. See the ransom analogy, discussed below.

64. All four Gospels strongly relate Jesus' death to the Passover, with its sacrificial lamb, but see especially the extended meditation on sacrifice by the author of Hebrews.

65. *ST* III 48 3.

66. See Douglas and Tenney, "Sacrifice and Offerings," 1262–65.

Within the demands of the Jewish Law, the Temple and its altar were filled, day after day, year after year, with a great procession of death. Slaughter, the draining and sprinkling of blood, the burning of the carcasses—some entire, some in part—and the sacrificial meals: this was daily life in Jerusalem, and it was paralleled in many, many ancient cities.

This great litany of blood, and its connection to the most central aspect of Christianity, has raised many questions and difficulties. What about the violent death of an animal could be pleasing to God? How could slaughtering something improve one's moral or religious state? Does the Jewish sacrificial system, and the cross, indicate that God is a sponsor and lover of violence?

René Girard's work especially has highlighted the destructive nature of much sacrificial logic.[67] His understandings of "mimetic desire" and "scapegoating" help to show the ways that cultic practices can represent deep—and dark—dynamics that underlie our societies. Mimetic desire, put simply, has to do with the way envy and jealousy often lie behind our ostensibly righteous personal and cultural practices; these destructive dynamics lead to a cycle of distortion in our societies that sets us against each other and alienates us from each other precisely through the common objects of our desire. Scapegoating has to do with the way that groups deal with the conflicts aroused by competitive desire by practicing violence on a marginalized individual or sub-group; instead of allowing competitive group members to destroy each other, a vulnerable individual or sub-group in the group will be identified, whose destruction releases the tension produced within the group by mimetic desire.

Girard's understanding of sacrifice points to what William Desmond terms a "dark origin."[68] The forces that occasion and shape the practice of sacrifice, by this assessment, are destructive in their origin. Rather than being the result of an originating love (what Desmond terms an agapeic origin), they flow from an empty and grasping desire (what Desmond terms an erotic origin).[69]

It must be admitted that many sacrificial systems function precisely this way, and that Girard has tellingly identified dynamics one can find in nearly any social group, including ancient Israel.[70] However, as Girard him-

---

67. See especially Girard, *Violence and the Sacred* and *Things Hidden Since the Foundation of the World*.

68. See Desmond, "Schopenhauer's Philosophy of the Dark Origin," 89–104; see also Simpson, *Deleuze and Theology*, 68–69.

69. Desmond, *Being and the Between*, 208, 231, 247–48 and 330; see also Simpson, *Religion, Metaphysics, and the Postmodern*, 104–12.

70. See Schwager, "Christ's Death," 111–22.

self saw, the logic of the cross is dynamic, overturning precisely the logic of this fallen world. In exactly the form and meaning of Christ's sacrifice, I will argue that we find a communication of meaning that overcomes violence, reconciling us to God and to the truth of what we are created to be.

This inversion can be seen, partially and in type, already in God's establishment of the Levitical sacrificial system.[71] Throughout Leviticus, the sacrifices enjoined are described as pleasing to God (Lev 1:9 and *passim*). Carefully read, though, what pleases God in this practice is not the blood of the sacrificial offering but the restoration of fellowship with his people.

This insight develops as one moves further into the Israelite prophetic period. Isaiah castigates the Jews for offering empty sacrifices, and he sarcastically tells them to cease the sacrificial system in favor of bringing to God upright and sincere hearts and practicing justice in their land (Isa 1:10–15). The double-mindedness of their worship, and their treatment of marginalized groups within their culture, would eventually lead God to take away from Israel Solomon's temple, the focal point for the sacrificial system. By exile, God re-educates his people as to what it means to be marginalized people themselves, called to worship in spirit and truth.

This dynamic intelligibility, that overcomes the dark origin that stalks this world, becomes fully real in the cross. Perhaps no one has stated more clearly or succinctly the logic of scapegoating and mimetic desire than Caiaphas: "You do not understand that it is better for you to have one man die for the people than to have the whole nation destroyed" (John 11:50). The Gospel of John indicates that Caiaphas speaks prophetically, although not according to his knowledge and intention. What Caiaphas intended according to the marginalizing and violent logic of this world, God would use to overcome exactly that order of violence and distorted desire.

One may still ask why God would work through the litany of blood every sacrificial system—including Israel's—entails. Perhaps God's wisdom allows through this violence a communication to us about the nature and seriousness of sin, namely, that sin always leads to death. More deeply, though, all sacrificial systems find their resolution in Christ, the symbol of God, in whom they are reconciled, redefined, purified, and inverted; it is in him, and in his sacrifice, that we have new life.

The Notion of Sacrifice

As foreshadowed by Isaiah and personified by Christ, the Christian understanding of sacrifice includes the state of the heart. Lonergan, in fact, defines

71. See Doran, "The Nonviolent Cross," 52–55.

a sacrifice as "a proper symbol of a sacrificial attitude."[72] He is by no means alone in this assessment of sacrifice. In Orthodox tradition, Maximus beautifully illuminates sacrifice's nature, also.

> By spiritual sacrifices is meant not only the putting to death of the passions, slaughtered by "the sword of the Spirit, which is the word of God" (Eph. 6:17), and the deliberate emptying out of all life in the flesh, as if it were blood; the term also signifies the offering up of the moral state we have gained through the practice of the virtues, together with all our natural powers, which we dedicate and offer [*prosagōgēn aphieroumenōn*] to God as whole burnt sacrifices, to be consumed by the fire of grace in the Spirit, so that they are filled with divine power.[73]

Likewise, the Syrian Orthodox tradition places the true meaning of sacrifice in the attitude of a pure heart.[74] All of these traditions explicitly or implicitly look to Paul's admonition in Rom 12:1 to present our bodies as living sacrifices, which is our spiritual or rational (*logikos*) act of worship. Paul himself drew on the Jewish tradition of the Psalter (Ps 50:19), and of Isaiah and Leviticus (as already mentioned).

This is not to say that the material nature of a sacrifice is irrelevant. Symbols, in Lonergan's terms, have a kind of dual-citizenship; that is, a symbol is "an image of a real or imaginary object that evokes a feeling or is evoked by a feeling."[75] Symbols, then, are tangible—in some way sensory—bridges to the world of meaning and value. They make present for our perception, are evoked by, and communicate to us the importance and reality of the world, and they animate and direct our minds and affectivity.

A symbol is proper, in Lonergan's terms, by being suited for its task.[76] In terms relevant to our consideration of the cross, a proper symbol represents a spiritual reality in terms of sense perception, not by a mere coincidental similarity but by "a certain analogical proportion."[77] Analogical proportion includes the natural aptitude of objects to evoke the requisite meanings and feelings, as well as the way that custom and social institution have conditioned us to make certain connections and responses. Preeminently, though, analogical proportion is brought about by real moral or physical connection between the symbol and what it symbolizes.

72. Lonergan, "The Notion of Sacrifice," 5.

73. Maximus, "Various Texts on Theology," 273, Greek transliterated.

74. See Brock, "Fire from Heaven," 231–32.

75. Lonergan, *Method*, 64.

76. Lonergan, "The Notion of Sacrifice," 6–10.

77. Ibid., 9–11.

A sacrificial attitude is one that springs from habits of intellect and will that are worshipful, addressed to God because of sins, thankful to God for benefits received, and petitionary to God for future benefits ("lauretic, propitiatory, eucharistic, and imperatory").[78] A proper sacrifice, then, has some kind of conventional or intrinsic connection to seeking God in spirit and truth, acknowledging that we have a relation of absolute dependence on him, petitioning him on account of sins, and beseeching his favor and pardon, indeed, his salvation. A perfect sacrifice, furthermore, by its action and existence, will have moral and physical connection to this attitude that it symbolizes.

Sacrifice and Communication

By his attitude on the cross and by the death he died, Christ both offered and was the perfect sacrifice for the human race. Again, to avoid the notion of a blood-thirsty God, we must examine this reality carefully. It was not the violence of the cross that made an acceptable sacrifice to God, but rather the communication of Christ to God made real in his very flesh.

Lonergan discusses the atonement holistically in terms of an act of communication.

> The redemption is the outstanding expression of God to man. "The Word was made flesh" was the incarnation. The words of St John refer primarily to the incarnation, to the fact that one person is both God and man. But it was not simply the fact of the second person of the Blessed Trinity assuming human nature; it was an act of communication. . . . And it is not only God communicating with us, it is God giving himself to us. The Gospels repeatedly affirm that the motive of Christ's coming was love.[79]

The *Logos* comes among us, for us and our salvation. He gave himself to us, and he is meaningful, the source of all meanings, and the one in whom all meanings cohere. The motive of this communication was love, and its purpose was to change us, transforming our histories, and uniting us to God.

Lonergan here powerfully extends both Abelard's moral analogy and Anselm's vicarious satisfaction analogy through his analogy of the cross as communication.[80] His analogy is complex and has two sections, one that

78. Ibid., 5.

79. Lonergan, "On Redemption," 5–6.

80. One should here note two recent (and excellent) dissertations explaining Lonergan's communication analogy, one by Mark Miller at Boston College ("Why the Passion?") and the other by John Volk at Marquette University (*Historical Causality of Christ*).

primarily involves communication to God, and one that primarily involves communication to us. In his own terms, the first part deals with vicarious satisfaction. Robert Doran's recent work, though, has connected Lonergan's insights to sacrifice, and I will do the same here.[81] The second part of Lonergan's analogy is moral, and I will draw on it in the section on the moral analogy, below, and in chapter 6's discussion of the saved life.

By concentrating exclusively on a legal analogy for the atonement, we can miss many of the other ways that Scripture specifies to bring about forgiveness of sin. Specifically, love covers over sin, zeal for God brings forgiveness, and God forgives those who repent (1 Pet 4:8; Num 25:11; Ps 106:30–31; Jonah 3:9–10; Luke 3:3; 15:3–7; 2 Cor 7:10). None of these factors have relevance in a court of law, and from the point of view of seeing sin as a matter of violating the divine law, it makes no sense to mention them; they can only be supplementary to the "real business," which is legal or commercial. But, the legal metaphor, while valid, is only a metaphor; it is one of the ways Scripture images our relation to God, and if we operate within it exclusively, or as a master narrative, we will tend to discount or ignore other valid relations that Scripture teaches.

Valid sacrifice does not operate within a legal environment, but rather it deals with the petition of the heart. As Mark Miller summarizes Lonergan's argument,

> Sin creates a rupture in the relationships between human persons and God, among human persons, and among all parts of creation. Christ's vicarious satisfaction flows from a non-ruptured relationship. It expresses a perfect concord of the human and the divine, through its threefold communication of (1) a perfect knowledge and love of God and humanity, (2) a perfect knowledge and sorrow for the offense that sin is, (3) and a perfect knowledge and detestation of the evil sin causes.[82]

This aspect of the communication of the cross is primarily from the human nature of Christ (informed, of course, by personal union with his divine nature) to God, and it constitutes the human race's finally getting it right.

This communication is performed in a high priestly way, in which Christ sacrifices himself for us. We have no such thing as even an adequate knowledge and love for God and humanity, apart from Christ's sacrifice,

81. See Doran, "The Non-Violent Cross," connecting Lonergan's communication analogy with Girard's theological work.

82. Miller, "Why the Passion?" abstract. Lonergan presented this theology at most length in *The Divine Redeemer*, which he described as a supplement to one of his Christology textbooks, *De Verbo Incarnato*.

let alone a perfect one. Also, as William Beveridge puts it, "My repentance needs to be repented of, my tears need washing, and the very washing of my tears needs still to be washed over again with the blood of my Redeemer."[83] But Christ, our high priest and perfect sacrifice, stands in our place and mediates between God and us.

Christ crucified became for us the perfect symbol of God. It was most fitting that Christ express the internal acts of love, knowledge, and detestation in communion with his physical being.[84] A complete human action is more perfect than one that is merely inner and private.[85] It is appropriate that Christ express the immensity of his love and knowledge of God in common with the gravity of his knowledge and detestation of sin and its effects by the most complete and noble action he could undertake; the supreme act of love is to lay down one's life for one's friends.[86] Furthermore, this communication endures when modern believers, in concert with those throughout the Christian centuries, contemplate the death of Christ; "what was meant long ago and is communicated truly today is precisely what Christ expressed by his passion and death."[87] Finally, by the real, moral and physical, connection between his inner love, knowledge, and sorrow, and his patience in suffering the destruction of his mortal body, Christ affects and becomes the most perfect symbol of a fully realized relationship between God and a human being. Again, we come to Christ crucified, true God and the one true man, enthroned on Calvary.[88]

Perhaps it need not be emphasized that the suffering and death of Christ was not the direct will of God, but was brought about proximately by the betrayal of Judas, his abandonment by his disciples, the conspiracy of the Jewish leaders, the complacency of Herod, and the governmental injustice of the Romans, all of whom succumbed to the temptation of the devil; remotely it was brought about by the sin of each of us, whom he came to save.[89] God directly wills only the good, and violence, suffering, and death are not goods. God did will the cross; in fact, he ordained and foreknew it (Acts 2:23). But God works through the evil of suffering (*malum poenae*) to achieve the greater good; he does not directly will even justly imposed evils,

83. Beveridge, *Private Thoughts*.

84. Lonergan, *The Divine Redeemer*, 196–201.

85. Ibid., 199. Lonergan here emphasizes the public and social nature of the cross.

86. Ibid., 199–200.

87. Ibid., 200.

88. See Behr, *Mystery of Christ*, 40–43.

89. See the analogy of the "three-lane highway" in chapter 3.

and wills penal evil only insofar as it is the consequence of a greater good. In the cross, we see God's judgment of violence, not his desire for it.[90]

For in the sacrifice of the cross, we find the great inversion of the logic of this world. The prophet Ezekiel cried to Israel, "Cast away from you all the transgressions that you have committed against me, and get yourselves a new heart and a new spirit! Why will you die, O house of Israel? For I have no pleasure in the death of anyone, says the Lord God. Turn, then, and live" (Ezek 18:31–32, NRSV). Christ, by his sacrifice, casts away from us all our sins, and by his perfect communication to God he opens the way to us for the perfect communication of God's own self.

The perfect communication of Christ is the gift of God to us for our purification.

> And He gave to mortals a twofold purification; one of the Eternal Spirit, and by it He cleansed in me the old stain, which comes from the flesh; and the other of our blood, for I call mine the blood Christ, My God, has poured, the redemption of the original infirmities and the salvation of the world. [91]

In his sacrifice, we see the closest union between Christ and sinners. For, by declaring himself to us and laying down his life for us, he makes us his friends (John 15:9–17). We also see the closest union between God and a human being, for in Christ the divine and human natures were personally united, and this union bore the noblest and deepest possible fruit in his willing sacrifice.

In the logic of sacrifice, Christ's death was a propitiation of God only in that it was addressed to God on account of sins. God is not intrinsically wrathful, and rather than pouring out punishment on Christ, he was receiving the noblest of communications from him. The dereliction of Christ was real, for he truly united his soul and body in suffering for our sake, and God permitted his unjust torture and death (Mark 15:34, quoting Ps 22:1). Yet, Christ's was a dereliction of hope, by which he would live, proclaim the Lord, and know the Lord's deliverance (Ps 22:29–31). By his sacrifice he made expiation for our sins, removing them from us and restoring us to God (Heb 2:17).[92]

---

90. See Doran, "The Non–Violent Cross," 51–52.

91. *Carmina* 1.1, ser. 11.4, ves. 24–92, quoted by Georges Florovsky in "Redemption," 300n98.

92. See Lonergan, "On Redemption", 15–16.

Moral Communication

Christ's death was not merely directed to change our legal standing before God, nor was it only communication addressed to God. The cross also brings about a change in *us*, communicating to our moral being, and calling us to love God and be like Christ. While some theologians, such as Peter Abelard, did see the moral theory of the atonement as a competitor to Anselm's satisfaction analogy, it is better to see moral motivation as a complementary aspect of the multiple intelligibility of the cross.

Abelard offers his moral analogy in his commentary on Rom 3:19–26.

> Now it seems to us that we have been justified by the blood of Christ and reconciled to God in this way: through this unique act of grace manifested to us—in that his Son has taken upon himself our nature and persevered therein in teaching as by word and example even unto death—he has more fully bound us to himself by love; with the result that our hearts should be enkindled by such a gift of divine grace, and true charity should not now shrink from enduring anything for him.[93]

The core of Abelard's claim is that Christ's death changes our hearts, bringing us to union with God by greater love. Because Christ entered our human condition and died for us, we have an example of love that both educates us and motivates us to be like Christ, as God works in our hearts by his grace.

Advocates of vicarious atonement (such as Anselm's satisfaction analogy) have often criticized Abelard for dealing only with our moral state and not with our guilt before God. However, Abelard had other theories of the atonement that addressed the problem of guilt.[94] Anselm's solution by itself, additionally, can leave one with the question of how our hearts, and not just our legal standing, are changed by the cross.

The Law of the Cross

The second half of Lonergan's communication analogy can be summed up by the phrase, "The Law of the Cross." It is an act of communication by a divine person that changes human history, teaching us who God is and changing us to be like him. It essentially expresses the way that God overcomes evil by good through sacrificial love. This analogy will be the basis of much of chapter 6, in which I will explore salvation, the divine life given to us.

93. Abelard, *Romans*, 2.3.

94. Namely, that God punished Christ for our sins, thereby absolving us from punishment. See Abelard's commentary on Rom 4:25 and 8:3.

This communication is a "mystery."[95] By this, Lonergan does not mean something completely beyond human understanding, for in the revelation of this mystery there is a meaning that changes the world. Rather, "mystery" connotes the secret plan of God, by which God has providentially ordered the ages, made manifest and revealed to us now in Christ.

This mystery, revealed to us in Christ, has a determinate content. In the section on sacrifice, we discussed Christ's act of communication that was primarily from human to God. The other half of Lonergan's analogy explains Christ's act of communication that was primarily directed to humans. Mark Miller again aptly summarizes Lonergan's thought.

> On the cross, Jesus wisely and lovingly transforms the evil consequences of sin into a twofold communication to humanity of a perfect human and divine (1) knowledge and love for humanity and (2) knowledge and condemnation of sin and evil. This twofold communication invites a twofold human response: the repentance of sin and a love for God and all things. This love and repentance form a reconciled relationship of God and humanity. Furthermore, when reconciled with God, a human person will tend to be moved to participate in Christ's work by willingly taking on satisfaction for one's own sin as well as the vicarious satisfaction for others' sins.[96]

Miller's last sentence does not indicate that humans in any way replace Christ's work, or that Christ's work was insufficient for our justification. It indicates that, on the basis of Christ's work, we join in Christ's ministry of reconciliation, motivated and changed by him (2 Cor 5:11–19).[97]

It is of utmost importance that the work of the cross is not something that comes to us only from the outside. The Holy Spirit works within us to remove our heart of stone, give us a heart of flesh, and make our character just like that of Jesus (Ezek 11:19; 36:26; 2 Cor 3:3; Gal 5:22–23).[98] Exactly what Christ communicates to us by the cross is inscribed in our inmost being by the gift of God's love, poured out in us by the Holy Spirit (Rom 5:5; 2 Cor 3:18).

The moral analogy emphasizes one of the most important aspects of the atonement. Our righteousness is not something that is merely imputed to us, somehow residing only in the mind of God and having no reality in

95. Lonergan, "On Redemption," 24–28.

96. Miller, "Why the Passion?" abstract.

97. Perhaps here there is something of Dostoyevsky's notion, expressed in *The Brothers Karamazov*, that we are each guilty for the sins of all, a knowledge that springs from and occasions love for our neighbor.

98. Lonergan, *Method*, 240–42; see Cone, "Transforming Desire."

this world. Being justified indicates that our beings have changed. On the basis of Christ's work on the cross, and through the ministry of the Holy Spirit, we are more and more empowered to live lives that are like that of Jesus. By living this transformed life, we come to know the Father and follow him, just as Jesus did; this is eternal life being imparted to us (John 17:3).

Within the limits of this life, the way we accept Christ's work, given to us by the Spirit, will always be dialectical.[99] That is to say, the Holy Spirit gives himself to us entire in salvation—for God has no parts—and where the Spirit comes, the Father and Son come, too; but we are not always faithful to the work and presence of God within us.[100] Even in the best of our hearts, there is some kind of ebb and flow. If we so desire, we can frustrate the work of God in us either entirely or for a time, for his gift does not abolish but elevates free will. Additionally, the message about Jesus will be preached and taught to us by some community, and that community will have both bright and dark parts. To the extent that our communities are inauthentic to the work of the cross, the work of the Spirit in our heart will conflict with them. But we are certainly affected by our communities and receive much of our knowledge of God—and of ourselves—through them.[101]

Luther's early explanation that we are both sinners and justified at the same time (*simil iustus et peccator*) helps illuminate the dialectical nature of saved human existence.[102] Those who are truly receiving the work of God are always the most conscious of their sin—a knowledge of sin must be revealed—yet they are also righteous by the reckoning of the merciful God. The reason they are accounted as righteous by God, even while sinners, is that God knows they will live completely righteous lives in the life of the world to come. God has promised to make them completely righteous, not just in his accounting but in their very lives and beings, and he knows he will be faithful to his promise. The promise of God, furthermore, is of more account than this present world; heaven and earth will pass away, but the word of Christ will not (Matt 24:35). God, therefore, is right to treat us and consider us according to reality, the reality he knows and he will bring about.

The moral analogy, then, expresses in a powerful way that true Christian life is eschatological. This does not mean we wait to the end of time to begin to live righteously; rather it means that eternal life has already begun in us. The past reality of the work of Christ has inaugurated the present reality of our saved lives that looks to and moves toward a future consummation

99. Lonergan, *Method*, 252.

100. *ST* I 43.5; II–II 23.2 ad 1; 24.5

101. Lonergan, *Method*, 299.

102. Luther, *Lectures on Romans*, 269.25–30; 272.3–21.

in the Second Coming.[103] By the communication of Christ to us, our lives and histories are changed to participate in the way that God is moving all of reality toward that last day.[104]

The Ransom for Sinners

The most influential model for understanding the atonement for most of the church, through most of its history, is that of the cross as a ransom. This model was so pervasive in the early church that Gustav Aulén could refer to it as the "classic solution."[105] What, exactly, it means needs to be explained carefully. The ransom analogy has, in fact, been criticized for intimating that God makes a deal with the devil, or propitiates him.[106] Rightly understood, however, the ransom analogy speaks of God's victory over evil, as Christ fulfills the righteous law of the Father.

Christ our ransom overcomes four aspects of evil. First, evil is in our bondage to death and to the devil. Hebrews 2:14–15 (NRSV) states, "Since, therefore, the children share flesh and blood, he himself likewise shared the same things, so that through death he might destroy the one who has the power of death, that is, the devil, and free those who all their lives were held in slavery by the fear of death."[107] As the great Christian teachers (such as Irenaeus) reflected on this, they concluded that through our acceptance of temptation—by which we credited the devil's testimony more than God's—instead of becoming free (what we wanted), we became slaves in a kingdom of darkness, living a life that moves, inexorably, toward death.[108]

Second, evil is in our disobedience to the Father. Our greatest problem is not that we are slaves to one of God's enemies. It is that we ourselves have become enemies of God (Eph 2:1–3). We have willingly joined the regime of the rebels against heaven. Therefore, we must fear the righteous judgment of God.

Third, evil is in our inner concupiscence and pride. The paths of our lives have become twisted, because our desires, our loves, have become disordered. Concupiscence is disordered desire, and as our lives are dominated

---

103. See Lowery, *Revelation's Rhapsody*.

104. See Lonergan, "Finality, Love, Marriage."

105. Gustav Aulén, *Christus Victor*, 4; see also Heine, *Classical Christian Doctrine*, 116–128.

106. McGrath, *Theology*, 72–75.

107. See also Rom 6:16.

108. Irenaeus, *Against Heresies*, 5.1.1; see also Origen, *Commentary on Matthew*, 16.8

by false love, every aspect of our inner being becomes distorted.[109] Finally, in our pride, we have desired to become God ourselves—ordering the universe around us in a disordered fashion.

Finally, evil is the subsequent corruption of our nature. It is only right that our whole beings, and the social orders of which we are part, become distorted, servants of destruction. The fruit of this ongoing state can be seen in the collapse of civilizations and societies, the breakdown of personal relationships, the distortions of envy and hate that mar our inner beings, and the final corruption of our physical bodies (Gen 2:16–17).

Into this world of woe comes Christ our ransom. Matthew 20:26–28 (NRSV) says, "It will not be so among you; but whoever wishes to be great among you must be your servant, and whoever wishes to be first among you must be your slave; just as the Son of Man came not to be served but to serve, and to give his life a ransom for many."[110] First Timothy 2:6, 1 Pet 1:18, and Rev 5:9 also explicitly speak of Christ's death as saving us by ransom.

M. H. Franzmann helpfully elucidates five aspects of Matthew's ransom saying.[111] First, it is a Saying of the Passion Road; that is, it is delivered at a point in the presentation of Matthew when the story has become more concentrated upon Jesus' death.[112] Christ has spoken of his passion three times prior to this in Matthew (16:21; 17:22; and 20:17), and has ascribed his journey to Jerusalem and its culmination to the will and counsel of God. "It is in this close and tense atmosphere, this air charged with destiny, that the ransom saying flashes forth and lightninglike illumines the Passion road of the Son of Man."[113] Second, it is a Suffering Servant saying. Matthew has already explicitly ascribed Jesus' ministry of exorcism and divine healing to the way that Isaiah 53's servant "took our infirmities and bore our diseases" (Matt 8:17). The servant language of this saying, as well as the qualification that his death is "for many," resonates with the many other echoes of Isaiah 53 in the passion account. Third, it is a Son of Man saying. The most frequent self-designation of Jesus, as Franzmann puts it, "The title 'Son of Man' contains the whole paradox, both of the total poverty and of the

---

109. See Snell and Cone, *Authentic Cosmopolitanism*, 87–104.

110. Parallel with Mark 10:45.

111. Franzmann, "A Ransom for Many," 497–504. Although the importance of form criticism has been overplayed in New Testament studies, there is a way that the structural components of a saying of Jesus, and those elements' connection to his other Gospel sayings, do help provide essential context for what he is communicating. See Hurtado, "New Testament Studies in the 20th Century," 43–57, for an overview and comment on developments in New Testament critical study.

112. Franzmann, "A Ransom for Many," 498.

113. Ibid.

uncompromising and unrestricted Messianic claim of Jesus. It is the nexus between the Passion and the *basileia*."[114] Fourth, it is also plausibly a kingdom saying, for the kingdom of the Danielic Son of Man is set in contrast to—and given conquering rulership of—the kingdoms of this world. Finally, it is an "I come" (*ēlthon*) saying. These sayings speak of Jesus' messianic self-consciousness and proclaim central aspects of his bringing of redemption and judgment. Jesus comes as the one who brings Spirit and fire (Matt 3:11), who fulfills the Law (Matt 5:17), and who calls not the righteous but sinners to repentance (Matt 9:13). The ransom saying, then, does not indicate a peripheral or secondary element of Jesus' ministry; rather, in it are drawn together the greatest of the messianic themes.

In explaining the ransom analogy, I will draw on the works of Irenaeus, Athanasius, Gregory of Nazianzus, and Gregory Palamas.[115] The theology of this pervasive analogy developed significantly over time, and each of these great theologians' efforts contribute something of significance. As developed by these theologians, Christ's ransom simultaneously acts in two directions. Toward God, it acts as a fulfillment; toward the enemy, it acts as persuasion and conquest.

According to Irenaeus, in our apostate state, we are subject to the tyranny of the devil not because the devil has any inherent rights over us, nor because God has placed us under his sway, but because the devil overcame us when we willingly submitted to his temptation.[116] God permitted this unjust domination, but he did not directly will it; instead, he wills to save us from the enemy's power. However, instead of mirroring the devil's tactics of rushing in to snatch the object of desire, God thought it fitting to rescue us from the enemy's grasp by means of justice. This is what Irenaeus means that Christ ransomed us through persuasion. Although the enemy could not understand God's plan, in his presumption he agreed to and arranged the death of Christ, thereby through what he intended for evil bringing about his own downfall (1 Cor 2:8).

Athanasius makes explicit, and a focal point, what Irenaeus also believed: the main work of Christ our ransom had not to do with the devil but with God.[117] We are subject to corruption, having violated the righteous law

114. Ibid., 501. Much recent scholarship has helped illuminate the context of messianic expectation in Second Temple Judaism plausibly connected with this Danielic title. See Kuhn, "One Like a Son of Man," 22–42.

115. The ransom analogy is also prominent in the history of the Western church, being used by both Augustine and Aquinas. See Augustine, *The Trinity*, 13.19; see also *ST* III 48.3.

116. Irenaeus, *Against Heresies*, 5.1.1.

117. Athanasius, *On the Incarnation of the Word*, 2.8–9.

of the Father. Christ, therefore, took on a body like ours so that he might present it to the Father in humility.

> Thus, taking a body like our own, because all our bodies were liable to the corruption of death, He surrendered His body to death instead of all, and offered it to the Father. This He did out of sheer love for us, so that in His death all might die, and the law of death thereby be abolished because, having fulfilled in His body that for which it was appointed, it was thereafter voided of its power for men. This He did that He might turn again to incorruption men who had turned back to corruption, and make them alive through death by the appropriation of His body and by the grace of His resurrection.[118]

Athanasius understood the law of corruption as the requirement of the Father that, because of our apostasy, needed to be satisfied; by offering his body, Jesus fulfilled the requirement completely. Since the requirement is completely met, it no longer has the ability to require anything of human beings.

Death and corruption are therefore destroyed in the body of Jesus. Christ destroys them by showing that they no longer pertain to humans; they have no just or intelligible relation remaining. Thus Christ demonstrates his divine power through establishing justice. Note that, as in Irenaeus, this is not just a so-called power encounter. God rescues through his power, but his power is the servant of his wisdom.

Gregory of Nazianzus refines the ransom analogy by pointing out the way that it, as any analogy, has limits.[119] In a human ransom, or redemption, there are four usual elements: a captive, a payment, a payer of the ransom, and one to whom the ransom is paid.[120] Yet, as with any analogy, when we apply a human situation to a divine reality, some aspects of it will be inappropriate or simply irrelevant.[121] For example, when we affirm that God is a shepherd (Ps 23), we do not mean to imply that God is a human being; but all the shepherds we know are, presumably, human beings.[122] Gregory argues that although in Christ's death we have a captive who is redeemed (all of us), a payment (his death on the cross), and a payer of the ransom (Christ

---

118. Ibid., 2.8.

119. Gregory of Nazianzus, *Oration 45*, 22.

120. McGrath, *Christian Theology*, 190.

121. For a significant examination of analogy in theological language, see Burrell, "Analogy, Creation, and Theological Language," 77–98.

122. McGrath, *Theology*, 20–21.

himself), it is inappropriate to designate a recipient for the payment.[123] God does not need to receive such a work as a payment, and the devil does not deserve it.[124]

What Gregory is emphasizing is that the logic of the ransom analogy operates in multiple ways. With respect to the paying of a price, it is right to understand the analogy according to a liberating transaction; but with respect to the recipient of a payment, it is better to understand the analogy, in one direction, according to the persuasion and destruction of the tyrant who held us captive, and in another direction, as fulfilling the righteous will and plan of God. We have fulfilled the Law in Christ, who conquers death and the enemy (Rom 8:1–4).

Gregory Palamas sums up this rich interpretive history in his magnificent sermon on the redemption.[125]

> As we had been justly handed over to the devil's service and subjection to death, it was clearly necessary that the human race's return to freedom and life should be accomplished by God in a just way. Not only had man been surrendered to the envious devil by divine righteousness, but the devil had rejected righteousness and become wrongly enamoured of authority, arbitrary power and, above all, tyranny. He took up arms against justice and used his might against mankind. It pleased God that the devil be overcome first by the justice against which he continuously fought, then afterwards by power, through the resurrection and the future Judgment. Justice before power is the best order of events, and that force should come after justice is the work of a truly divine and good Lord, not of a tyrant.[126]

Gregory here emphasizes that the devil had no just dominion over us, but that God permitted our subjection, so that the work of his justice would bring about our resurrection into eternal life.

123. Alister McGrath and Lonergan both agree that looking for a recipient of the payment is stretching this analogy too far. McGrath, *Christian Theology*, 190–95, and Lonergan, *The Divine Redeemer*, 112.

124. Gregory's friend and ally, Gregory of Nyssa, followed Origen in believing that the death of Christ was a ransom offered to the devil (see Gregory of Nyssa, "Greater Catechism," Chapters 23–24). However, even in this working of the analogy, Nyssa's emphasis is on the way that the pride of the devil brought about his own downfall, as God displayed his superior wisdom.

125. Gregory Palamas, "On Redemption."

126. Ibid., 81.

The Cross and Evil: First Reflection

In chapter 3 of this work, the explanation of God's providence and the place of evil (using Lonergan's analogy of a three-lane highway) had two main points. First, God does not directly will natural evil or penal evil; those are both not part of God's direct will for any person. Second, these evils, and even moral evil that God forbids, are accounted for by God's wisdom. They are not outside of God's plan in terms of being something God cannot account for.

What the three-lane highway analogy never said is that evil (of any sort) is ever God's friend. Evil is an enemy. It is not capable of truly breaking free of God—to do that is to lose all relation with existence. Nor is evil an original creator, a power or thing on its own. It is a rebellion, a falling away, from God's wisdom and love.

By ransoming us, Christ rescues us from evil, fulfilling the righteous law of the Father. Christ's ransom thereby shows that in pardoning us, God is just. He did not merely overwhelm the devil by might, for mere might does not make right, and God's goal is an ultimate righteousness. God overcame the devil by persuasion in the death of Christ. Therefore, in the conquest of the devil, the devil cannot claim that God is unjust. Moreover, Christ our ransom has satisfied the righteous demands of God's law, making peace for us with God.

The reign of darkness is thereby overthrown by the deeper wisdom of God. Death is an enemy (1 Cor 15:26); it is the whale that would devour us. It is also the mark that we have made ourselves enemies of God. In so doing, we have made ourselves enemies of ourselves, for we pursue an apostasy that will destroy us.

By ransoming us, Christ destroys the reign of the whale of death that would swallow us. That is, he himself swallows up and destroys the wickedness of the devil, the flesh, and the world (Luke 11:29–32; 1 Cor 15:54–57). As John Meyendorf puts it, "The point was not to satisfy a legal requirement, but to vanquish the frightful cosmic reality of death, which held humanity under its usurped control and pushed it into the vicious cycle of sin and corruption. . . . God alone is able to vanquish death, because He 'alone has immortality' (1 Tim 6:16)."[127] By ransoming us, Christ overcomes the spiritual wickedness that would hold us in bondage and the evil we have in our beings: the old man who must die, the enemy who tempts and accuses us, and the world order that is shaped as a result of these two.[128]

---

127. Meyendorf, *Byzantine Theology*, 161.

128. See Maximus, *Ambiguum 10*, 9, in which he declares that Christ seized sin through the cross and killed its king, the devil.

God thereby shows that his wisdom and justice are superior to the devil's. The devil's justice knows only sin and death, but the justice of God knows righteousness and resurrection. In the logic of this world, there are three moral cause-and-effect relationships. Good is rewarded by good, a retributive justice that awards merit for righteousness. Evil is rewarded by evil, a retributive justice that awards punishment for unrighteousness. Evil sometimes follows upon good, and this is the choice of moral evil. But the Law of the Cross is a truly supernatural relation, in which God overcomes evil by good; this is a distributive justice by which the providence of God, through Christ our ransom, transforms that which the enemy and our foul intentions intended for evil into the source of our righteousness and resurrection. Retributive justice is not thereby annulled; rather it is fulfilled, for Christ pays everything that was owed, nailing the writ that was against us to the cross, and thereby leading us in triumphal procession over our enemies (Col 2:8–15).

Having demonstrated the absolute superiority of his wisdom and justice, Christ completes our ransom by his power. Evil does not want to let us go. The devil is a thief, a liar, and a murderer (John 8:44; 10:10). The part of us that loves him does not want to die (Rom 7). Yet, as Meyendorf states,

> One discovers in the [Byzantine liturgy of Holy Week] the ultimate, soteriological reason why Cyril's theopaschite formula became the criterion of orthodoxy in sixth-century Byzantine theology: death has been vanquished precisely because God Himself tasted it hypostatically in the humanity which he had assumed. This is the paschal message of Christianity.[129]

Cyril, against the apparent dictums of philosophy, maintained the biblical witness that though the Son suffered in his person (*hypostasis*)—and this a divine person—he was nonetheless fully God.[130] Christ died, yet showed himself free of corruption; by death he trampled death.[131] This world moves toward decline with an inexorable inertia, but we may be of good cheer, for Christ has overcome the world (John 16:33).

That Christ has become our ransom means that rightly, justly, God through might and persuasion delivers us from the enemy. He delivers us from the enemy's power, visiting divine wrath upon him (Rev 19:20–12;

---

129. Meyendorf, *Byzantine Theology*, 164. He refers to Cyril's conclusion that in Christ, God "suffered impassibly." See Cyril of Alexandria, *Scolia on the Incarnation*, and *Christ Is One.*

130. See O'Keefe, "Impassible Suffering," 39–50, and Smith, "Suffering Impassibly."

131. The Byzantine paschal troparion.

20:7–15). The unrepentant evil one receives the only good he will accept, the application of retributive justice in eternal punishment.

Here again, though, we can see the action of a God who does not love violence, but who acts reasonably, and in persuasion, even toward an enemy. Lonergan notes that one good of the ransom analogy is it makes clear, again, that it was not God, but the enemy, who demanded the death and suffering of Jesus.[132] Robert Doran has, furthermore, drawn on the work of Girard to show that, in more concrete terms, one of the central meanings that Christ has laid bare our apostate nature and redeemed it is in his exposure of the cycle of violence we perpetuate, overcome by his refusal to return evil for evil and his enactment of forgiveness.[133]

In our liberation, God begins to make this world new (Rev 21:5). Maximus shows the dynamic intelligibility of the cross in this way:

> [Jesus] restores nature to itself not only in that having become man he kept a free will tranquil and undisturbed in the face of nature and did not allow it to become unsettled in its own movement in a way contrary to nature even in the face of those who were crucifying him; he even chose death at their hands rather than life, as the voluntary character of the passion shows, which was accomplished by the disposition of love for men by the one who underwent this passion. But even more than this, he abolished enmity in nailing to the cross the bond by which nature waged implacable war against itself, "reconciling" us through himself to the Father and with each other in such a way that we no longer have a will opposed to the principle of nature and that thus we be as changeless in our free decisions as we are in our nature.[134]

By ransoming us, Christ heals and elevates our human nature. Before his advent we were caught in the destructive cycle of irrational (a-logos) movement in which we denied both our true nature and our creator. But Christ voluntarily and in love submitted himself to death for our sake; he thereby both abolishes any claim our old nature has on us and elevates our nature to free and reasonable communion with the Father.[135]

---

132. Lonergan, "On Redemption," 18–19. See also Wright, *Jesus and the Victory of God*, 540–611, for a biblical exegesis of the reasons for Jesus' crucifixion.

133. Doran, "The Non-Violent Cross," 51–52.

134. Maximus, "Commentary on the Our Father," 2.

135. See Hart, *The Doors of the Sea*, 45–104.

The Recapitulation of the Human Race

Jesus Christ draws together and sums up the history of the human race. Because humans are the microcosm of the universe, he thereby recapitulates the meaning of the entire cosmos. This teaching draws on the proclamation and prayer of the Apostle Paul in Ephesians 1:3–14 (NRSV). This is one long sentence in Greek, and it is worth quoting in full.

> Blessed be the God and Father of our Lord Jesus Christ, who has blessed us in Christ with every spiritual blessing in the heavenly places, just as he chose us in Christ before the foundation of the world to be holy and blameless before him in love. He destined us for adoption as his children through Jesus Christ, according to the good pleasure of his will, to the praise of his glorious grace that he freely bestowed on us in the Beloved. In him we have redemption through his blood, the forgiveness of our trespasses, according to the riches of his grace that he lavished on us. With all wisdom and insight he has made known to us the mystery of his will, according to his good pleasure that he set forth in Christ, as a plan for the fullness of time, to gather up all things in him, things in heaven and things on earth. In Christ we have also obtained an inheritance, having been destined according to the purpose of him who accomplishes all things according to his counsel and will, so that we, who were the first to set our hope on Christ, might live for the praise of his glory. In him you also, when you had heard the word of truth, the gospel of your salvation, and had believed in him, were marked with the seal of the promised Holy Spirit; this is the pledge of our inheritance toward redemption as God's own people, to the praise of his glory.

"To gather up all things," in Greek, is one word—*anakephalaiosis*, or "recapitulation." Recapitulation deals with how Christ, our prototype and the Second Adam, transforms our historical being. As our exemplar, as our prototype, as Adam—a second, better Adam—Christ sums up and reenacts human history; and he gets it right. By getting it right, Christ changes the meaning of human history. After Adam, the history of the human race is the litany of death one finds in Genesis. In Christ, the second Adam from above, human history leads toward resurrection.[136]

Just as we descended to death through the work of unrighteous Adam, so we ascend to life through the righteous Jesus Christ. Just as death conquered us in Adam, so we receive victory over death, if we are in Christ.

---

136. See the discussion of recapitulation in chapter 2.

> In the recapitulation of human history in Christ, we find again
> the beauty we originally had with the Father. Because the true
> story of the world has been lost in the seemingly endless epic
> of sin, Christ must retell—in the entire motion and content of
> his life, lived toward the Father and for his fellows—the tale
> from the beginning. . . . First and foremost, Christ recapitulates
> humanity's struggle against evil, and in doing so achieves the
> victory humanity could not (5.21.1); he who from the beginning
> is the head of all things recapitulates the human entirely, in the
> shape and substance of a whole life lived for the Father, never
> lapsing into sin, never yielding to the temptation to turn from
> God, enacting in every instant the divine figure of the human
> (5.21.1–3).[137]

This retelling—which is a transformation of human historical being—works
to restore the likeness of God we lost in our apostasy.

Recapitulation in Christ

John Meyendorf emphasizes the way that the Chalcedonian definition
helps us understand how Christ could recapitulate each and every human
existence.[138] Chalcedon proclaims that Christ was consubstantial with the
Father (with respect to his divine nature) and also consubstantial with us
(with respect to his human nature). Christ is a divine person (*hypostasis*),
and in that he is only one person (neither a divided person, nor two persons,
nor a fusion of different types of person), that indicates that there is not
a human person (*hypostasis*) in the Christ. He is one person, the Second
Person of the Trinity, and acknowledged in both human and divine natures.
Because he has no human person, Christ is able to have a relationship with
each human being that he otherwise could not have: no human person can
fully be in another. "But Jesus' hypostasis has a fundamental affinity with
all human personalities: that of being their *model*."[139] That we are created
in God's image indicates we are created in the image of the *Logos*. "When
the Logos became incarnate, the divine stamp matched all its imprints: God
assumed humanity in a way that did not exclude any human hypostasis,
but which opened to all of them the possibility of restoring their unity in

---

137. Hart, *Beauty of the Infinite*, 325–26. Hart's parenthetical references are to Irenaeus, *Against Heresies*.

138. Meyendorf, *Byzantine Theology*, 159.

139. Ibid., emphasis original.

Himself."[140] In Christ, the Second Adam, each of us finds the meaning of our lives realized perfectly, for he is able to exist toward us in a way that is possible for no merely human personality.[141]

According to Irenaeus, Christ's recapitulation is progressive in character and has three main themes. First, Christ restores creation, bringing together the economies of creation and redemption. Second, Christ sums up creation, incarnating its meaning and achieving its goals. Third, Christ reiterates—goes over again—human history, being victorious where Adam and the people of Israel failed.[142] All of this happens according to the economy of God; in fact, it is exactly in Christ's recapitulation that all the different economies that compose human and cosmic history are gathered together in one.

In his typological understanding of Genesis, Irenaeus assigned clear significance to the fact that just as Adam ate of the fruit on the sixth day of creation, leading to his death, so also Christ was crucified on the sixth day of the week.[143]

> For by summing up in Himself the whole human race from the beginning to the end, He has also summed up its death. From this it is clear that the Lord suffered death, in obedience to His Father, upon that day on which Adam died while he disobeyed God. Now he died on the same day in which he did eat. For God said, "In that day on which ye shall eat of it, ye shall die by death." The Lord, therefore, recapitulating in Himself this day, underwent His sufferings upon the day preceding the Sabbath, that is, the sixth day of the creation, on which day man was created; thus granting him a second creation by means of His passion, which is that [creation] out of death.

By his passion, Jesus summed up all of human death, thereby making us a new creation no longer subject to the rule and fear of death. As recapitulated in Christ, the horizon of human existence is not death, but resurrection and eternal life (John 11:23–27).

Maximus drew on Irenaeus' themes (and those of many others, such as Basil the Great and Gregory of Nazianzus) to present the truly cosmic nature of Christ's recapitulation.

---

140. Ibid.
141. Ibid.
142. Kurz, "Gifts of Creation," 118–19.
143. Ibid., 121.

> For the wisdom and sagacity of God the Father is the Lord Jesus
> Christ, who holds together the universals of beings by the power
> of wisdom, and embraces their complementary parts by the sa-
> gacity of understanding, since by nature he is the fashioner and
> provider of all, and through himself draws into one what is di-
> vided, and abolishes war between beings, and binds everything
> into peaceful friendship and undivided harmony, *both what is
> in heaven and what is on earth* (Col. 1:20), as the divine Apostle
> says.[144]

Maximus here indicates again the significance of the fact that the wisdom
by which the universe is made (the *Logos*) is the personal being that enters
its history and draws all its meanings together. Whereas the universe would
exist in a state of war if left to its own terms—for it would be intrinsically
a-logos, irrational, and inescapably at enmity with itself and every other existence—in the very being of Christ, by his wisdom, there is peace.

Although we are made according to the image of the *Logos*, with the
coming of Christ an entirely new way of being human appeared.[145] All of
our history reflects the divine economy, but our renewal did not come about
by an intelligibility or agency immanent in that natural order. God's intention in creation was to provide a way we could have union with him, and
he gave us capacities of reason and free will that would enable us to live a
life with him. In that we misused those abilities, God provided in Christ
another way, "more marvelous and more befitting of God than the first," that
we would come into union with him.[146]

According to God's salvific economy, the rational and volitional powers of the created order were not annulled, but they were purified, elevated,
and redirected, having been recapitulated in Christ.

> God took on himself both [the *logos* of creaturely origin and the
> *tropos* of birth] for our sake and thus renewed our nature, or
> better yet he created our nature anew, and returned it to its pri-
> mordial dignity of incorruptibility through his holy flesh, born
> of our own flesh and animated by a rational soul. What is more,
> he generously provided our nature with the gift of deification,
> which he could not possibly have failed to bestow since he was
> himself God incarnate, indwelling the flesh in the same manner

144. Maximus, *Ambiguum 41.*
145. Ibid. *7*, 4.
146. Ibid.

that the soul indwells the body, that is, thoroughly interpen-
etrating it in a union without confusion.[147]

The *logos* of creaturely origin refers to dependence on the *Logos* for one's being, whereas the *tropos* of birth refers to the way we who come into existence
do so, not in a state of rest, but in a state of change and motion. Christ's
human nature, as every human nature, depended on his divine nature for its
meaning and being; and, because his human will always perfectly submitted
to his divine will, the motion of his being was always in accord with his
divine nature. What is more, this ontological state had an effect. Created
nature, joined in a union without confusion with the divine nature, receives
the dignity of incorruptibility, and the nature that the *Logos* assumed is
elevated and healed.

In Lonergan's discussion of recapitulation, he turns first of all to the
absolutely bountiful nature of the divine wisdom and then to the way that
the concrete order of the universe displays and manifests that wisdom.[148]
He also notes the special way that the wisdom of God is made manifest by
the cross.[149] It is in this world-order, in which evil exists and is overcome by
divine love, that we see the wisdom of God. The basis of our participation in
this wisdom is nothing that we are owed but is only the bounteous wisdom,
goodness, love, and mercy of the Lord.[150]

The Cross and Evil: Second Reflection

The recapitulation of human history by Christ is our victory over sin and
the devil, and it is the source of our inner renewal and resurrection. "He
has therefore, in His work of recapitulation, summed up all things, both
waging war against our enemy, and crushing him who had at the beginning
led us away captives in Adam, and trampled upon his head."[151] The best
revenge against evil is a life lived well, an abundant life that evil has wanted
to poison.[152]

The Christian answer to evil is the resurrection. The Christian answer
to evil is the apocalypse and eternal life—God makes all things new, and in
this life we will know Jesus Christ (Rev 21:5). Because Christ has re-done

147. Maximus, *Ambiguum* 42.

148. Lonergan, *The Divine Redeemer*, 97–98.

149. Ibid., 102.

150. *ST* I 21.4 ad 1.

151. Irenaeus, *Against Heresies*, 5.20.1, referring to Gen 3:15.

152. Herbert, *Jacula Prudentium*.

and summed up human history in himself, restoring it to what God planned for it to be, the meaning of human history now includes resurrection. This resurrection is not merely in the future, though, but also is real now as the life, death, and resurrection of Christ give significance to the events of our lives, to our suffering, to the meaninglessness we war against.[153] This is true to the extent that Christ truly becomes our life.

As Paul wrote to the Philippians, "I want to know Christ and the power of his resurrection and the sharing of his sufferings by becoming like him in his death, if somehow I may attain the resurrection from the dead" (Phil 3:10–11). Together, as humans bound together with Christ, we move in a history that glimpses and foretastes the most abundant life. We will reach it fully someday, when the meaning of human history—shaped and drawn by God—will be complete. Evil will be no more, righteousness will shine like the noonday sun, and we will walk, together, with God.

Conclusion

The meaning of the cross, then, overflows all our formulations as Christ brings peace to this dark world. We approach God's wisdom, expressed in our words, as a spectrum of great beauty, not as a laser with which we may penetrate to the core. Yet, we are enlightened, and transformed, as the gift of Christ, crucified and resurrected, penetrates us (1 Cor 1:18–31; 2 Cor 3:18).

According to the analogy of satisfaction, Christ died because in his death he offered to God the perfect willingness to atone for our situation, fulfilling and declaring the divine justice, going the whole way and holding nothing back. In this way, the retributive justice of God was satisfied and a new order of the world—a distributive justice—put into effect (Rom 5:6–11; 8:31–38).

According to the analogy of ransom, Christ died to fulfill the righteous law of the Father, and to persuade and conquer the enemy. Because his death is the fulcrum upon which God decisively condemns and punishes sin, it is the perfect combination of persuasion (acting justly toward the devil and the flesh) and conquest (showing the superiority of God's justice and wisdom, that can overcome evil with good (Matt 20:27–28; Rom 6:5–11; 1 Pet 1:18–20).

According to the analogy of sacrifice, Christ died to become for us the perfect symbol of God. Because sin always leads to death, the cross shows us the seriousness of sin, and the perfection of the reconciliation by which the Father is pleased. The suffering of Christ participates in the perfect

---

153. See Williams, *The Resurrection*.

contrition he showed for sins, and a perfect knowledge and love for God. Christ willingly accepted suffering and allowed it to the full, that his repentance on our behalf might be complete. The suffering was not demanded of him by God, but was inflicted on him by the enemy and by human beings; but Christ turned this work of evil into an occasion of great good, using the suffering that the betrayal, false trials, torture, and crucifixion wrought to offer a perfect sacrifice of contrition, knowledge, and love on our behalf (Matt 9:13; 1 Cor 5:6–8; John 1:29–34).

According to the analogy of recapitulation, Christ died because by taking on our fallen story entirely, yet without sin, he redefines it. Because it was impossible for death to keep its hold on him, he makes the human story to end not in death, but in resurrection. Thereby the original intention of creation is fulfilled, first in the glorified Christ himself and then in the deification of those he came to save (John 17:20–24; 19:30; Phil 2:1–11; Eph 1:3–14).

6

Standing Forth a Radiant Being

SALVATION

The incarnation is the principle instance of grace and prototype of what we are called by grace to become. We often take the command to conform to Jesus only in human terms—Jesus was the perfect man, and we should therefore become perfected human beings. This is true. But the greater truth is that we are called to grow into the whole measure of the maturity of Christ (Eph 4:13; Matt 5:48). What Jesus is by nature, we are called to become by grace. By nature, Jesus is a personal union of the human and the divine. By nature, we are human, but by grace, we are called to and given life that is divine.

Salvation is having our life (our persons) personally united with God's life. We receive God's life in such a way that we become little christs—growing to be like the Son of God because we have been begotten from above (John 3:3). This must be understood carefully, but in a way that does not sap its power. We continue to have a human life (received as children of Adam and Eve). Our human life is healed by God's healing grace (justification, and the aspect of sanctification that restores us to being truly human). Yet we receive the fulfillment of that created human life, the likeness of God—God's life—which grows to become the new principle, and fulfillment, of our life and being.

Those who have read C. S. Lewis' *Mere Christianity* have heard this story before.[1] Imagine that a statue, human-shaped but made of inert stone, should come alive—receive a human life. It is the story of the myth Pygmalion. A lesser kind of being, shaped like us, in our image, becomes one of

1. Lewis, *Mere Christianity*, 153–59.

163

us by receiving human life. But we are made in the image of God. We begin to become by grace what Jesus is by nature. We do not become the divine nature—that is absolutely impossible—but we come to the culmination of human life by receiving God's life, by grace. From the very beginning the purpose of human life was not to remain merely human. It was to come to share the life of love and wisdom, of personal communion, of true life, that is the life of God (John 17:20–24).

The work of the Holy Spirit is to create the Christ-life in us, thereby giving us communion with the Father. The Eastern Christian tradition, and much of the Western tradition, identifies this new life as divinization, or deification (*theosis*). Divinization is an image, an analogy by which we can come to organize and understand what it means that we have been saved, are being saved, and await our ultimate salvation. This chapter will explore its meaning in three ways. First, it will present the most significant biblical, patristic, and medieval evidence. Second, it will use Bernard Lonergan's systematic definition to give clarity to its discussion. Finally, it will extend that definition, in the light of the Law of the Cross, to give a spectrum of the manifold ways that God transforms us, our histories, and our world, as he draws us to become like him.

Scriptural and Patristic Foundation

Because of the somewhat unfamiliar nature of the analogy of deification to many Western readers, it is worth reviewing some of its biblical foundations, as well as the way that those foundations were interpreted by central figures in the Christian tradition.

The Language and Logic of Scripture

Following a prayer for grace and peace to be ours in abundance through the knowledge of God and our Lord Jesus Christ, 2 Pet 1:3–4 (NRSV) says,

> His divine power has given us everything needed for life and godliness, through the knowledge of him who called us by his own glory and goodness. Thus he has given us, through these things, his precious and very great promises, so that through them you may escape from the corruption that is in the world because of lust, and may become participants of the divine nature.

This language, coming from a Jewish monotheist, is striking. The apostle goes on to exhort us that our minds, our character, and our very lives must transformed, renouncing our sinful past, and entering the kingdom of God provided by Christ's grace (2 Pet 1:5–11).

Having warned against the work of antichrist, and proclaiming that the anointing of Christ abides in us, 1 John 3:1–2 (NRSV) states,

> See what love the Father has given us, that we should be called children of God; and that is what we are. The reason the world does not know us is that it did not know him. Beloved, we are God's children now; what we will be has not yet been revealed. What we do know is this: when he is revealed, we will be like him, for we will see him as he is.

The apostle then warns us to pursue purity and turn from the work of the devil, loving one another (1 John 3:3–11).

In the great, culminating, theological conclusion to the first half of the Epistle to the Romans, Paul declares (Rom 8:15–19, NRSV),

> For you did not receive a spirit of slavery to fall back into fear, but you have received a spirit of adoption. When we cry, "Abba! Father!" it is that very Spirit bearing witness with our spirit that we are children of God, and if children, then heirs, heirs of God and joint heirs with Christ—if, in fact, we suffer with him so that we may also be glorified with him.
>
> I consider that the sufferings of this present time are not worth comparing with the glory about to be revealed to us. For the creation waits with eager longing for the revealing of the children of God.

The apostle continues to proclaim the way that our present suffering, like labor pains, will lead to our resurrection, as the Spirit intercedes for us and works in us, conforming us to the image of the Son, according to the will of God (Rom 8:20–30).

The analogy of deification has roots in the Old Testament, as well. Psalm 82:6 (NRSV) states, "I say, 'You are gods, / children of the Most High, all of you.'" Jesus quotes this Psalm in John 10:34–36, applying it to those who received the word of God. He, thereby, confounded the Jewish leaders by the declaration of his own divinity, as confirmed by the miracles he performed (John 10:37–39).

One can see the dynamics of deification in many New Testament descriptions of salvation. For example, Paul's enumeration of the fruit of the Spirit (Gal 5:22–23) gives a picture of new life. The fruit of the Spirit are the attributes of God, received in human form. In our salvation, the loving God creates in us his love. His blessedness is echoed in our joy. The divine impassibility is received in us as peace. His eternity becomes patience in we who wait. God's condescension and compassion become kindness, given to us. Goodness is the reception of God's moral nature, which is also the full expression in action of who he is. His constancy grounds our faithfulness. His omnipotence is seen in us as gentleness, and his wisdom in our self-control.

All of these are the work of the Spirit, enlivening us by giving us God's life; and they are the exact character of Jesus. Jesus' life was a life of complete love, for Jesus is God, and God is love. As we are changed to love what and how we did not love before, we are made like him. Jesus was a man of sorrows and acquainted with grief, yet his life was a life filled with the joy of the blessedness of God himself. As we find joy in the midst of suffering in the Christian life, we become like him. Jesus is the Prince of Peace, who came to make peace between God and sinful human beings. As we become ministers of reconciliation, and as we find peace ourselves with God, we become like Jesus. He is also the most patient one, who came in the fullness of time, to fulfill the times. Time did not master him; he was the maker of and master of time. As we live more by God's grace and less by our human schedules and timetables, as we seek first the kingdom of heaven with what we do and care about, we more and more live out the character of Jesus. How great the kindness, furthermore, of the one who sacrifices himself on our behalf! He was also good the way only God can be good. In his faithfulness, he will never leave us nor forsake us. In his gentleness, he drew even the little children to himself. And, has anyone ever been mature the way Jesus is, truly of a sound mind, never controlled by his desires, but desiring the Father's way and will?

The whole fullness (*plērōma*) of deity dwells in Jesus in bodily form, and we have received fullness (*peplērōmenoi*) in him, the head of all rule and authority (Col 2:9–10). It is in imitating Jesus, the exact image of God, that we become truly human ourselves, and recipients of the divine life. This new life has aspects of being and aspects of action, and all of the fruit of the Spirit share this dual nature. For it is as we are drawn away from our old life and transformed that we are able to love in a way that we did not formerly love, walk in a way that responsibly chooses the good, and know that which (without God's help) we could never know.

The Patristic Tradition

Trying to express the comprehensive and supernatural nature of this transformation, the patristic authors spoke of Jesus' work in us in the language of deification. As I noted in chapter 1, such language does not indicate any eliding of monotheism or assertion of pantheism. Rather, it puts into words the fullness (*plērōma*) of life we have received in Christ. As Norman Russell's work shows, deification as a doctrine developed in a complex philosophical and religious context and came to be a distinctively Christian formulation of salvation that occupied a central place in the most prominent Eastern theologians.[2] Christensen and Wittung's edited volume shows, as well, how deification became a central element in both Eastern and Western traditions, including many key figures of the Protestant Reformation.[3]

In Irenaeus' arguments against the Valentinians, who despised the matter of our human flesh, he argues,

> For it was for this end that the Word of God was made man, and He who was the Son of God became the Son of man, that man, having been taken into the Word, and receiving the adoption, might become the son of God. For by no other means could we have attained to incorruptibility and immortality, unless we had been united to incorruptibility and immortality. But how could we be joined to incorruptibility and immortality, unless, first, incorruptibility and immortality had become that which we also are, so that the corruptible might be swallowed up by incorruptibility, and the mortal by immortality, that we might receive the adoption of sons?[4]

Irenaeus then goes on to affirm most clearly that only Jesus, among humans, ever had or ever will have true divinity; he also speaks of the way that, because of Christ's death and resurrection, we are bound together with God in our resurrection.[5]

Athanasius built on Irenaeus' account, declaring,

> [The Word], indeed, assumed humanity that we might become God. He manifested Himself by means of a body in order that we might perceive the Mind of the unseen Father. He endured shame from men that we might inherit immortality. He Himself was unhurt by this, for He is impassable and incorruptible; but

2. Russell, *Deification*.

3. Christensen and Wittung, *Partakers in the Divine Nature*.

4. Irenaeus, *Against Heresies*, 3.19.1.

5. Ibid., 3.19.2–3.

by His own impassability He kept and healed the suffering men
on whose account He thus endured.[6]

It is important to note that for both Irenaeus and Athanasius, the reason
that God became a human being is for our salvation, that we might be deified—beginning now, but fully achieved in the resurrection.

In this way, the classic christological doctrines have always been linked
to soteriology.[7] In his interpretation of Athanasius, John Behr notes the central way that patristic tradition saw the incarnation as something only truly
knowable through the cross.[8] The Word did not come for his own sake, but
for ours, and by his crucifixion he gives us his life.

Gregory of Nazianzus, then, followed Athanasius' lead in his criticism
of the Apollinarians, who taught that the divine *Logos* took the place of
Christ's human mind. Christ's human nature, according to this false teaching, consisted only of material, not intellectual or spiritual being.

> If anyone has put his trust in [Christ] as a Man without a human
> mind, he is really bereft of mind, and quite unworthy of salva-
> tion. For that which He has not assumed He has not healed; but
> that which is united to His Godhead is also saved. If only half
> Adam fell, then that which Christ assumes and saves may be
> half also; but if the whole of his nature fell, it must be united to
> the whole nature of Him that was begotten, and so be saved as
> a whole.[9]

Gregory's thought presages the dogmatic precision of Chalcedon, in which
the unity of Christ's person, acknowledged in two natures, is seen to be the
exact basis for our salvation. We are united to Christ, and this union is not
merely to half of him, for it is not merely half of us who needs to be saved.
Christ assumes human nature to heal us, and this healing—or salvation—
can only be accomplished by our elevating union with his divine nature.[10]

Augustine preaches deification with his typical pleonastic clarity in his
sermon on Psalm 50.

> See in the same Psalm those to whom he saith, "I have said, Ye
> are gods, and children of the Highest all; but ye shall die like
> men, and fall like one of the princes." It is evident then, that He

---

6. Athanasius, *On the Incarnation of the Word*, 54.

7. Lossky, *Mystical Theology*, 7–22.

8. Behr, *The Nicene Faith*, 1:185.

9. Gregory of Nazianzus, "To Cledonius the Priest Against Apollinarius (Epistle
101)."

10. See McGuckin, "Strategic Adaptation of Deification," 101–4.

hath called men gods, that are deified of His Grace, not born of His Substance. For He doth justify, who is just through His own self, and not of another; and He doth deify who is God through Himself, not by the partaking of another. But He that justifieth doth Himself deify, in that by justifying He doth make sons of God. "For He hath given them power to become the sons of God." If we have been made sons of God, we have also been made gods: but this is the effect of Grace adopting, not of nature generating. For the only Son of God, God, and one God with the Father, Our Lord and Saviour Jesus Christ, was in the beginning the Word, and the Word with God, the Word God.[11]

Augustine thus reinforces the link between the advent of the Christ, who is true God, and our deification, in which we are adopted as children of God.[12]

The theme of deification is often, not surprisingly, present in a significant way in connection with Christ's birth.[13] In a sermon on Christmas, Augustine again refers to our deification by the incarnation of the Word, using the traditional formula, "God became man so that man might become God."[14] His point here was not simply to declare the doctrine of this special day, though, or at least not to do so in a way restricted to the Gospel depictions of Bethlehem. His special reference is to the way that, by his incarnation, death, and resurrection, Christ meets with us and changes us; Augustine enriches that understanding by referring to the way that we have participation with Christ in Holy Communion.

Maximus and Aquinas

Few theologians have spoken of divinization as movingly and penetratingly as the defender of Chalcedon, Maximus the Confessor. Although Maximus never assembled his reflections into a systematic theology, through an examination of his various writings one can find a synthetic and purifying understanding of the harvest of patristic theology. As chapter 1 of this work explained, Maximus saw the purpose of the universe not just to include or allow but to be centered on the incarnation of Christ, who draws the ages together, both fulfilling the Father's purpose, and uniting us to God.

11. Augustine, "Psalm L."

12. See Hallonsten, "*Theosis* in Recent Research," 283; see also Meconi, *The One Christ*, on the way that Augustine's understanding of divinization interpenetrated his understanding of soteriology; and Gordon "Deifying Adoption;" I thank Joe Gordon for pointing me to Meconi's fine work.

13. Ibid., 283–84.

14. Augustine, *Sermon 13*.

Maximus' explanation of divinization can conveniently be organized around his symbolic reading of the days of creation in Gen 1:1—2:3. In particular, he speaks of the existence and destiny of human beings according to the sixth, seventh, and eighth days of creation.[15] The "eighth day of creation" is a patristic theme that extends at least back to Basil the Great, and it indicates the way that the life of the world to come transcends the life of the present universe.[16] This progression of the days of creation is closely tied to Maximus' theme, already mentioned by this work in chapter 3, that we progress from being, to well-being, to eternal being.[17]

According to the Genesis account, God made human beings on the sixth day of creation (Gen 1:26–27). By analogy with this sixth day, Maximus explains human existence according to the mode in which we are created, before elevation by supernatural grace.[18] In this day we are made in the image of God; that is, through the two-fold natural birth as body and soul we have a being that is absolutely dependent upon, and that expresses, participation in the essence of God.[19] Life according to the sixth day includes the accomplishments of the life of natural virtue.[20] Such virtues are the excellence of merely natural existence, but they exist as types and foreshadow the fullness of life to come.[21] We are created as beings in motion—that is, as those who have desire, who are moved by the senses, motivated through the passions, and who are subject to becoming and change. If confined to the level of created being, then, and not renewed and directed by well-being, we become enemies of ourselves, for we do not live according to the *logoi* of our own existence.[22] We also are, thereby, enemies of God, for the *Logos* is him, and our *logoi* are what they are by participation in him. We are created out of nothing, with an existence that is real but not yet stabilized by eternal rest in God; we exist, then, in a radical dialectic between falling back into the darkness and moving forward to union, by supernatural grace, with the source of our being.[23]

15. Maximus, *Chapters on Knowledge*, 1.51, 55–56, 60; *Ambiguum 65*; *Questions and Doubts*, 191.

16. See Baghos, "St Basil's Eschatological Vision," 85–103.

17. Maximus, *Chapters on Knowledge*, 1.56.

18. Ibid., 1.51, 55–56, 60; *Ambiguum 65*.

19. Maximus, *Questions and Doubts*, 156–57; *Ambiguum 42*. See chapter 1 of this work.

20. Maximus, *Questions on Knowledge*, 1.55.

21. Maximus, *Ad Thalassium 22*.

22. Maximus, *Ambiguum 42*; *Ambiguum 7, 2*.

23. Maximus, *Ad Thalassium 22*; *Ambiguum 7, 2*.

The seventh day of creation is the Sabbath rest of God, and in Maximus' typology it indicates the life of salvation in the present age (Gen 2:1–3).[24] By baptism, we have entry into a second birth by the Holy Spirit that gives us access to a new way of life.[25] In the seventh day, God's grace works in concert with human free will.[26] This is the age in which our being becomes well-being—moving more and more according to the *logoi* by which we are made—and in which we begin to achieve the likeness of God that we have potency toward by being made in his image. By grace, we become accustomed to the free choice of the good and receive the knowledge of God.[27] In this day, Christ orders our minds to the characteristics of the mind of God, in the meekness that acts by resolution and self control, in the detachment that is not owned by this world, and in the long-suffering that overcomes evil with good. The Holy Spirit also creates in us God's love, making us receptive of his character. Just as we have existence in relation to God's essence, by voluntary deliberation we come to participate in God's energies: his mighty wisdom, love, and power.[28]

In the eighth day of creation, our well-being is made eternal. This does not indicate a mere extension of the temporal life of salvation; rather, we are made complete and transcend the life of this world, becoming, as far as is possible for a merely created being, like Jesus. In our ultimate deification,

> [The soul] becomes a radiant abode of the Holy Spirit and receives, if one can say it, the full power of knowing the divine nature insofar as this is possible. By this power there is discarded the origin of what is inferior, to be replaced by that of what is superior, while the soul like God keeps inviolable in itself by the grace of its calling the realization of the gifts which it has received. By this power, Christ is always born mysteriously and willingly, becoming incarnate through those who are saved.[29]

In this way, Christ completes

> His mystical work of deifying humanity in every respect, of course, short of an identity of essence with God; and he will assimilate humanity to himself and elevate us to a position above

24. Maximus, *Chapters on Knowledge*, 1.37–39.

25. Maximus, *Ambiguum 42.*

26. Ibid.

27. Maximus, *Questions and Doubts,* 156–57.

28. Maximus, *Chapters on Knowledge,* 2.83; *Questions and Doubts,* 156–57; in Maximus' understanding, God's energies are nothing less than his complete and real divinity, understood by an analogy with motion.

29. Maximus, "Commentary on the Our Father," 4.

all the heavens. It is to this exalted position that the natural magnitude of God's grace summons lowly humanity, out of a goodness that is infinite.[30]

By deification, we receive a third birth, by resurrection, into the ultimate rest of God. This is a rest in which our desires are active, but totally directed and fulfilled by moving only toward God himself, their ultimate source and goal.[31] We also receive immortality, incorruption, and impassibility as God interpenetrates our beings, minds, and wills.[32] Following the perichoretic logic of Chalcedon, we become partakers of the divine nature, interpenetrated by him, except at the level of being.[33] We do not become the divine essence; rather, the deification we receive is the ultimate fulfillment of the human species.

While it may seem more usual to see Gregory Palamas as the heir of Maximus' theology, the understanding Maximus has of divinization may also fit naturally with the theology of Thomas Aquinas. Palamas prominently uses the language of God's energies and essence, as does Maximus, but Thomas, as part of the Augustinian tradition, eschews this terminology.[34] However, an examination of the meanings of Maximus and Aquinas may show significant consonance, albeit expressed quite differently by theologians who had significantly different idiomatic expressions and historical situations.

One central issue has to do with the way in which we come to know God. With Palamas, we might ask whether we know God in a way that is immediately accessible to us now, and that will continue, though to a much higher degree, in the world to come.[35] The theological consequence of God's accessibility is then that God's being (essence) always remains unknown to us, even in heaven, for we cannot know God's essence now. Palamas' distinction of essence and energies seems to defend the reality of present Christian experience by making something like this trade. Aquinas, on the other hand, wondered whether we know God in a way that is mediated to us now by faith, and that with respect to experience and knowledge will have an essentially different character in the life of the world to come.

Under the first view, experience of God is knowing something that we directly have in this life—God's energies, the uncreated light of the

30. Maximus, *Ad Thalasium* 22.

31. Maximus, *Ambiguum* 42.

32. Maximus, *Ambiguum* 7, 3.

33. Maximus, *Ambiguum* 41.

34. See Finch, "Neo-Palamism," 233–49.

35. See Florovsky, *Bible, Church, Tradition,* 105–20.

transfiguration—and this experience transforms us in a dynamic way. Prior to this experience, we may have had to rely on God's grace to purify us and conform us to him by the disciplines of prayer and asceticism.[36] Under the second view, we relate to God most directly in this life by being changed by God, that is, by becoming a person who has faith in God and is in love with him.[37] In this case, what we directly experience is God's effects; especially, we experience that our lives, and this whole cosmos, can never be the same. This is an experience of God, because God has made this change in us directly by the gift of the Spirit.

The knowledge we have of God in this life, according to the second understanding, is mediated by faith, and we will know and experience God in a fundamentally different way in the life of the world to come.[38] We will know God's essence then, which we cannot do at all now.[39] The love that we have for and from him, though, is already a direct participation in the life of the world to come.[40]

Although some modern authors differ over whether Thomas taught the doctrine of deification, he is explicit in affirming it: "The Only-begotten Son of God, wanting us to be partakers of his divinity, assumed our human nature so that, having become man, he might make men gods."[41] Far from being a peripheral teaching for Thomas, it is central and indispensable for his doctrine of grace and salvation.

With respect to the habit of charity, by which we have friendship with God and which is the form—the undergirding intelligibility—of every other virtue, Thomas said,

> The Divine Essence Itself is charity, even as It is wisdom and goodness. Wherefore just as we are said to be good with the goodness which is God, and wise with the wisdom which is God (since the goodness whereby we are formally good is a participation of Divine goodness, and the wisdom whereby we are formally wise, is a share of Divine wisdom), so too, the charity whereby formally we love our neighbor is a participation of Divine charity.[42]

36. See Palamas' defense of hesychasm in *The Triads*.

37. *ST* II–II 23.1; 23.6 ad 1.

38. *ST* II–II 1.1; 4.1.

39. *ST* I 12.1, 4.

40. *ST* II–II 26.13.

41. Aquinas, *Opusc. 57*, in festo Corp. Christi, 1; quoted by John Paul II, "Spirit Enables Us to Share in Divine Nature," and cited as doctrine by the *Catechism of the Catholic Church*, 1.2.2.3.1, 460.

42. *ST* II–II 23.2 ad 1.

The friendship of charity is that by which God communicates to us his happiness.[43] "Happiness," or "beatitude," in Thomas essentially has to do not with transitory feelings but with a state of well-being.[44] Friendship, furthermore, requires a certain mutuality. We are utterly unable to attain any kind of mutuality with God on our own terms; knowing and loving God, however, is the reason for our being. By God's gracious gift, we are given relationship with him, and transformed to achieve the goal of our created nature.[45]

The gifts of faith and hope likewise participate in our elevation. Aquinas states concerning hope,

> As stated above (Article 1), the hope of which we speak now, attains God by leaning on His help in order to obtain the hoped for good. Now an effect must be proportionate to its cause. Wherefore the good which we ought to hope for from God properly and chiefly is the infinite good, which is proportionate to the power of our divine helper, since it belongs to an infinite power to lead anyone to an infinite good. Such a good is eternal life, which consists in the enjoyment of God Himself. For we should hope from Him for nothing less than Himself, since His goodness, whereby He imparts good things to His creature, is no less than His Essence. Therefore the proper and principal object of hope is eternal happiness.[46]

Faith, also, is that by which eternal life has already begun in us, for it contains virtually (although not yet actually) the transforming vision of God's essence we will have in eternity.[47]

The active agent bringing about our deification can be nothing other than God himself.

> Nothing can act beyond its species, since the cause must always be more powerful than its effect. Now the gift of grace surpasses every capability of created nature, since it is nothing short of a partaking of the Divine Nature, which exceeds every other nature. And thus it is impossible that any creature should cause grace. For it is as necessary that God alone should

---

43. *ST* II–II 23.1.

44. *ST* I–II, 3.8; I–II 4.3; See Cone, "Aquinas' Charity and Lonergan's Religious Conversion"; see also Snell and Cone, *Authentic Cosmopolitanism*, 131–45; Wieland, "Happiness," 57–68; and Schockenhoff, "Charity," 244–58.

45. *ST* I–II 1.8.

46. *ST* II–II 17.2.

47. *ST* II–II 1.4.

deify, bestowing a partaking of the Divine Nature by a participated likeness, as it is impossible that anything save fire should
enkindle.[48]

The goal of our created nature is the supernatural order of communion with
God. This goal is disproportionate to what we (or any other created agent)
can achieve; yet our natures have potency to know God and be like him.
In grace, God's gift to us of himself actuates this obediential potency as we
receive his life.[49]

Our deification proceeds equally from the mission of the Word and
the mission of the Spirit, bringing us into communion with the Father. The
divine missions indicate the way that the Son and the Spirit, through whom
the Father creates the world, enter into relation with this world in a way that
is analogous to their eternal intra-Trinitarian relations.[50] The Father, Son,
and Spirit have always interpenetrated each other in infinite and eternal
relations of mutual self-giving, for God's being is a relationship of wisdom
and love.[51] The visible mission of the Son is the incarnation of Jesus, his
actions and teaching, and his death and resurrection; the invisible mission
of the Son consists of the gift of faith by which we have eternal life. The
visible mission of the Spirit is such miraculous signs as tongues of fire and
a divine wind; the invisible mission of the Spirit (in which Thomas is much
more interested) is the transformation of our hearts by the gift of charity,
the strengthening of our wills by hope, and the creation in us of the fruit
of the Spirit. We can conceive of the Word as having an analogy with an
unlimited act of understanding, and the faith that proceeds in us has an
analogy with the eternal begetting of the Son.[52] Likewise, we can conceive
the Spirit as having an analogy with an unlimited act of love, and the love
that transforms us has an analogy with the eternal love by which the Spirit
proceeds from the Father and the Son.[53]

While all of creation shows vestiges of the Trinity, for an effect is
always similar to its cause, and the Trinity is the universe's cause, the Word

---

48. *ST* I–II 112.1.

49. See chapter 2's discussion of obediential potency.

50. *ST* I.43; see Emery, "Trinity and Creation," 58–76. See also Lonergan, *The Triune God: Systematics.*

51. *ST* I 28.2; 29.4; 32.3.

52. *ST* I 27.2; 34.1–3.

53. ST I 27.4; 37 and 38. Aquinas here employs and develops Augustine's psychological analogy for the Trinity. See Wilkins, "Why Two Divine Missions?," 1–30; and
"Trinitarian Missions and the Order of Grace according to Thomas Aquinas," 689–708.

and Spirit are sent only according to sanctifying (that is, saving) grace.[54] This means that the orders of creation and redemption, the divine providence that flows from the love and wisdom of God, brings this world about and enters into it for the purpose of having eternal communion with us. All other graces, though real, are ordered to this purpose, which is the glory of God. Such is the foundation of our being, and such is the only possible culmination of this universe's long drama.[55] By the gift of themselves to us in our creation and redemption, the Son and the Spirit create themselves in us, thereby giving us entry into the life of self-giving love and wisdom they have always had with the Father.

By creation, God causes us and brings us into relationship with himself according to his essence, power, and presence: by essence, because we have being by a relation of absolute dependence on his eternal being; by power, because he is the efficient cause that makes us; by presence because he knows us, acts in us, and includes us in his providence.[56] By salvation, though, God comes to exist in us in a new and different way, for he comes to dwell in us as in a temple.[57] The infinite act of wisdom, that is the Word, and the infinite act of love, that is the Spirit, come to dwell in us—have an abiding and elevating relationship with us—in a way that brings us to know and love like them. The desire of our minds is superabundantly fulfilled by the knowledge of God, and the motion of our souls finds joyful rest in him, the true object of every desire.[58]

We do not thereby become the divine essence, nor does the state of our knowledge and love ever exactly come to equal God's. As in any Christian theology of divinization, we become as much like God as is possible for a creature, and knowing and loving exactly as God does would require us actually to be the divine essence.[59] Nor does this elevation by God abrogate human free will, for the love by which we have beatitude must be freely chosen.[60] Rather, this similitude to the divine operations is the ultimate fulfillment of the human potencies of intelligence and will.

54. *ST* I 32.1; 43.3.

55. See Merriell, "Trinitarian Anthropology," 123–42.

56. *ST* I 8.3.

57. *ST* I 43.3.

58. *ST* I–II 4.1.

59. *ST* I 12.7, 8.

60. *ST* I–II Introduction and 1.1. See chapter 4 of this work.

Communication of the Divine Nature

In Lonergan's early work, "The Supernatural Order," he extends Thomas' theology of divinization. While Lonergan's argument continues the project of his dissertation and earliest published theological works, the basic insight it provides can help one to consider the truly comprehensive and transformative nature of salvation.[61] Lonergan's later theology of the atonement, in a complementary way, helps give specificity to the content and dynamics of the divine life created in us.[62]

The first thesis of "The Supernatural Order" specifies that, "There exists a created communication of the divine nature, which is a created, proportionate, and remote principle whereby there are operations in creatures through which they attain God as he is in himself."[63] Each element of this thesis deserves careful examination.[64] Taken briefly, the thesis posits a communication, a principle, operations, and an attainment.

First, a communication is "that by which something becomes common or shared, which otherwise would be proper (not common, restricted to itself)."[65] For example, loving the way that God loves and knowing the way that God knows are proper only to God, for they are attributes of the divine nature and not of any finite and contingent nature. That there is a created communication of the divine nature indicates that, by God's gracious action, finite and contingent beings come to participate in the divine nature in a way they have no ability to do on their own. That this is a communication of God's nature indicates that God's grace affects us in a way that impacts our being; the remainder of Lonergan's thesis specifies just how grace affects our being.

Second, a principle is "that which is first in some order."[66] This principle is a communication of nature, and it becomes the principle of operations. Therefore, grace provides us with a new orienting set of relations, both in the order of our being and in the order of our doing. In *Insight*, Lonergan specifies that the operation of salvation does not involve a change

---

61. See Lonergan, *Grace and Freedom*; Michael Stebbins' *The Divine Initiative* has become the indispensible companion to and interpreter of Lonergan's early work on grace.

62. See chapter 5 of this work.

63. Lonergan, "The Supernatural Order," 65.

64. In addition to Stebbins' excellent work, this text is published, with annotation and translation, in volume 19 of Lonergan's collected works, *Early Latin Theology*.

65. Lonergan, "The Supernatural Order," 67.

66. Ibid., 65.

in the human species.[67] Human beings are saved; they are not changed into something else and then saved. The potencies of human nature, however, are fulfilled by grace in a way that we could not achieve in our own created terms; this becomes the basis of a change in how we are able to live in the world. That these changes happen by communication indicates that the mechanism by which we are changed is the work of grace to bring us into a new relationship with God. Because we are created for eternal friendship with God, grace gives us entry into a new order of relationship with God that fulfills the purpose of our being, and this new supernatural relationship has a necessary connection to transforming the way that we live.

Operations specify exactly how we live in the world.[68] In their ultimate term, the operations Lonergan speaks of are knowing God in the beatific vision and loving him in the fullness of the life of heaven.[69] That these operations are created indicates that they are finite, and the work of finite beings; we do not become the divine essence. Yet the life of the world to come is truly knowing and loving God—directly, without mediation, and in the totality of his being.

That we thereby attain God means that we come to be in relationship with him as he truly is.[70] For, it was not an angel that God sent to save us, but he came himself in the person of the Son (Heb 1:1–14). God was not content with a relationship that would hold us always at a distance from him; therefore the mediator between God and human beings is God himself. By entering into saving relationship with him, our entire being is completely transformed—not, again, with a change in our species or the loss of our personal identities, but with the absolute fulfillment of everything we were ever made to be.

Through faith, hope, and charity, and through every other operative and cooperative grace ordered to our salvation, we come to participate in the life of heaven even now. Such forms the basis of the life of witness and service, worship and sacrifice, by which any truly Christian life is lived. Hereby we cast off everything that hinders, resist the work of the enemy, and live the heavenly life now, awaiting the fulfillment of the new heavens and new earth.

The supreme and perfect example of this communication is Jesus.[71] Because Jesus is both God and a human being, he claims and has the fullness

67. Lonergan, *Insight*, 693–96.
68. Lonergan, "The Supernatural Order," 65.
69. Ibid., 69.
70. Ibid., 67.
71. Ibid., 69–71.

of the divine operations by right, and he lives them out with fullness and perfection as a human being. In the way that his human will always cohered with his divine will, even when tempted, and in the way that his human intellect was always enlightened by the beatific vision, even in his suffering, Christ shows exactly and perfectly what it means to receive in created form the fullness of God.[72]

Lonergan also explained Christ's work on the cross by analogy with communication.[73] As Lonergan explains it, Christ's communication on the cross was directed both to God and to us. Toward God, Christ communicated, "(1) a perfect knowledge and love of God and humanity, (2) a perfect knowledge and sorrow for the offense that sin is, (3) and a perfect knowledge and detestation of the evil sin causes."[74] Toward us, Christ communicated "a perfect human and divine (1) knowledge and love for humanity and (2) knowledge and condemnation of sin and evil."[75] God's nature cannot be changed in any way, and thus the purpose of the communication toward God was to affect a different relation between God and human beings. Our natures, however, can be fulfilled. The purpose of the communication, toward us, then, was to make proper for us that which is proper only for God, inaugurating us into a new relationship with God in which we know and love him as we ought, and in which we come to detest and overcome the evil that afflicts our natures and that plagues this world.

By receiving this communication from Christ, we come to be like him. Specifically, the work of the Holy Spirit is to change us to receive the work of Christ.[76] Together, they bring us to the Father. In that Christ by his death trampled death, our lives no longer bear the stamp and ultimate horizon of death. Instead, we begin already, by communion with the Trinity, to live the life of resurrection, animated, in a preliminary but real way, by the love and wisdom that attain God himself.

Participation in God

Because life in Christ and the Holy Spirit changes us with respect both to our nature and to our operations, the Christian life is a life, lived out of relationship with God, in which God's wisdom and power become real in the world through us (Phil 2:12–13; Eph 2:10). This is, of course, not the only

72. *ST* III 10.1; 15.6, 10; 18.1, 5.

73. See chapter 5 of this work.

74. Miller, "Why the Passion?" abstract.

75. Ibid.

76. See Cone, "Aquinas' Sanctifying Grace and Lonergan's Religious Conversion."

way in which God acts in the universe or in human history; the Spirit blows where it wills, and his Word is not chained (John 3:8; 2 Tim 2:9). But God has given us the privilege of cooperating with him in his work of bringing the universe to its completion.

Any exposition of the nature of Christian life can be only exemplary, not exhaustive. That is, in examining the manifold ways that God works in us and through us, it is the complete totality of our beings and doings that is changed. Everything that is righteous for humans to do, from the dawn of creation to the very end of time, is included in the transformation God both intends and brings about. We do not know the fullness of what God intends to do, and even the life we do know has a complexity whose totality eludes our grasp (2 Cor 2:9). But, we do have an anchor for our considerations in the communication to us of Jesus. Whatever God intends to bring about, it will cohere with him. We will therefore look especially for the ways that Christ becomes present to us and in our lives.

In order to specify the shape and contour of the saved life, this chapter will briefly consider different aspects of the way that we participate in God as we are changed by the communication of Christ and the work of the Holy Spirit. Thereby we both make more specific what we mean by the communication of the divine nature and clarify that no single aspect of Christian existence has totalizing importance. The master *Logos* is only Jesus himself, in whom all the universe's economies are drawn together and summed up.

Justification

In justification, we are set right with God through the forgiveness of our sins and through receiving the righteousness of Christ. God receives satisfaction for our sins, pardoning us because of the perfect willingness of Christ to suffer on our behalf. Christ's communication to God instantiates the love, knowledge, and sorrow for sin by which his perfect sacrifice expiates our sins. The claim against us of the evil one is shown to be the illegitimacy of an unjust tyrant, and Christ triumphs over him by the cross; Christ's ransom for us thereby fulfills the perfect will of the Father. Christ's death and resurrection also recapitulate the human struggle against evil. While we fail according to the natural logic of our being (that is, as we are in Adam), Christ's work succeeds. If we are in Christ, then, our lives are no longer defined by death—the whale that would swallow us, the wound that limits the destructive nature of our being—but we are brought into a horizon as wide as eternity and as limitless as the very love of God itself.[77]

77. See chapter 5 of this work.

Our justification cannot merely be an accounting of our guilty or innocent status in the mind of God. Even according to a purely legal analogy, ancient legal theory demanded that the dictates of law correspond to reality; Scripture was written, and all the classic christological analogies were composed, long before Ockham's nominalism insisted in separating the real status of something from the label the law applies to it.[78] Our justification must therefore necessarily include the way that Christ changes our lives, to live like him, and the way that this transformation will be complete in the life of the resurrection.[79]

Christ knows our hearts, and even the least turning to him is precious in his sight; yet a complete and unremitting refusal of the life and character transformation he offers us must put us in danger of refusing Christ himself (Matt 25:31–46; Luke 15:1–32; Luke 18:9–14; Rom 2:9–11; 2 Tim 2:11–13; Jas 2:14–26). This is because the transformation Christ offers is to conform us to his very self through the work of the Holy Spirit (Rom 12:1–2).[80] The communication of Christ to us, therefore, is also part of our justification, for truly being righteous is a right relationship with God that includes every aspect of our lives and beings (Rom 5:1–5), and he himself will complete this work in eternal life (Rev 21:9–22:7). In this relationship, we can have great confidence in the grace of God to supply strength in our weaknesses and work through the dialectical nature of our being (Mark 9:24). But, the road of justification is one that we must walk, stumbling and wandering though our steps may be, as we journey with our savior.[81]

Our justification is by faith, but saving faith is a relationship by which the Word, Jesus Christ, creates himself in us and transforms our lives.[82] Origen's understanding of judgment by deeds is instructive in this respect.[83] Origen did not believe that God's final judgment indicates that God keeps a tally-sheet, recording our good and evil deeds. Judgment by deeds indicates God's assessment of our minds as we stand before him.[84] Each moral decision we make leaves a mark on us, and at the end, the shape of our lives either bears the fruit of Christ's transformation or denies him to his face

---

78. See Kilcullen, "The Political Writings," and King, "Ockham's Ethical Theory;" see also McGrade, *The Political Thought of William of Ockham*.

79. See Wesley, "The Scripture Way of Salvation."

80. See Snell and Cone, *Authentic Cosmopolitanism*, 105–30.

81. See Baker, *Diagonal Advance*.

82. See chapter 4 of this work on the relation between grace and faith.

83. Origen, *Commentary on Romans*, 2.10.1.

84. I thank Justin Schwartz for this insight.

(Matt 12:30; Luke 11:23).[85] That we are admitted into heaven is by nothing but God's grace, but receiving God's grace requires *truly* being with him, as his grace transforms all that we do and are.

In the context of the Protestant tradition, Kierkegaard makes a strongly consonant point.

> In every human being there is an inclination *either* to want to be meritorious when it comes to works *or*, when faith and grace are to be emphasized, also to want to be free from works as far as possible. . . . Christianity's requirement is this: your life should express works as strenuously as possible, then one thing more is required—that you humble yourself and confess: But my being saved is nonetheless grace.[86]

Does our existence bear the mark of Christ? This is the question of justifying faith, and it is the way that God normatively makes his grace operative in us. We are saved simply by trusting Jesus, but that very trust indicates the purchase on our hearts whereby the law of the Spirit of life can set us free from the law of sin and death (Rom 8:1–4).

Saving faith communicates to us the set of dynamics identified by the Law of the Cross. It is exactly in faith in Christ that we come to know God; this knowledge requires the commitment of our being.[87] Because of our love for God, saving faith places us in a horizon by which our moral beings are edified and strengthened.[88] The wretchedness of evil is revealed to us, along with our participation in it, as we are motivated to cast it off and pursue true life with the God who calls us, even in the face of suffering and cost, overcoming evil by good (Heb 12:1–3).

Regeneration

In regeneration, our human nature is healed and elevated by the reception of God's life, a second birth normatively given to us in baptism.[89] Baptism is the second birth from above, which comes from the Holy Spirit (John

---

85. Cf. Max Scheler on love *versus ressentiment*. Scheler, *Ressentiment*.

86. Kierkegaard, *For Self Examination*, 16–17, emphasis original. See Simpson, *The Truth Is the Way*, 171–77.

87. See Simpson's discussion Kierkegaard in *The Truth Is the Way*, 45–49.

88. See Cone, "Transforming Desire"; see also Snell and Cone, *Authentic Cosmopolitanism*, 105–30.

89. See Campbell, "Lunenburg Letter." See also Hicks and Taylor, *Down in the River to Pray*, for a historical and systematic understanding of baptismal life.

3:5).[90] At baptism, God forgives our sins and inaugurates us into the life of the Holy Spirit (Acts 2:38).[91] "God Himself stakes His honor, His power, and might" that, through it, the power of death and the devil over us is destroyed, and we gain entry into the kingdom of God to live forever with him (Titus 3:5).[92]

Two New Testament images have been especially prominent as Christians have tried to understand this mystery: the baptism of Jesus, and his death and resurrection.[93] Jesus' baptism is narrated or referred to by all four Gospels (Matt 3:13–17; Mark 1:9–13; Luke 3:21–22; John 1:29–34). Christian teachers have consistently affirmed that Christ was not baptized because he himself needed something; rather, *we* need something, and he brought sanctity to the baptismal waters.[94] When we are baptized, we are united to Christ; we too are declared to be God's beloved and pleasing children, his Spirit descends upon us, and we are empowered and sent into ministry. In baptism, we are also united to Christ in his death and resurrection (Rom 6:1–14). By being united to Christ's death, we gain all the benefits that he merited for us by his sacrifice and mighty victory. More than this, though, our lives become cruciform, simultaneously living out his death and resurrection (Gal 2:19–21; 2 Cor 4:6–16; Phil 1:18–21).

Baptism is strongly connected to faith (Acts 2:38; 16:30–34), and just as in faith, the Law of the Cross becomes operative in us both by God's free gift and by our participation.[95] Maximus linked baptism to the voluntary aspects of our deification; the Holy Spirit by sheer gift creates in us a new birth by baptism, but he actuates the reality of that birth in our lives by converting our wills.[96] Maximus also emphasized that baptism gives us entry to the church, and in this community we come to experience a life together in which the disorder of our passions is put to death, our minds are enlightened by Christ, and our wills are directed to him; we are thereby

90. See Maximus, *Ambiguum 42*. See also Castelein, "Christian Churches/Churches of Christ View."

91. *ST* III 69.1, 8.

92. Luther, *The Large Catechism*, 4.13.

93. See McDonnell and Montague, *Christian Initiation*, 93–103. See Ferguson, *Baptism in the Early Church*, for a magisterial overview of baptism in the patristic period. See also World Council of Churches, *Baptism, Eucharist, and Ministry*, 2.

94. *ST* III 39.1. In this response, Aquinas indicates he is following the theology of Chrysostom, Gregory Nazianzus, Ambrose, and Augustine. As with the rest of Christ's life, in his baptism he came not to be served, but to serve.

95. *ST* III 66.1; Luther, *The Large Catechism*, 4.13.

96. Maximus, *Ad Thalassium 6*; *Ambiguum 42*. See Vishnevskaya, "Divinization as Perichoretic Embrace," 139.

strengthened to endure the suffering of this world with joy, accepting it and offering healing to the world, because we have become united to Christ.[97]

By our regeneration, rather than being subject to physical and spiritual death, we receive immortality (John 11:25–26). Rather than having a body and spirit subject to physical and moral decay, we receive incorruption (Rom 8:1–11). These are both characteristics of the kind of life God has natively. They become ours by grace, as we are given participation in the divine nature, as God's life is communicated to us.[98] What was once not natural to us becomes natural, in a preliminary way now and in fullness at the resurrection, for our nature is being elevated and changed. Irenaeus, however, emphasizes that our regeneration is not merely a fact that has become true about us. Recalling Luke 7:42–43, he shows the way that God's overcoming of our apostate state, in which we are swallowed by the whale of death, should create in us great gratitude and draw us to love the God who saves us.[99]

Communion: Body and Spirit

The Christian life is a life of communion with God and with each other. Just as baptism is the great symbol of our regeneration, the Lord's Supper is the great symbol of our life together (Matt 26:26–29; Mark 14:22–25; Luke 22:14–23; 1 Cor 11:23–26).[100] The original context of the Lord's Supper was a Jewish Passover meal, and the Lord's Supper thereby draws on all of the rich imagery of the exodus (Exod 12). The Lord God kept vigil for Israel, sparing and delivering them from the angel of death by the blood of the paschal lamb, and leading them out of the land of slavery to become his covenant people. In Christ, though, we have a new and better covenant, which is based on the sacrifice of Christ for the forgiveness of our sins and the new command to love as Jesus loves (Jer 31:31; Luke 22:20; 1 Cor 11:25; 2 Cor 3:6; Heb 8:7–13). The superiority of the new covenant is especially that it is written on our hearts, not on tablets of stone, indicating that God gives us new life (his own life), which changes us and moves us to respond to him, through the gift of the Holy Spirit. The celebrations of Communion in the early church, therefore, appropriately celebrated the entire ministry of Jesus,

97. Maximus, *Mystagogia*, 24.

98. Irenaeus, *Against Heresies*, 2.29.2; 3.19.1; 3.20.2; 3.23.7; 5.3.2; 5.13.3.

99. Ibid., 3.30.2. See Presley, "Irenaeus and the Gnostics on 1 Corinthians 15:53–54."

100. See Hicks, *Come to the Table*, for a helpful discussion of the celebration and meaning of the Lord's Supper. For an intellectually converted interpretation of the Lord's Supper from a Roman Catholic perspective, see Mudd, *The Eucharist and Critical Metaphysics*.

including his whole incarnation, and culminating in his death, resurrection, and gift to us of the Holy Spirit.[101]

The exact metaphysical status of the elements of Communion has been a source of significant controversy during the history of the church. Whatever the status of Christ's corporality in the elements of Communion, it must be upheld that Christ communes with and communicates himself to us in our corporality. That is, Christ gives himself to us in such a way that the total reality of our life in space and time becomes progressively incorporated into him. In receiving the gift of his presence, we come to share in God's life, dying to our old way of life, overcoming the work of the enemy, and rising to walk in the strength and fullness of Jesus Christ.[102]

Concerning the sacraments, John Calvin stated, "I say that Christ is the matter, or, if you rather choose it, the substance of all the sacraments, since in him they have their whole solidity, and out of him promise nothing."[103] In the Lord's Supper, Calvin affirmed that the totality of Christ becomes present to us, for us, by the work of the Holy Spirit.[104] By this affirmation, Calvin did not mean the transubstantiation of the elements of Communion (which he denied), but he rather affirmed the way that Christ in Communion meets with us and gives himself to us completely, by the power of the Holy Spirit, thereby communicating himself to us and drawing us into his life.[105]

In his evangelical re-appropriation of the historic faith of the church, Robert Webber writes concerning this mystery,

> When bread and wine are received by faith, we are transformed. Bread and wine nourish our union with Jesus. It transforms us into his image and likeness.
>
> The testimony of the early church fathers is clear: the Christian faith is a supernatural vision of reality. God is known to us through bread and wine, for these elements, together with the prayers that surround their celebration disclose Christ in all of his saving and transforming presence, both as he is prefigured in the Old Testament and as he is anticipated in his future final victory over all that is sin and death in the world. . . .
>
> Therefore, while the Bible discloses the story of the world in words, the same story is enacted at bread and wine.[106]

101. See Hippolytus, *The Apostolic Tradition*, 1.3.

102. Luther, *The Large Catechism*, 5.14.

103. Calvin, *Institutes*, 4.14.16.

104. Ibid., 4.17.4.

105. See Hesselink, "The Reformed View," 59–71.

106. Webber, *Ancient-Future Worship*, 140.

From a non-Reformed perspective, Dinelle Frankland echoes Webber's insight that God makes himself present to us in his mighty power and love by the symbols through which he gives himself to us, calling for our response and drawing us back to himself in love.[107]

Maximus thought it important that just as Adam sinned by food, so Christ in recapitulating the human race restores us by food.[108] Christ becomes for us the bread from heaven, who strengthens us and brings about the kingdom of heaven on this earth (Matt 6:11; John 6:51; 1 Cor 10:1–4). In the church's celebration of Communion, we receive the "grace and familiarity" by which we are united to God and deified.[109] In the present age, we receive the work of the Holy Spirit, transforming our hearts to love with Christ's love, and we conform our wills to follow God's commands. This life of "the seventh day," however, is penultimate. By these realities we have a foretaste of eternal life, and in the resurrection God by his grace will give to us the full reality of what the church and sacraments symbolize, and in a way already enact, here below.[110]

In Kierkegaard's discourses on the Lord's Supper, he meditates upon the way that we receive the Law of the Cross in Communion. For it is in the Lord's Supper that Christ communicates to us and awakens in us the heartfelt longing for eternity by which we can overcome the meaninglessness of this world.[111] In the cross, we see the brutality of sin, as our betrayal of him leads to his abasement and suffering; Christ's communication to us reveals to us our need for a savior and motivates us with a love, stirred by his suffering on our behalf, from which we would otherwise turn aside.[112] The meal by which we remember Christ, therefore, becomes a meal of love and reconciliation, as God's love for us, which is manifest in Christ, covers over all our sins.[113] Yet it is also a meal of blessing, for by his blessing of this meal, Christ overcomes the meaningless against which we struggle and our impotence to live rightly in this world on our own terms.[114] And the blessing

---

107. Frankland, *His Story, Our Response*, 43–44.

108. Maximus, "Commentary on the Our Father," 4.

109. Maximus, *Mystagogia*, 24.

110. Ibid. See Vishnevskaya, "Divinization as Perichoretic Embrace," 138–39. See also Linman, "Martin Luther," 193–96, for Luther's understanding of the relation of both baptism and Eucharist in divinization.

111. Kierkegaard, *Discourses at the Communion on Fridays*, 45–46.

112. Walsh, "Introduction," 22–23.

113. Ibid.

114. Kierkegaard, *Discourses at the Communion on Fridays*, 85–87.

is *him*, his gift to us of himself, who moves us with the joy that receives and transforms the suffering of this world.[115]

The communion we have with God includes, in a central way, the elevation of our intellectual and moral nature. Lonergan's exposition of intellectual, moral, and religious conversions indicates the thoroughgoing nature of the transformation of our conscious being by God.[116] Intellectual conversion has to do with the rectitude of the human relationship with knowledge, in which we both eradicate the myth that we know the world merely through experiencing it and come to realize that our knowledge reflects judgments we make based on sufficient evidence. In Christian terms, intellectually converted life believes and accepts that the reality of the world is mediated to us through the message of the gospel. Moral conversion has to do with committing ourselves to that which is actually most choice-worthy, and not just to that which is of benefit for our group or ourselves. In Christian terms, morally converted life understands and commits itself to the Law of the Cross as the most choice-worthy way of life, in which we do not turn aside from following the good in the face of suffering but accept that we must overcome evil through good. Religious conversion means to be grasped by the love of God, placed in the horizon of faith, in which we have a saving relationship with God, the source of all this world's value and the ultimate good that transforms the world. In Christian terms, religious conversion means to receive the gift of the Holy Spirit, who transforms our hearts by giving us God's love (Rom 5:5).

Lonergan's notion of conversion extends and transposes the insights of Aquinas' notion of habits and his psychological account of grace.[117] By grace, our minds become informed by faith, believing and understanding divine truth that sets all earthly truth in its proper order and context; our wills become set on an eternal hope, the hope of heaven that moves us to live here in ways that only make sense in light of the resurrection; and our lives become transformed by God's love, in which we receive a love relationship with the infinite God who draws us to his very heart and makes us vessels to pour out his love here.[118] Lonergan is thus a significant modern proponent

115. Ibid., 106.

116. Lonergan, *Method*, 238–44; "Self–Transcendence: Intellectual, Moral, Religious."

117. Lonergan, *Method*, 27–34; *Grace and Freedom*, 54–58.

118. See Snell and Cone, *Authentic Cosmopolitanism*, 66–86, 105–30. Specifically on religious conversion, see Petillo, "The 'Experience of Grace' in the Theologies of Karl Rahner and Bernard Lonergan"; on religious and moral conversion, see Cone, "Transforming Desire"; on intellectual conversion, see Snell, *Through a Glass Darkly*; see also Walter Conn's excellent works, *Conversion*, and *Christian Conversion*.

of the psychological analogy for the Trinity; in this conversion of our heart and mind one can see the reception, in human form, of the infinite act of understanding that is the Word and the infinite act of love that is the Spirit.

Our communion with God also consists of the Christian life of prayer. Prayer is communication with the one who knows and loves us, and who has given himself for us. It is a journey into the heart of God. The primary purpose of prayer is not to present God with a wish-list, although petitionary prayer is not just authorized but commanded by the New Testament (Matt 6:9–13; Phil 4:6; Eph 6:18). The foundational work of prayer is instead to receive divine significance in what had been ordinary human lives.[119] Because we are joined with the divine life, growing into God and seeking God becomes the way we know our own true selves.[120] The language of truth and love, a divine conversation, becomes for us a way of life in which we seek out the one who has found us.

One can see this emphasis displayed in Maximus' commentary on the Lord's Prayer. Introducing his comments to the unidentified "lord," or "master" who had requested him to write, he states,

> If then the realization of the divine counsel is the deification of our nature, and if the aim of the divine thoughts is the successful accomplishment of what we ask for in our life, then it is profitable to recognize the full import of the Lord's prayer, to put it into practice and to write about it properly.[121]

As many commentators have recognized, in the prayer Jesus gives us we do not have a simple list of requests, but rather we have, in kernel, the whole business of God in redeeming this world.[122] As we come to know the Blessed Trinity, as we recognize that the economy of this world is his becoming present to it and drawing it to himself, as we join our wills and ourselves to this divine work, as we recognize our absolute dependence on God and our ability to trust in him, as we replicate the work of forgiveness that he gives to us, and as we discipline our matter to resist temptation and trust in God to deliver us from all evil, we come to participate in the life of the Trinity.

In the Eastern tradition of prayer, the early Russian *starets*, Nil Sorsky, wrote a kind of monastic rule to teach the monks gathered around him the importance of this battle against temptation and the enemy, and to help them in their struggle. His *Ustav* is a seminal work on the spiritual warfare

119. Augustine, *Confessions*, 10.27.

120. Ibid., 1.1.

121. Maximus, *Commentary on the Our Father*, 1.

122. For example, *ST* II–II 83.9, in which Aquinas cites Augustine, *Epistle 130*, 12.22.

that essentially consists of conforming the mind and will to God.[123] The *Ustav's* primary concern is what it terms mental activity, which is a reference to the world of our inner thoughts and desires.

Right mental activity involves the cleansing of heart and mind that allows a person to have thoughts and intentions that are fully pure and under control, offering pure worship to God in spirit and truth. The proper form of this mental activity is prayer, for it is in devoting ourselves fully to God that we become single-minded and pure in heart. Knowing God is the point of life, the meaning and goal of human existence. External prayers and religious activities—said with the mouth but not penetrating to the heart—do not suffice for this. Knowledge of God must permeate us, it must come to characterize us, so that we are truly in communion with him.

Nil, along with the tradition of prayer he followed, believed that our minds are arenas of combat in which the enemy strives to oppose the spiritual progress that would bring us close to God. By winning this battle, great freedom from sin is gained, the whole soul is filled with light, and God adorns it with many spiritual graces. By losing this battle, we succumb to the darkness. Nil saw the mind as a vineyard to be cultivated, and cleansed of the vices, so that the virtues of the heavenly kingdom would grow. It is a work that we begin now with the help of God, that we will see the full fruit of in eternal life. Nil waxes quite eloquent about the glories of this prayer of true communion with God. In it, our reason is freed and our minds are able to experience the unutterable God. A person who has found this true home of prayer—a precursor of the life of heaven—will be truly satisfied only with it and will rest content and know peace.

It is the context of communion, then, that gives asceticism and spiritual disciplines their proper context (2 Pet 1:5–8). Spiritual formation consists of our participation in the trinification of the universe.[124] Asceticism and spiritual disciplines are primarily positive, directed toward communion with God. Yet our flesh, to use the Pauline phrase, resists this work, as does the work of the accuser (Rom 7:14–25; Eph 6:10–17). Maximus placed great emphasis on our need to discipline our bodies through ascetic self-denial in order to receive the fullness of the life of heaven.[125] Again, his emphasis is primarily positive. Of our own free will we offer up and submissively direct our wills to their true ultimate end, which is God.[126] Because we have come into existence as material beings, out of non-being, it is necessary that the

123. Sorsky, *Ustav.*

124. I thank Neal Windham for this insight.

125. Maximus, *Chapters on Knowledge,* 2.94–100.

126. Maximus, *Ambiguum 7,* 1.

way we join our beings to the *Logos* does not merely include inner contemplation but also includes ascetic disciplines by which we conform ourselves to God.[127]

Among Evangelicals, the work of Richard Foster and Dallas Willard has helped to reintroduce the life-giving practice of the spiritual disciplines during the last two decades.[128] Both of these authors draw on a range of traditional sources and emphasize the varied nature of the way God works in our lives to draw us to him.[129] Foster's comments on the discipline of celebration are instructive, however, on the essentially positive nature of spiritual life, "Celebration is the heart of the way of Christ."[130] As Foster here goes on to note, Christ entered the world on a note of jubilation, and he bequeathed his joy to his disciples at the end of his public ministry (Luke 2:10; John 15:11). The reception of the Law of the Cross necessarily has to do with suffering, and Jesus promised this to his disciples (John 16:33). But the point of our transformation by Jesus is that in the midst of suffering, there is joy.[131]

Communion: Life Together

The life of truth and love by which we have communion with each other and with God is especially seen in the church (*ekklēsia*). Biblical images for the church include the body of Christ (Rom 12:25; 1 Cor 12:27), the bride of Christ (Rev 19:7; 21:2, 9), the people of God (2 Cor 6:16; Heb 4:9; 8:10; 1 Pet 2:9–10), the temple or building of God (Eph 2:21, 1 Pet 2:5), and the New Jerusalem (Rev 21:9). With reference to the Old Testament, the people of God gathered together at Sinai are called a church (Acts 7:38). The word *ekklēsia* itself indicates the way that God calls us out of our former existence to life in a new community. All of these indicate ways that our natural existence is sublated by eternal life, as we are drawn into the heavenly life together.

Augustine, in fact, considered the start of the church—God's sojourning people—to be in Abel, who did not build an earthly city and who made an acceptable offering to God, and Seth, the child of Adam who called on the name of the Lord (Gene 4:1–26); here is the beginning of God's undoing

127. Ibid., 2.

128. Foster, *A Celebration of Discipline*, and Willard, *The Spirit of the Disciplines*.

129. See, for example, Willard, *Spirit of the Disciplines*, 158, on the need for practical wisdom to learn the forms of spiritual discipline God is calling us to emphasize in the different times of our lives. Sorsky also emphasized the benefit of varying one's approach to spiritual devotion.

130. Foster, *A Celebration of Discipline*, 190.

131. See Simpson, *The Truth Is the Way*, 175.

of the evil of sin and the first move of his saving purpose in human history.[132] In another way, though, the church begins with the gift of the Holy Spirit at Pentecost (Acts 2).[133] Augustine has a complex understanding of the church that included both the church as a "sociological entity and as a lived relationship with Christ and the Holy Spirit."[134] Both of these are the result of grace, as God brings this world into existence and arranges it justly in a great symphony of peace.[135]

By Augustine's definition, a people is "an assembled multitude of rational creatures bound together by a common agreement as to the objects of their love."[136] The church exists, therefore, because of the communication to us of the Law of the Cross, both in Jesus' gift to us and in the Holy Spirit's work in our hearts. That God makes us his people, his heavenly city, means that he brings into existence the sociological entity of the church and works to transform those in it by his grace, binding them together and moving them by the gift of his love and truth. The goal and true reality of this work is eschatological, both in the sense that it will exist in its fullness only at the end of time and in the sense that all of time is transformed by being ordered toward this consummation.

Maximus saw in the church, by grace and the cooperation of human free will, the achievement of God's purposes in history. Pointing out the great differences among individuals that compose the church, he states,

> All are born into the Church and through it are reborn and recreated in the Spirit. To all in equal measure it gives and bestows one divine form and designation, to be Christ's and to carry his name. In accordance with faith it gives to all a single, simple, whole, and indivisible condition which does not allow us to bring to mind the existence of the myriads of differences among them, even if they do exist, through the universal relationship and union of all things with it. It is through it that absolutely no one at all is in himself separated from the community since everyone converges with all the rest and joins together with them by the one, simple, and indivisible grace and power of faith. "For all," it is said, "had but one heart and one mind." Thus to be and to appear as one body formed of different members is really worthy of Christ himself, our true head, in whom says the

132. Augustine, *City of God*, 15.17–18.

133. Van Bavel, "Church (*ecclesia*)," 169–70.

134. Ibid., 169.

135. Augustine, *City of God*, 19.23.

136. Ibid., 19.24. See Peters, *Logic of the Heart*, 23–102, for Augustine's embedded sense of reason; see also Snell and Cone, *Authentic Cosmopolitanism*, 15–43.

divine Apostle, "there is neither male nor female, neither Jew nor Greek, neither circumcision nor uncircumcision, neither foreigner nor Scythian, neither slave nor freeman, but Christ is everything in all of you."[137]

The work of Christ is to reconcile the divisions in the universe, not by assimilating all to uniformity but by a unity in difference that mirrors his perichoretic being.[138] Humans, who are the microcosm of the universe, achieve the divine intention for creation by Christ's grace and the work of the Holy Spirit. We participate in this work as God calls us together and constitutes us as the church, which itself becomes the symbol of unity in diversity of the reconciled soul, and of the atonement of the world.[139]

In the church we receive the Scriptures, by whose meaning we are renewed in our minds to receive the image and likeness of God.[140] By an informed study of Scripture, we are able to rise up to the fullness of all good things and the treasures of knowledge brought by communion with the Holy Spirit.[141] As we come to see the way that Scripture preaches Christ, and as this meaning informs us, God himself becomes written on our hearts, as we are united to him.

Calvin, like Maximus, stressed the indispensable role of the church in our deification.[142] "For Calvin, participation in Christ is inseparable from the active participation in the love and unity of the body of Christ."[143] Calvin especially connected the church's celebration of Communion with the koinonia (communion) we have with Christ and each other.[144] Because we each share in Christ, we come to have unity with each other. The church, both visible and invisible, is the way that God brings this reality about in human history, realizing his saving purpose and will.

As received in Catholic, Orthodox, and Protestant tradition, then, the corporate worship of the church, in which the Scriptures are preached and

137. Maximus, *Mystagogia*, 1. Maximus refers to Acts 4:32 and Gal 3:28.

138. See chapter 1 of this work.

139. Maximus, *Mystagogia*, 4.

140. Ibid., 6. Forcing on Maximus the weight of Protestant *versus* Catholic and Orthodox understandings of the relation of the Scriptures and the church is anachronistic. He simply did not have in mind the situation of the Protestant Reformers in their quest reconstitute a church whose hierarchy had rendered itself effectively immune to scriptural correction.

141. Ibid., 7.

142. For the further historical development of Reformed thought about union with Christ, see Evans, *Imputation and Impartation*.

143. Billings, "John Calvin," 209.

144. Ibid. 209–10.

the sacraments celebrated, is of central importance for our life in Christ. In considering the church's life of corporate worship, or common prayer, there seem to be two possible relations between our worship services and the rest of our lives: either there is no difference between the rest of our lives and our corporate celebrations of worship, or there is some difference. That there would be no difference seems contradicted by the author of Hebrews' admonition not to forsake the gathering of ourselves together (Heb 10:25). If there is a difference, then, there seem two likely relations between the church's common prayers and the rest of our lives: either our common worship is a reflection and distillation of our everyday lives, or the common prayers of the church set the agenda for, provide the meaning of, and empower us for the rest of our lives. By the first understanding, what we receive in corporate worship is what we bring to it, and garbage in will lead to garbage out; by the second, our lives become purified, ordered and reoriented by drawing together to worship God. The second understanding seems to reflect more clearly the Law of the Cross, for by Christ's communication we are reoriented and transformed.

Catherine Pickstock argues that the liturgical life of the church provides the essential context and answers practical wisdom's search for how to live in this world.

> First of all, the liturgical relativises the everyday without denying its value. Personal joys are not allowed to become over-inflated because they are placed within the context of collective enjoyment and are seen as but specific manifestations of a continuous collective celebration. Inversely, personal sorrows are shared with others and are viewed in the context of cosmic patterns which include such tragic eventualities. . . . By contrast, a modern individual may alternate between seeking refuge from public misery in private delight, or escaping personal sorrow through absorption in the impersonal world of the media. . . . People cannot readily live with themselves and in public at the same time. But this co-dwelling is exactly what liturgy renders possible.[145]

Liturgy also satisfies philosophy's quest for wisdom, because it is as the transcendent goodness of God makes itself manifest in worship, and as human beings, by doxology, participate in this superabundant giving of God's self to us, that the right relationship between creation and its transcendent source is both made real and revealed.[146] In consonance with Maximus, Pickstock

145. Pickstock, "Liturgy, Art, and Politics," 161.
146. Pickstock, *After Writing*, 199–211.

points to the way that Christ gives himself to us, especially in Communion, and to the way that his very person in his gift to us overcomes the divisions and dichotomies of the created world.[147]

In an Evangelical context, Robert Webber speaks of the way that by celebrating the church's traditional liturgical calendar we can come to participate in the work that God has once and for all done in Christ.[148] Webber emphasizes the way that the worship of the church gives a redeemed and redeeming order to time. Rather than being tossed about by our own personal desires and agendas, or by the exploitative efforts of the corporate and political agendas of this world, the traditional cycles of Advent, Lent, and the rest of the church calendar give an order to our existence in time that comes from the gospel.[149]

The Orthodox Church has preserved a powerful sense of the way that heaven interpenetrates earth in Christian worship, and does so in a way that draws us into the worship that is ever contemporary and ongoing before God's throne.

> Byzantine liturgical texts filled with profound theological and mystical content, alternate with the prayerful incantation of the psalms, whose every word resonates in the hearts of the faithful. Even the elements of "choreography" characteristic of Orthodox services, such as solemn entries and exits, prostrations and censing, are not intended to distract from prayer but, on the contrary, to put the faithful in a prayerful disposition and draw them into the *theourgia* in which, according to the teaching of the Fathers, not only the Church on earth, but also the heavenly Church and even the angels participate.[150]

In this way, the Orthodox understand the church's worship to be a time when we breathe the air of heaven. The offering of our hearts that we make to God participates in the "Holy, Holy, Holy" of the four living creatures, as we join the twenty-four elders in falling before the throne (Rev 4:1–11). This doxology will have no end.

---

147. Ibid., 252. See Wybrew, *The Orthodox Liturgy*, 89–101, on liturgy in the time of Maximus.

148. Webber, *Ancient Future Time*, 19–34.

149. Ibid., 35–178.

150. Alfeyev, "Orthodox Worship as a School of Theology."

Action

The practice of Christian ethics must grow out of the way that we have received the life of God. It will then be an expression of the communion we have with God, and a way that our justification and regeneration are made present in the world. Of great importance for Christian ethics, the Law of the Cross communicates to us both love and knowledge, and the faith, hope, and love by which we participate in it grounds us in a horizon in which we are drawn to live authentically toward ourselves and each other. Authenticity is the culmination of the life of love, for we best fulfill the responsibilities we have to each other and know the truth that makes us who we are as we live out the character of Jesus.

In *Works of Love*, Kierkegaard reminds us of the cruciform shape of life together, by which we receive the image of the Trinity. In his prayer to begin this great work on Christian ethics, he says,

> How could one speak properly about love if you were forgotten, you God of love, source of all love in heaven and on earth; you who spared nothing but in love gave everything; you who are love, so that one who loves is what he is only by being in you! How could one speak properly about love if you were forgotten, you who revealed what love is, you our Savior and Redeemer, who gave yourself in order to save all. How could one speak properly of love if you were forgotten, you Spirit of love, who take nothing of your own but remind us of that love-sacrifice, remind the believer to love as he is loved and his neighbor as himself![151]

In the first meditation of this work, Kierkegaard identifies love as the bond between temporality and eternity.[152] Eternity reveals the selves that we truly are, and it is in the life of eternity that we receive the selves, by receiving or refusing grace, by knowing or refusing the truth, that we have become. But, we only become our true selves by the life of love, in the genuine self-transcendence of love of God and love of neighbor. It is therefore great grace that love of neighbor is commanded to us (Matt 22:39), for God thereby "wrenches open the lock" of the preoccupation with ourselves by which we so easily lose who we really are.[153] Only thereby are we liberated from the despair—the loss of ourselves—that we would "gain" as we try to live a life

151. Kierkegaard, *Works of Love*, 3–4.

152. Ibid., 6–16.

153. Ibid., 17–43.

enclosed only in ourselves and our desires, instead of "losing" ourselves in a life given toward others (Matt 16:26).

Kenneth Melchin's account of Christian ethics flows out of Lonergan's theological insight that we are incarnate acts of meaning, radically compromised by sin, but even more radically redeemed by grace.[154] Moral knowledge must account both for facts (the realities of the world, and especially the usual operation of human affairs) but also for values (the goodness and evil of the world, including the relative worth of different moral options). By living in a morally responsible way, we are not responding (primarily) to factors imposed from outside us, but rather we are fulfilling the exigencies of our internal desires to know what reality is and choose what is best.[155] While fulfilling the requirements of our beings, moral knowledge has an essentially social character; the practical knowledge we have and the values we adhere to have significant relation to our groups, both in their genesis and in their development.[156] With respect to moral obligation, however, input does not equal output. While our intrinsic and unrestricted quest for truth and goodness provides the criterion for a correct grasp of moral obligation, we now grasp the reality of the world and its value only partially—in a mirror, a riddle—and we live dialectically toward the good and truth we know. Moral systems do not produce righteous living, though bad ones can hinder it; rather, virtuous people must choose virtue in every case, and we do so as members of societies that both constitute us and are the domain of our responsible choice.[157]

As the present work noted in its discussion of the relation of grace and faith, the authenticity or unauthenticity of our groups has an effect on how we ourselves will understand what is good and true.[158] Aside from our own personal moral limitations (which are both radical and real), we are subject to structural evil through elements of decline present in our societies.[159] Put simply, although our natural being contains all the exigencies to the realization of natural virtue, we are circumscribed from realizing that life of virtue by the effects of sin.

154. Melchin, *Living with Other People.*

155. Ibid., 33–34.

156. Ibid., 60.

157. Ibid., 78–80.

158. See chapter 4.

159. Melchin, *Living with Other People*, 105–6; see also chapter 3 of the present work on decline.

In this context, Melchin adverts to the importance of the gift of faith.[160] Christian faith does not merely pit good against evil with a hopeful conviction that the good must somehow be stronger; in faith we meet, personally, the power of grace that overcomes evil with good. This encounter heals and elevates us to be responsible agents in the world, origins of good who participate in the power and mystery of Christ's resurrection.

A Christian understanding of social responsibility will then identify three factors active in the processes of our cultures and histories: progress, decline, and redemption.[161] Progress indicates the way that, in terms explainable by our created origin, we pursue truth and virtue. Decline indicates the personal and societal ways we fail in those pursuits. If there is any concrete conclusion to take from the doctrine of original sin, it is that if the contest is purely between progress and decline, over time decline *always* wins. But thanks be to God, for he gives us victory in Jesus Christ (Rom 7:25).

The communication to us of the Law of the Cross has both a personal and a social character. As Lonergan emphasizes, symbols are both personal and social realities.[162] They have a foundation in our intelligent, feeling, and bodily nature, but they also express our human need to express our thoughts and feelings to each other. Christ crucified and resurrected, the perfect symbol of God, communicates God's infinite perfection in and to the finite order of space and time.[163] The Law of the Cross therefore manifests and makes possible the fulfillment of the potencies of our created nature, both personally and in the social order.[164]

Lonergan thus speaks of the way that God's love, through faith, has the power to overcome decline.

> Without faith, without the eye of love, the world is too evil for God to be good, for a good God to exist. But faith recognizes that God grants men their freedom, that he wills them to be persons and not just his automata, that he calls them to the higher authenticity that overcomes evil with good. So faith is linked with human progress and it has to meet the challenge of human decline. . . . Faith places human efforts in a friendly universe; it reveals an ultimate significance in human achievement; it strengthens new undertakings with confidence. Inversely,

160. Melchin, *Living with Other People*, 105.

161. Ibid., 105–6.

162. Lonergan, "The Notion of Sacrifice," 7.

163. Ibid., 9.

164. See Snell and Cone, *Authentic Cosmopolitanism*, 131–45.

progress realizes the potentialities of man and of nature; it reveals that man exists to bring about an ever fuller achievement
in this world; and that achievement because it is man's good
also is God's glory. Most of all, faith has the power of undoing decline. . . . It is not propaganda and it is not argument but
religious faith that will liberate human reasonableness from its
ideological prisons. It is not the promises of men but religious
hope that can enable men to resist the vast pressures of social
decay. If passions are to quiet down, if wrongs are to be not ex-
acerbated, not ignored, not merely palliated, but acknowledged
and removed, then human possessiveness and human pride
have to be replaced by religious charity, by the charity of the
suffering servant, by self-sacrificing love.[165]

Progress and decline both have roots in human self-transcendence, progress
in its attainment, decline in its failure.[166] Because of the communication to
us of Christ's love, the concrete realities of personal and social evil do not
have to have the final word about us or our societies. But, truly to participate
in Christ's victory, we ourselves will have to take on the character and truth
that is communicated to us. We ourselves will have to sing the Song of the
Servant, overcoming evil through redemption.

Even before Aristotle formalized the relation, ethics and politics were
closely related to each other.[167] Defining a Christian politics is an exceeding-
ly difficult task. At the least we may say that it will oppose the totalitarianism
by which humans (knowingly or unknowingly) follow the tyrant, the devil.
It will also eschew the reborn spirit of paganism Milbank has effectively
exposed in Machiavelli.[168] In that God's grace works with our free will, it
will support the personal liberties of society's members; and in that God in
the cross makes us his friends, it will see the function of the institutions and
roles of the society to foster personal relations (not to subsume personal
relations as only having validity in service of institutions or even of the good
of order).[169] Certainly it will never coerce conversion, and the tyrannical
logic of "error hath no right" will not exist within its bounds. If the church
has a special place in a society, that place must definitively be to serve, not
to "lord it over" as the pagans do (Luke 22:24–27).

Because there is no completely converted society, and because each of
our societies, even among their converted elements, are not free from the

165. Lonergan, *Method*, 117.

166. Ibid.

167. Aristotle, *Nicomachean Ethics*, 1.2.

168. Milbank, *Theology and Social Theory*, 23.

169. Lawrence, "The Human Good and Christian Conversation," 251–52.

work of sin, a Christian politics will need to take into account the complex intelligibility of the cross.[170] The application of practical wisdom will be required to see the ways in which the cruciform life practically is applied in each situation.

Recognition that our societies include the absurd nature of sin may lead to a Christian political position that, in some respects, seems allied with Reinhold Niebuhr's Christian realism, in which the end we seek in political action is justice, not charity.[171] The present work, however, prioritizes justice in political action for different reasons, and it envisions the concrete form of justice differently than Niebuhr's realism. Niebuhr spoke out of a lively awareness of the Reformed doctrine of original sin, and in his context, this retrieval was a significant advance. It seems better, though, to view political theology through the lens of Maximus' deifying logic of the three days of creation.

A Christian politics, if Christian, will work from the logic of what Maximus spoke of as the seventh day, the reality based on the advent of Christ to bring salvation; it will also know that history is interpenetrated by the realities of the eighth day, in which we will achieve final deification, but that it has not achieved them yet. Because politics necessarily works in concert with unconverted individuals, it will often aim at the goals of the sixth day of creation, that is, at the practice of the intellectual and moral virtues (but not the theological ones). The way of existence of the sixth day is a radically incomplete one, and therefore those working from the standpoint of the seventh day will be aware of the absurdity of sin in the situations addressed. However, the proximate goal of the Christian politician will be to encourage the practice of justice and practical wisdom that is indicated by the gift of created being.

From a Christian perspective, these virtues are radically incomplete without the work of supernatural grace. Politics will always be the art of the possible. But a Christian politician can see where the practice of the natural virtues is supposed to go, and therefore introduce an intelligibility and moral compass that actually does fulfill the demands of justice and prudence, because justice and prudence in actuality achieve their immanent goals as informed by charity. She cannot expect that the unconverted ones she works with to recognize the full shape and import of why the solutions given are the best ones. But she can expect God to be active in every human

170. See Kierkegaard, *Attack upon "Christendom."* As noted in chapter 5 of this work, the complex character of the cross indicates that the redemption is a wisdom that deals with the effects of sin, which is unintelligible and a strict privation of meaning.

171. Niebuhr, *Christian Realism and Political Problems.*

heart, and she can argue, on mutually accepted bases of intelligibility, for prudential and just solutions to this world's problems.

Such a political logic will necessarily involve the right use of power. Practical wisdom is about getting things done; justice is about the achievement of a right good of order. Christianity, if it is the true expression of the divine economy, must be able to serve as the basis and main support of a society, not merely as a protest against it. To understand the prophetic element of Christianity to limit the work of Christians and the church to critique of those in power is to embody the slave morality Nietzsche criticized.[172] It is also to see Christians as less able receive the exercise of divine authority than those who set themselves up against the cause of Christ (Rom 13).

Because of the surd of sin, a Christian politics will sometimes support and even carry out the use of force in retributive justice.[173] It will never do so as an end in itself, though, but only in support of and as a part of a more comprehensive distributive justice. Especially, it will never do so as a work of hatred or anger, as a part of a totalitarian or imperialistic ambition, or in the Machiavellian (or is it Caiaphistic?) expediency that to make an omelet one must break a few eggs. It will also be suspicious of the work of bias in the distortion of our societal pursuit of the good, and of the way that mechanisms of mimetic violence and scapegoating lead us to make victims of convenient parties (Rev 13). We must not return evil for evil, but we must overcome evil with good (Matt 5:38–48).

In this way we will follow the example of our savior, who gives to evildoers retributive justice only in the last resort, if they will receive no other participation in the good, and who works by distributive justice to create a world order in which the designs of the divine justice are realized. Insofar as is possible, the wounds of justice will be given only to reform and heal, with restraint of evildoers always preferred to their annihilation, if possible, in hopes of their eventual repentance. For the work of Christian power should always be exercised in the hope that God is working to move those in the sixth day of creation to the seventh, and to be humble, knowing that we ourselves are not so secure in having the mind of Christ that we can yet be the judges of the world.

In order to use power in a way befitting our savior, a Christian politics must necessarily pursue compassion.[174] Because of the way that we are given in this world as members of each other, the concrete form of justice will be compassion. A Christian politics, then, will always see and treat others

172. Nietzsche, *On the Genealogy of Morals*, 20–25.

173. *ST* II–II 40.1.

174. ST II–II 31, 32, 33.

as destined for eternal friendship with God, for that is what they actually are according to the design of their creation.[175] The perceptive reader will notice here reference to Aquinas' teaching on charity, which may seem to conflict with the earlier logic of Christian realism; and, it does, if taken on Niebuhr's terms. But by the logic of Maximus' days of creation, charity is the well-being of justice that the world cannot see, and it is here that a Christian politics must decisively witness to the logic of this world.[176]

A Christian politics must necessarily include a Christian economics; this economics must also be shaped by the communication of the cross. Economics, again, is a field fraught with complexity, but one can find a significant achievement of understanding economics in terms of the human potencies of intelligibility and love—and the dynamics of progress, decline, and redemption in relation to our economic being—in Lonergan's work.[177] Frederick Lawrence has, thankfully, provided an excellent summary and explanation of Lonergan's core insights.[178] Lonergan's economics, as Lawrence points out, are reducible neither to pure capitalism nor to socialism, but look at the intelligible relation of both egalitarian and anti-egalitarian dynamics in cycles of economic progress; they also analyze the way that failing to understand or act responsibly with respect to these dynamics leads to economic stagnation or collapse. Three factors of Lonergan's analysis bear special mention here.

First, because human history is composed of intelligible sets of relations, economics will not deal primarily with the blind forces of the universe but with the way that human beings realize or fail to realize their created potencies to intelligence and responsibility.[179] Human economic systems, therefore, are concrete realizations of the way that human intelligence and responsibility function or fail to function in this world. Specifically, we must realize the structure of the human good that is being realized in cycles of economic progress, and we must have the responsibility to act in a way that privileges the overall good of society rather than purely looking at our own good.

Second, because economics deals with an intelligible process, the right ordering of economics is aided by education.[180] Just as Irenaeus insisted that the overall economy of the created order is pedagogical, so Lonergan insists

175. *ST* II–II 25.1.

176. Such as in Wesley, "On Visiting the Sick"

177. Lonergan, *Macroeconomic Dynamics*; Lonergan, *For a New Political Economy*.

178. Lawrence, "Between Capitalism and Marxism," 941–59.

179. Lawrence, "The Human Good and Christian Conversation," 248.

180. Ibid.

that much of our problem—in economics or otherwise—is ignorance. He hereby rejected the notion that the greed of powerful individuals alone occasions the breakdowns of our economic well-being; rather, our economy's propensity to inequity and collapse results in large part from lack of knowledge, especially ignorance of the basic dynamics of economic expansion.[181] But, the education Lonergan envisioned must lead us truly to be more attentive, intelligent, reasonable, responsible, and loving beings; it will not be the mere function of providing more data or conceptual tools for thinking machines.[182] We must learn to reverse the language of nihilism we have imbibed as children of modernity, and come to grasp and be grasped by the new ideas that help us understand this world and live in it successfully.[183]

Finally, we will not succeed in this project by human resources alone, but only by the grace of God (Matt 4:4).

> In principle and in practice, [Lonergan] was a champion of both modern science and modern scholarship. And yet reflecting on what he called the third historical plateau or stage of meaning, he was utterly convinced of the intractability of the human condition by human resources alone. For Lonergan, our damaged overall human environment requires a healing that far transcends human creativity and originality. In a strictly technical sense, the evils in this universe constitute a mystery of iniquity since they are disproportionate to our human powers to solve them sufficiently.
>
> But Lonergan was also a person struck to his core by an even greater disproportion or incommensurability: that God so loved the world that he gave his only-begotten Son . . . (Jn. 3:16). He could not repeat often enough St. Paul's statement about God's love having been poured into our hearts by the Holy Spirit (Rom. 5:5).[184]

Especially, Lonergan thought that regularly to make the pivot from the anti-egalitarian "thrift and enterprise" appropriate to one aspect of an economic cycle to the egalitarian "benevolence and enterprise" appropriate to another aspect will require not just the motivation of humanly-informed desire and justice, but of desire and justice informed by divine charity.[185] Therefore,

---

181. I thank Ryan Hemmer for this insight.

182. See Snell and Cone, *Authentic Cosmopolitanism*; see also Smith, *Desiring the Kingdom*, and Smith, *Imagining the Kingdom*.

183. Lawrence, "The Human Good and Christian Conversation," 249.

184. Lawrence, "Fragility of Consciousness," 208.

185. Lawrence, "Between Capitalism and Marxism," 959.

while the economic processes of this world promote such particular goods as technology, production of wealth, and elevation of the societal standard of living, in order to be intelligent and reasonable—thereby attaining their goals—they must be radically open to the perfection of love.[186]

Also, as John Zizioulas clearly expresses, it is by knowing ourselves as the priests of creation that we keep the economic cycles of human growth and progress from destroying world God has made, and in which we see the right development of the natural world.[187] A Christian ecology, which will interpenetrate a Christian politics and economics, follows the Law of the Cross. As Christ is offered for us through his created being, so we also present the created being of this universe as an offering to God. Obviously, here as elsewhere, "politics," "economy," and "ecology" do not just operate at a massive corporate level, but include each of our personal lives and our individual attitudes.

Whereas, "stewardship," may link us to creation only functionally, and "conservation" may link us to it only managerially and passively, a true understanding of our common priesthood, based on Christ, knows us to be related to creation existentially, in our very being.[188] We develop nature because we are linked with it to assist it in fulfilling the divine intention. Because we approach nature as priests of God, we will have toward it an attitude conformed to its creator. Rather than seeing our ecological being as a necessary exploitative enterprise, in which the rest of creation exists to serve our needs, we will see in the natural world another aspect of the divine economy, in which all things are to be summed up under Christ.

Christian participation in the action of God in this world is often understood under the rubric of ministry. As this section hopefully has clarified, "ministry" is a banner as wide as God's providence, and it is the provenance of all believers (1 Pet 2:5). It is nothing less than our participation in the ongoing life and work of Jesus, empowered by the Holy Spirit, reconciling this world to God.

Only God can do the work of God. How can we be ministers of reconciliation, offering peace with God to the world? Only insofar as the work of our lives becomes living out the life of Jesus. Christian ministry, in all of its forms, must then flow from the Law of the Cross.

Preaching has always had a special connection with the Holy Spirit, and a number of the great sermons in Acts are described as resulting from the preacher being filled with the Holy Spirit (Acts 2:4; 4:8; 5:32; 7:55; 8:29).

186. See Hemmer, "What Is a Man in Nature," 205–16.

187. Zizioulas, The Eucharistic Communion and the World, 137–39.

188. Ibid., 139.

The work of the Holy Spirit in preaching is two-fold. There is a work in the preacher, teaching him or her the truth about Jesus and emboldening the preacher's heart (John 15:26–27; Acts 1:8). There is also the work of the Spirit in the hearers, convicting them and using the message that is preached to speak of Jesus (Mark 13:11; John 16:7–11; Gal 3:1–6).

Luther and Calvin held that Christ is really present in the preaching of Scripture. Luther, in fact, considered the preached word of God to be of more importance than the written word, though preaching must be the explication of the written word.[189] The written word, by itself, is not as powerfully presented to us as it is through the ministration of a minister God has ordained to speak it.[190] Inpreaching, Christ speaks to us "to feed the soul, make it righteous, set it free, and save it, provided it believes the preaching."[191] The outer word of God speaks to us and occasions the inner word of God's edification and conversion.[192] Christ accomplished our salvation on the cross, but that salvation is communicated and distributed to us through the word of God proclaimed to us.[193] Some Lutheran traditions have strongly connected Luther's understanding of the communication of Christ to us in preaching with the doctrine of deification.[194]

In fact, Luther paralleled the real presence of Christ in preaching with his real presence in the sacrament of Communion.[195] Luther's theology of sacraments depended on the promise and command of God—God's word.[196] Just as in Communion we receive and meet God through a physical action and element, so also in preaching.[197]

> To be sure, I do not hear this with my ears or see it with my eyes; all I hear is the voice of the preacher, or of my brother or father, and I behold only a man before me. But I view the picture correctly if I add that the voice and words of father or pastor are not his own words and doctrine but those of our Lord and God. It is not a prince, a king, or an archangel whom I hear; it is He who declares that He is able to dispense the water of eternal life.[198]

189. Beach, "Real Presence of Christ," 80–81.

190. Ibid.

191. Luther, *The Freedom of a Christian*, in *Luther's Works*, 31.346.

192. Beach, "Real Presence of Christ," 81–82.

193. Luther, *Against the Heavenly Prophets in the Manner of Images and Sacraments*, in *Luther's Works*, 40.214.

194. See Jensen, "Theosis and Preaching," 432–37.

195. Beach, "Real Presence of Christ," 80.

196. Ibid., 81–82.

197. Ibid., 79.

198. Luther, *Sermons on the Gospel of St. John*, in *Luther's Works*, 22.526–27. See

The seriousness with which Luther viewed preaching was therefore comparable to that with which he viewed the celebration of Communion, for in true preaching we meet Christ himself under the external form of human words.[199]

Calvin also paralleled the presence of Christ in preaching with his presence in the Lord's Supper. Calvin held that Christ was not present in Communion by transubstantiation of the elements but by the communication of his being to the recipient's soul through the power of the Holy Spirit.[200] While Lutherans and Catholics have disputed whether this is a doctrine of Christ's real presence, Calvin certainly intended it to be one; by the work of the Holy Spirit, the communicant truly receives Jesus.

Preaching, according to Calvin, is the primary way that God's presence becomes real and actual in us.[201] Pointing to proclamations of the Old Testament prophets, Calvin argued that while God often did choose to work through a human intermediary, in their prophecies it was the Lord himself who spoke. "Preaching, then, is part of God's saving presence; even more, it is *the vehicle* of that saving presence!"[202] Calvin saw the preaching of the gospel as the means that God chooses to communicate to us all the blessings of his saving presence and power.[203]

In *Practice in Christianity*, Kierkegaard reinforces the connection between the preaching of the gospel and the Law of the Cross. He makes clear that a sermon (and those who hear and preach it) must not just "observe" Christ; it (and they) must come before him, either in faith or in offense.[204] What Kierkegaard means by this is two-fold. First, the message about Jesus is one that involves us personally. Preaching cannot be an abstract or speculative matter, but it must call for and involve meeting Jesus. Second, Christ does not call for admirers, but for imitators. By coming in lowliness, by saving through a cross, he leaves human ingenuity no room for excuses. We, too, must take up our cross and follow him, or we must turn away in denial.

The work of the Holy Spirit also empowers evangelism. The Spirit motivates us and empowers us to communicate the good news about Jesus (Rom 15:13–21). The Spirit also opens effective doors for ministry, shaping

Beach, "Real Presence of Christ," 83–84.

199. See Wilson, "Luther on Preaching as God Speaking," 63–76.

200. John Calvin, *Institutes*, 4.17.10.

201. Beach, "Real Presence of Christ," 92.

202. Ibid., 93, emphasis original.

203. Calvin, *Institutes*, 3.5.5.

204. Kierkegaard, *Practice in Christianity*, 378–84.

circumstances and working in the hearts and minds of those who are being evangelized (Acts: 16:6; Eph 6:18–19).

Some authors, in fact, have considered that the evangelistic mission of the church to the master key to understanding Scripture.[205] At the least, we may say that there is certainly foundation for mission in both Old and New Testaments.[206] God's initial blessing to Abraham contained universal intent (Gen 12:1–4), and this work is not finished until the gospel is proclaimed to all nations, to the very ends of the earth (Matt 28:18–20; Acts 1:8).

Leslie Newbingin connects the mission of the church to the missions of the Trinitarian persons. Although traditional Christian theology does not speak of the Father as "sent," Newbingin connects mission to the Father in that it is the fulfillment of the meaning and destiny of the cosmos as the Father chose to create it.[207] In the mission of the Son, God's mission can no longer be treated as an abstraction or a mere concept, for it acquires a face and a name in Jesus. Jesus embodied God's kingdom in his person, and in him we see incarnate the basis of the mission: God's love.[208] In the Holy Spirit, the mission of the church acquires the certainty of hope, for it is the Spirit that both convicts the world and leads the church toward the fullness it does not yet have.[209]

The practice of Christian mission must inculcate the Law of the Cross due to its incarnational character. Just as Jesus came among us, so he sends us (John 20:21). A truly Christian mission will not imperialistically impose the gospel on non-Christian persons or cultures, and it will not confuse the transcendent work of Christ with the norms and practices of any human culture. It will necessarily declare Jesus, his person, his perfect knowledge and love for God and humankind, and his knowledge and detestation of human sin; more than declare, it must embody, as far as possible, these very things. Then, and only then, will it rightly proceed in the confidence that it is joining in the work of the Spirit to declare Christ.

While a consideration of Christian ministry could continue almost without limit, for God owns and intends to claim every aspect of this universe, we will conclude with a consideration of the church's ministry of education. Christian education has to do with joining in God's work of transforming the universe. It is properly grounded in seeking and promoting conversion (intellectual, moral, religious), and in working to promote

---

205. Wright, *The Mission of God.*

206. Glasser, *Announcing the Kingdom.*

207. *ST* I 43.4; Newbingin, *The Open Secret*, 30.

208. Newbingin, *The Open Secret*, 40–41.

209. Ibid., 57–59.

the flourishing of the human person in the image of God.[210] It will take account of and use every facet of human intellectual and cultural gain in that process.[211]

In Lonergan's analysis of decline in *Insight*, he identifies the most destructive dynamic of decline as the way that the ideas and loves of our cultures become distorted to reflect not responsibility and intelligence but absurdity.[212] In this way, the logic inherent in our social groups itself becomes allied with the forces that bring about our downfall, instead of empowering us for progress. Especially dangerous is capitulation to the tyranny of time, in which long-term solutions can no longer be accepted because they do not fit the shape of our cultural logic and the desires that animate it. Our situation becomes a case of, "If water sticks in our throat, what can we wash it down with?" Our cultures are supposed to be the engines by which we collaborate to overcome our difficulties. But, a tyranny of desire focused on short term-gains can set up a self-reinforcing network, effectively reducing a culture to an organ of what Kierkegaard termed the aesthetic sphere of existence.

Lonergan identified the solution to this problem as "cosmopolis."[213] Reaction to cultural decline—which is exactly a species of cultural change— is likely to run in three different directions. There will be the conservative rearguard that tries to live in a world that no longer exists. There will be the so-called progressives, who see freedom simply in casting off the old order without dissociating themselves from its ultimately nihilistic logic. In cosmopolis, however, Lonergan defined a "not numerous center, big enough to be at home in both the old and the new, painstaking enough to work out one by one the transitions to be made, strong enough to refuse half measures and insist on complete solutions even though it has to wait."[214] The primary features of cosmopolis will be the development of a theoretical viewpoint and an unwavering commitment to discover and state what is true.[215] A theoretical viewpoint is necessary because only the development of theory allows the relations of different elements of cultural progress and decline to be identified and correctly related to each other. An unwavering commitment to what is true is necessary because only truth sets free, and only in pursuing what is true without limit do we join ourselves to the purposes of

---

210. See Snell and Cone, *Authentic Cosmopolitanism*.

211. See Estep and Kim, *Christian Formation*.

212. Lonergan, *Insight*, 261–62.

213. Ibid., 263–64.

214. Lonergan, "Dimensions of Meaning," 245.

215. Lonergan, *Insight*, 264.

God. It is also exactly truth—not the dictates of the culture of decline—that will overcome the tyranny of the moment in which human practicality becomes a death knell to itself.[216]

Christian education must work to create cosmopolis, to foster it, and to protect it (Rom 12:1–2; 2 Cor 10:15). Where else will the love of Christ so animate us to follow what is true and give ourselves to it without reserve or fear? Where else will the fullness of being human be pursued, with the motivation to make the sacrifices required to overcome decline? In this way the Law of the Cross comes to be true in us, for in truly pursuing human flourishing, we are pursuing the mission of Christ in this world. Or in refusing it, we are failing in that which we are supposed to hold most dear.

Destiny

In our salvation, our destiny becomes the same as that of Jesus (Rom 8:32; Rev 22:1–5). We will be with him (John 14:3; 17:24). The promise of the Garden of Eden is restored to us, fulfilled as we become the New Jerusalem, in whom there is no darkness at all, and in whom God fully dwells (Rev 21:7–27). Already this new life has begun in us; not yet is it fulfilled. Still, it is really here, and we can scarcely conceive the fullness of its glory (2 Cor 2:9).

Just as Jesus was resurrected bodily, so we will be, too (1 Cor 15:20–22).[217] In the church's long confession of and reflection on the bodily resurrection, it has found in this doctrine affirmation that the life of the world to come will include our continued personal identity, our being's restoration to wholeness, and our purification and elevation as God remakes us to be fit for eternal life.[218] Bodily resurrection is the ultimate affirmation of materiality, for God uses the material world as a locus of his creative and saving power (Rom 8:18–25).

Our materiality—and through us, the universe's microcosm, the materiality of all of creation—is included in the process of our deification, which does not dispense with matter but transforms it. The Law of the Cross is not just a law of crucifixion, but looks through the cross to the empty tomb. The same dynamics of love, knowledge, and the detestation of evil will not only continue but be intensified in the life of the resurrection (Rev 21:5–8). Through the transformed ones, and, signally, through Jesus our resurrected Lord, creation itself comes to exist on a whole new footing (1 Cor 15:42–49).

216. See Snell and Cone, *Authentic Cosmopolitanism*, 146–81.

217. Wright, *The Resurrection of the Son of God.*

218. Bynum, *Resurrection of the Body.*

What now is the implicit logic of creation will become its manifest and completely present reality, as material being itself is invested with participation in the vision of God.

Leslie Newbigin links the literal nature of Christian eschatology to the reality of our current hope.[219] That there should be a literal "last" in the series we call time boggles our minds, but if true, its reality effects every moment of our present. If the reality thus brought about is the judgment of God, whose rectitude and love we know, then the hope that we cling to, and by which we live, has all the reality of the justice and love of God. As we contemplate this Day, two realities may strike us with special force. The first is our continued need for forgiveness, the way that we clutch to egoism and the last shreds of decline. The second is Christ's unfathomable compassion, by which we are saved.

Christian eschatology, however, does not just have to do with the end of time but suggests a relation of which our current reality is a part. As Lawrence suggests, we know the shape of history in an explanatory way when we realize a proportion: as nature is to supernature, so history is to eschatology.[220] "Nature" is the world of created being as proportionate to the (non-obediential) potencies of its created logic; "supernature" is creation as elevated by God in deification. "History" is the effect of human creativity and love (and its lack) in moving this universe in progress or decline; "eschatology" is the way that the gift of God's grace, and of his very self in Christ, transforms the horizon of our intelligence and love, making us live in a new way, and bringing forth his purposes in the economy of this world.[221] All of these realities are present simultaneously. The purpose of apocalypse, as a genre of literature, is to unveil the meaning of the world, for the ultimate truth of it is the way it is being transformed by God.[222] The meaning of Christ's death and resurrection is the ultimate key to the meaning of the world, in all its shape and destiny, and Christ's power reaches us still through baptism, Holy Communion, and the whole of the Christian life, communicating to us the Law of the Cross.[223]

The meaning of this world, then, is most truly known in anticipation of Christ's Second Coming (Matt 25:31–46; Mark 14:52; Acts 1:11; 1 Cor 15:51–52; 1 Thess 4:13–18; 2 Thess 1:5–12; 1 Pet 1:3–9; 2 Pet 3:8–13; Rev 22:7–20). The personal, bodily return of Christ indicates that

219. Newbigin, *Signs amid the Rubble*, 38–45.

220. Lawrence, "Philosophy, History, and Apocalypse," 95.

221. Ibid., 96–97.

222. Ibid., 99–100.

223. See also Williams, *The Resurrection*.

the consummation of human history will be brought about not without the unmediated presence of Christ, but with it and according to it. At his Second Coming, Christ will not abolish the goods of the present age but overcome the evils, transforming and elevating the goods brought about through human history to be fit for and participate in the life of the world to come.[224] In the resurrection of the righteous, individual and bodily, all those who have participated in the redemption wrought by Christ in history will come to share in the completed and fulfilled blessedness of eternal life. In the resurrection of the damned, those who have refused this redemptive purpose will receive participation in as much good as they have been willing to receive, the retributive justice that gives a true account of their lives and metes out to them their own choices.[225] The present world will be sublated into a supernatural mode of existence—the eighth day of creation spoken of by Maximus and the patristic authors. This higher mode will not negate the goods of the natural order but will fulfill the potencies by which natural existence is ordered to the divine.

Herein lies the meaning, perhaps, that John the Revelator communicated as the millennial reign of Christ (Rev 20:1–10).[226] In our present age of history, Christ reigns in the church, and his reign effectively brings about redemption that sublates progress and overcomes decline. To slay the primeval dragon, though, and not merely temporarily restrain him, requires that the history brought about through the church on the basis of the cross be brought to a head. The dark aspects of our nature, in which the whale of the natural order's brokenness seeks continually to swallow us, and in which we are subject to temptation and attack by our ancient enemy, must be finally overcome. In doing so, Christ personally and finally completes his work, not against the choices of human freedom and intelligibility that his redemption liberates and allows, but as a final, culminating, validation of them. In this way, the *Parousia* does not violently interrupt human history as a force coming to it from without, but enacts a great transformation in which the universe realizes its own inmost meaning. The source of its *esse* liberates it, creating and fulfilling in it the radiant goodness of its own true self.

The notion of the tribulation, then, is that just as there is a limit to the patience of God with evildoers, so there is a limit to the suffering that God is willing to countenance, endured by his faithful ones, in bringing about

224. Wright, *Surprised by Hope.*

225. Kierkegaard, *Works of Love*, 5–8.

226. See Hoekema, *The Bible and the Future*, on amillennial interpretations of Revelation 20. See also Lowery, *Revelation's Rhapsody.*

the ultimate good (Matt 24:21–22). In redemption, God overcomes evil by absorbing it, working through the transformative endurance of suffering to bring about an ultimate good. By becoming part of Christ's redemption, we participate in the suffering of Christ, enduring evil in this world as we cooperate with Christ's grace to overcome it with good. It would be possible that God would institute a world order in which the work of Christ through the church would eventually in and of itself bring about total redemption and reconciliation of the universe, by the testimony about Jesus and the blood of the saints (Rev 12:11). But, it seems that the world order that God's wisdom brings about is one in which he eventually says, "Enough!" The bodily and personal return of Christ indicates that God is not content to let evil inflict horrendous wrong without limit. By his return, Jesus sums up all things under one head, nullifying the ability of the dynamics driving decline to inflict harm, forever uprooting their foul sources, and bringing into the light of day the fullness of humanity. In this way, Christ's work in the church is seen to be part of a cosmic drama, of which the cross is the center, but whose boundaries reach to the end of the age (Matt 28:16–20).

Reflection

This is our salvation.

One may see here the universal extent of God's work, operative centrally in the death and resurrection of Christ, giving us salvation. Perhaps the greatest way that we see the new life operative in us, though, is in the everyday lives of love and service that we share with each other: in true friendship, in forgiving, in hoping and working for the good, in quietly doing one's part, in the big and small decisions of choosing righteousness, in the love we have for family, country, and our fellow human beings. Salvation is not primarily "doing something special"; it is "doing something impossible," on merely human terms, living out in the present age a precursor of the life of the world to come, in all that we are and all that we do.

One may also see how different this view is from a view of salvation that focuses mainly on our legal status before God, on the heart of faith being made to assent to propositions, on good works being done simply because God commands it, on ministry as a set of skills we sharpen and use, and on worship that is mainly the proclamation of right doctrine about God and the production of emotion reinforcing that doctrine. Divinization includes our justification; it is the necessary condition for our regeneration. Likewise, in divinization we will assent to propositions; our belief in Christ is one of the necessary conditions of the Christ life in us, and a result of our regeneration. Divinization joyfully receives God's commands to do good works, for these are precisely the works the regenerated heart longs to do. Divinization develops skills for ministry, for every true advance in knowledge is an advance in God's wisdom, yet the skills find their meaning as useful means for expressing the life that has been given us and that we cannot keep inside. Divinization likewise proclaims the truth about God in worship, and since our whole human beings are drawn into participation with the Spirit of God, our emotions are elevated along with our minds.

Yet there is an infinite beauty we are drawn to, a transforming vision of divine love. The living flame of God's love wounds our soul in its deepest center, bringing us from death to life.[227] Because God's Spirit dwells in us, we ourselves become spiritual, and we send forth God's grace to others.[228]

In this regard, C. S. Lewis poignantly reflects,

> Morality is indispensable: but the Divine Life, which gives itself to us and which calls us to be gods, intends for us something in which morality will be swallowed up. We are to be remade. . . . we shall find underneath it all a thing we have never yet imagined: a real man, an ageless god, a son of God, strong, radiant, wise, beautiful, and drenched in joy.[229]

Conclusion

The story of this universe is a great narrative in which God brings into existence a created world for the purpose of ultimate fellowship with him (Gen 1:26–31). At the center of this story is Christ, in whom the fullness of deity dwells bodily, and who communicates this blessedness to those he came to save (Col 1:15–23). Christ is truly the beginning and end of creation; it is made according to him, and finds its consummation in him (John 1:14). And, in that consummation, the purpose of creation is completed and the dynamics of death are overcome (Rev 1:17–18). The completion of creation is its deification, as those whom Christ saves are changed to live a life in communion with the Trinity (John 17:3).

As Christ transforms us, through his Spirit, to have communion with the Father, every aspect of our existence in history is transformed by receiving the Law of the Cross (Col 2:8–15). God forgives our sins and gives us Christ's righteousness (Rom 5:1–5); he regenerates us in body and spirit

---

227. John of the Cross, *The Living Flame of Love*.

228. Basil, *On the Holy Spirit*.

229. Lewis, "*The Grand Miracle*," 85.

(Rom 8:1–11); we receive communion (*koinonia*) with him and, thereby, with each other (1 Cor 12:12–27); the active life we live comes to express the divine happiness (*eudaimonia*) (Matt 5:3–12); and, we live most truly when we live lives that are grounded in our coming resurrection (1 Cor 15:58). In this way, Christ recapitulates creation, bringing every aspect of it in submission to God's plan, and fulfilling in it the fullness of the divine intention (Eph 1:3–14).

To this end, we may echo the doxology of the brother of Christ (Jude 1:24–25, NRSV).

> Now to him who is able to keep you from falling, and to make you stand without blemish in the presence of his glory with rejoicing, to the only God our Savior, through Jesus Christ our Lord, be glory, majesty, power, and authority, before all time and now and forever. Amen.

Bibliography

Abelard, Peter. *Commentary on the Epistle to the Romans*. Washington, DC: Catholic University of America Press, 2011.

Acar, Rahim. *Talking about God and Talking about Creation: Avicenna's and Thomas Aquinas' Positions*. Leiden: Brill, 2005.

Aden, Ross. "Justification and Sanctification: A Conversation between Lutheranism and Orthodoxy." *St. Vladimir's Theological Quarterly* 38.1 (1994) 87–109.

Alfeyev, Hilarion. "Orthodox Worship as a School of Theology: Lecture Delivered at the Kiev Theological Academy on September 20, 2002." Translated by William Bush. No pages. Online: http://orthodoxeurope.org/page/12/1.aspx.

Anselm. *Cur Deus Homo (Why God Became Man)*. No pages. Online: http://www.fordham.edu/halsall/basis/anselm-curdeus.asp.

Aquinas, Thomas. *Aristotle: On Interpretation. Commentary of St. Thomas and Cajetan.* Translated by Jean T. Oesterle. Milwaukee: Marquette University Press, 1962.

———. *Commentary on the Metaphysics of Aristotle.* 2 vols. Translated by J. Rowan. Chicago: Regnery, 1961.

———. *Lectures on the Letter to the Romans.* Translated by F. Larcher. Edited by J. Holmes. Online: nvjournal.net/files/Aquinas_on_Romans.pdf.

———. *On the Truth of the Catholic Faith: Aquinas' Summa Contra Gentiles.* Translated by Anton C. Pegis (Bk. 1), J. F. Anderson (Bk. 2), and Vernon J. Bourke (Bk. 3), C. J. O'Neill (Bk. 4). 1955. Reprint. Notre Dame: University of Notre Dame Press, 1975.

———. *Quaestiones Disputatae De Potentia Dei.* Translated by English Dominican Fathers. London: Burns, Oates and Washburn, 1923.

———. *Scriptum super libros sententiarum magistri Petri Lombard Episcopi Parisiensis.* 4 vols. Edited by P. Mandonnet and M. F. Moos. Paris: Lethielleux, 1929–47.

———. *The Summa Theologica.* Translated by Fathers of the English Dominican Provence. Chicago: Encyclopaedia Britannica, 1955.

———. *Truth.* 3 vols. Translated by Thomas Mulligan et al. Indianapolis: Hackett, 1994.

Aristotle. *Aristotle Physics.* Edited by R. Waterfield and D. Bostock. Oxford: Oxford University Press, 1996.

———. *The Ethics of Aristotle: The Nicomachean Ethics.* Edited by J. A. K. Thomson and Hugh Tredennick. New York: Penguin, 1976.

———. *The Metaphysics.* Edited and translated by Hugh Tredennick and G. Cyril Armstrong. Loeb Classical Library. New York: Putnam's Sons, 1933.

Armstrong, John, editor. *Understanding Four Views on Baptism*. Grand Rapids: Zondervan, 2007.

Ashton, John. *In Six Days: Why 50 Scientists Choose to Believe in Creation*. Frenchs Forest, Australia: New Holland, 1999.

Athanasius. *On the Incarnation of the Word*. No pages. Online: http://www.ccel.org/ccel/athanasius/incarnation.html.

Augustine. *Against Two Letters of the Pelagians*. No pages. Online: http://www.ccel.org/ccel/schaff/npnf105.xviii.iii.html.

———. *Augustine: Confessions*. Oxford: Oxford University Press, 2012.

———. *Augustine: The City of God against the Pagans*. Cambridge: Cambridge University Press, 1998.

———. *Letter 130*. No pages. Online: http://www.newadvent.org/fathers/1102130.htm.

———. *On Free Choice of the Will*. Translated by T. Williams. Indianapolis: Hackett, 1993.

———. *On Genesis: A Refutation of the Manichees, Unfinished Literal Commentary on Genesis, The Literal Meaning of Genesis*. Translated by E. Hill. Hyde Park, NY: New City, 2002.

———. *On the Predestination of the Saints*. No pages. Online: http://www.newadvent.org/fathers/1512.htm.

———. *The Literal Meaning of Genesis*. Edited by John Hammond Taylor. New York: Paulist, 1982.

———. "Psalm L." In *St. Augustine: Exposition of the Book of Psalms*, edited by P. Schaff. No pages. Online: http://www.ccel.org/ccel/schaff/npnf108.ii.L.html.

———. *Saint Augustine, Anti-Pelagian Writings*. Edited by P. Schaff. Grand Rapids: Eerdmans, 1971.

———. *Sermon 13*. No pages. Online: http://www.newadvent.org/fathers/160313.htm.

———. *The Trinity*. Translated by E. Hill. Hyde Park, NY: New City, 2012.

Aulén, Gustaf. *Christus Victor: An Historical Study of the Three Main Types of the Idea of the Atonement*. Translated by A. Habert. New York: Macmillan, 1951.

Baghos, Mario. "St. Basil's Eschatological Vision: Aspects of the Recapitulation of History and the 'Eighth Day.'" *Phronema* 25 (2010) 85–103.

Baker, Anthony D. *Diagonal Advance: Perfection in Christian Theology*. Veritas. Eugene, OR: Cascade, 2011.

Baker, Mark D. "How the Cross Saves." *Direction* 36.1 (2007) 43–57.

Basil of Caesarea. *On the Holy Spirit*. Edited by David Anderson. Crestwood, NY: St. Vladimir's Seminary Press, 1980.

Beach, J. Mark. "The Real Presence of Christ in the Preaching of the Gospel: Luther and Calvin on the Nature of Preaching." *Mid-America Journal Of Theology* 10 (1999) 77–134.

Behr, John. *Asceticism and Anthropology in Irenaeus and Clement*. reprint ed. The Oxford Early Christian Studies. New York: Oxford University Press, 2000.

———. *The Mystery of Christ: Life in Death*. Crestwood, NY: St. Vladimir's Seminary Press, 2006.

———. *The Nicene Faith*. Formation of Christian Theology 2 (2 Parts). Crestwood, NY: St. Vladimir's Seminary Press, 2004.

———. *The Way to Nicaea*. Formation of Christian Theology 1. Crestwood, NY: St. Vladimir's Seminary Press, 2001.

Berkhof, Louis. *Systematic Theology*. Grand Rapids: Eerdmans, 1996.

Beveridge, William. *Private Thoughts on Religion: And a Christian Life. In Two Parts.* Glasgow: Collins, 1827.

Billings, J. Todd. "John Calvin: United to God through Christ." In *Partakers of the Divine Nature*, edited by Michael J. Christensen and Jeffery A. Wittung, 200–218. Grand Rapids: Baker Academic, 2008.

Blanchette, Oliva. *Philosophy of Being: A Reconstructive Essay in Metaphysics.* Washington, DC: Catholic University of America Press, 2003.

Blowers, Paul, and Robert Wilken. *On the Cosmic Mystery of Jesus Christ: Selected Writings from St. Maximus the Confessor.* Crestwood, NY: St. Vladimir's Seminary Press, 2003.

Bluefarb, Sam. *The Escape Motif in the American Novel: Mark Twain to Richard Wright.* Columbus, OH: Ohio State University Press, 1972.

Boethius. *The Consolation of Philosophy.* Translated by V. Watts. New York: Penguin, 1999.

———. *The Trinity Is One God, Not Three Gods.* No pages. Online: http://www.ccel.org/ccel/boethius/tracts.iv.i.html.

Bouteneff, Peter. *Beginnings: Ancient Christian Readings of the Biblical Creation Narratives.* Grand Rapids: Baker Academic, 2008.

Briggman, Anthony. *Irenaeus of Lyons and the Theology of the Holy Spirit.* New York: Oxford University Press, 2012.

Brock, Sebastian P. "Fire from Heaven: From Abel's Sacrifice to the Eucharist: A Theme in Syriac Christianity." In *Studia patristica Vol. 25*, 229–43. Louvain: Peeters, 1993.

———. *Fire From Heaven: Studies in Syriac Theology and Liturgy.* Burlington, VT: Ashgate Variorum, 2006.

Brown, Walter T. *In the Beginning: Compelling Evidence for Creation and the Flood.* Phoenix, AZ: Center for Scientific Creation, 2008.

Burrell, David B. "Analogy, Creation, and Theological Language." In *The Theology of Thomas Aquinas*, edited by Rik Van Nieuwenhove and Joseph Wawrykow, 77–98. Notre Dame: University of Notre Dame, 2005.

———. *Knowing the Unknowable God: Ibn-Sina, Maimonides, Aquinas.* Notre Dame: University of Notre Dame Press, 1986.

Bynum, Caroline Walker. *The Resurrection of the Body in Western Christianity, 200–1336.* New York: Columbia University Press, 1995.

Calvin, John. *Institutes of the Christian Religion.* No pages. Online: http://www.ccel.org/ccel/calvin/institutes.toc.html.

Campbell, Alexander. "The Lunenburg Letter with Attending Comments." Nashville: Disciples of Christ Historical Society, 1966.

Cassian, John. *Conferences.* No pages. Online: http://www.ccel.org/ccel/cassian/conferences.toc.html.

Castelein, John. "Christian Churches/Churches of Christ View: Believers' Baptism as the Biblical Occasion of Salvation." In *Understanding Four Views on Baptism*, edited by J. Armstrong, 129–44. Grand Rapids: Zondervan, 2007.

Chandler, Raymond. *The Long Goodbye.* New York: Vintage, 1988.

Christensen, Michael J., and Jeffery A. Wittung, editors. *Partakers of the Divine Nature: The History and Development of Deification in the Christian Traditions.* Grand Rapids: Baker Academic, 2007.

Clement of Alexandria. *The Stromata, or Miscellanies.* No pages. Online: http://www.ccel.org/ccel/schaff/anf02.vi.iv.html.

Collins, C. John. *Did Adam and Eve Really Exist? Who They Were and Why You Should Care.* Wheaton, IL: Crossway, 2011.

Cone, Steven D. "Aquinas' Sanctifying Grace and Lonergan's Religious Conversion: Exceptions that Prove the Rule." In *Grace and Friendship: A Festschrift for Frederick Lawrence*, edited by M. Shawn Copeland and Jeremy Wilkins. Milwaukee: Marquette University Press, forthcoming.

———. "Transforming Desire: The Relation of Religious Conversion and Moral Conversion in the Later Writings of Bernard Lonergan." PhD diss. Chestnut Hill, MA: Boston College, 2009.

Conn, Walter E. *Christian Conversion: A Developmental Interpretation of Autonomy and Surrender.* Eugene, OR: Wipf and Stock, 2006.

———. *Conversion, Perspectives on Personal and Social Transformation.* New York: Alba House, 1978.

Craig, William Lane. *The Problem of Divine Foreknowledge and Future Contingents from Aristotle to Suarez.* Leiden: Brill, 1988.

Crysdale, Cynthia, and Neil Ormerod. *Creator God, Evolving World.* Minneapolis, MN: Fortress, 2013.

Cunningham, Conor. *Darwin's Pious Idea: Why the Ultra-Darwinists and Creationists Both Get It Wrong.* Grand Rapids: Eerdmans, 2010.

———. "*Natura Pura*, the Invention of the Anti-Christ: A Week with No Sabbath." *Communio: International Catholic Review* 37 (2010) 243–54.

Cyril of Alexandria. *S. Cyril, Archbishop of Alexandria: Five Tomes against Nestorius; Scholia on the Incarnation; Christ Is One; Fragments against Diodore of Tarsus, Theodore of Mopsuestia, the Synousiasts.* Oxford: Parker and Rivingtons, 1881.

Davis, Stephen T., Cobb, John B., editors. *Encountering Evil: Live Options in Theodicy.* Atlanta: John Knox, 1981.

Desmond, William. *Being and the Between.* Albany, NY: State University of New York Press, 1995.

———. *God and the Between.* Malden, MA: Blackwell, 2008.

———. "Schopenhauer's Philosophy of the Dark Origin." In *A Companion to Schopenhauer*, edited by B. Vandenabeele, 89–104. Malden, MA: Wiley-Blackwell, 2012.

Doran, Robert M. "The Nonviolent Cross: Lonergan and Girard on Redemption." *Theological Studies* 71.1 (2010) 46–61.

———. *Theology and the Dialectics of History.* Toronto: University of Toronto Press, 1990.

Dostoyevsky, Fyodor. *The Brothers Karamazov: A Novel in Four Parts with Epilogue.* Translated by Richard Pevear and Larissa Volokhonsky. New York: Farrar, Straus and Giroux, 2002.

Douglas, J., and Tenney, M. "Sacrifice and Offerings." In *Zondervan Pictorial Bible Dictionary*, edited by J. D. Douglas and Merrill C. Tenney, 1262–65. Grand Rapids: Zondervan, 2011.

Emery, Gilles. "Trinity and Creation." In *The Theology of Thomas Aquinas*, edited by Rik Van Nieuwenhove and Joseph Wawrykow, 58–76. Notre Dame: University of Notre Dame, 2005.

Enns, Peter. *The Evolution of Adam: What the Bible Does and Doesn't Say about Human Origins.* Grand Rapids: Brazos, 2012.

Enûma Eliš: The Babylonian Epic of Creation. Edited by W. G. Lambert, and S. B. Parker. Oxford: Clarendon, 1966.

Estep, James Riley, and Jonathan H. Kim. *Christian Formation: Integrating Theology & Human Development*. Nashville: B. & H. Academic, 2010.

Evans, William B. *Imputation and Impartation: Union with Christ in American Reformed Theology*. Studies in Christian History and Thought. Reprint. Eugene, OR: Wipf & Stock, 2009.

Farrell, Thomas J., and Paul A. Soukup. *Communication and Lonergan: Common Ground for Forging the New Age*. Lanham, MD: Rowman & Littlefield, 1993.

Ferguson, Everett. *Baptism in the Early Church: History, Theology, and Liturgy in the First Five Centuries*. Grand Rapids: Eerdmans, 2009.

———. *Doctrines of Human Nature, Sin, and Salvation in the Early Church*. New York: Garland, 1993.

Finch, Jeffrey D. "Neo-Palamism, Divinizing Grace, and the Breach between East and West." In *Partakers of the Divine Nature*, edited by Michael J. Christensen and Jeffery A. Wittung, 233–49. Grand Rapids: Baker Academic, 2008.

Florovsky, Georges. *Bible, Church, Tradition: An Eastern Orthodox View*. Collected Works of Georges Florovsky, 1. Vaduz, Liechtenstein: Buchervertriebsanstalt, 1987.

———. *Creation and Redemption*. Collected Works of Georges Florovsky, 3–4. Belmont, MA: Nordland, 1976.

———. "Redemption." In *Creation and Redemption*, Collected Works of Georges Florovsky, 3–4, 95–162 (notes, 280–309). Belmont, MA: Nordland, 1976.

Foster, Richard J. *Celebration of Discipline: The Path to Spiritual Growth*. San Francisco: Harper & Row, 1988.

Frankland, Dinelle. *His Story, Our Response: What the Bible Says about Worship*. Joplin, MO: College, 2008.

Francis, Samuel Trevor. "O the Deep, Deep Love of Jesus." No pages. Online: http://www.hymnary.org/hymn/TH/535.

Franzmann, Martin H. "A Ransom for Many: Satisfactio Vicaria." *Concordia Theological Monthly* 25.7 (1954) 497–515.

Fredriksen, Paula. *Sin: The Early History of an Idea*. Princeton: Princeton University Press, 2012.

Gerson, Lloyd P. "Plotinus." In *History of Western Philosophy of Religion, Volume 1, Ancient Philosophy of Religion*, edited by Graham Oppy and Nick Trakakis, 211–22. New York: Oxford University Press, 2009.

Giberson, Karl, and Francis S. Collins. *The Language of Science and Faith: Straight Answers to Genuine Questions*. Downers Grove, IL: InterVarsity, 2011.

Girard, René. *Things Hidden Since the Foundation of the World*. Edited by J.-M. Oughourlian and G. Lefort. Stanford: Stanford University Press, 1987.

———. *Violence and the Sacred*. Baltimore: Johns Hopkins University Press, 1977.

Glasser, A. F., et al. *Announcing the Kingdom: The Story of God's Mission in the Bible*. Grand Rapids: Baker Academic, 2003.

Gordon, Joseph. "Deifying Adoption as Impetus for Moral Transformation: Augustine's Sermons on the Christological Ethics of 'Godhood.'" *Stone-Campbell Journal* 16 (2013) prepress document.

Goris, Harm. "Divine Foreknowledge, Providence, Predestination." In *The Theology of Thomas Aquinas*, edited by Rik Van Nieuwenhove and Joseph Wawrykow, 99–122. Notre Dame: University of Notre Dame, 2005.

Graham, Daniel W. "Heraclitus." *The Stanford Encyclopedia of Philosophy* (Summer 2011 Edition). Edited by Edward N. Zalta. Online: http://plato.stanford.edu/archives/sum2011/entries/heraclitus/.

Greek Orthodox Archdiocese of North America. "Repentance and Confession—Introduction." No pages. Online: http://www.goarch.org/ourfaith/ourfaith8493.

Gregory of Nazianzus. *The Second Oration on Easter (Oration 45)*. No pages. Online: http://www.ccel.org/ccel/schaff/npnf207.iii.xxvii.html.

———. *To Cledonius the Priest against Apollinarius (Epistle 101)*. No pages. Online: http://www.ccel.org/ccel/schaff/npnf207.iv.ii.iii.html.

Gregory of Nyssa. *Great Catechism*. No pages. Online: http://www.ccel.org/ccel/schaff/npnf205.xi.ii.i.html.

Gregory Palamas. "On Redemption." In *The Saving Work of Christ: Sermons by Saint Gregory Palamas*, edited by Christopher Veniamin, 80–100. Waymart, PA: Mount Thabor, 2008.

———. *The Triads*. Edited by John Meyendorff. New York: Paulist, 1983.

Grenz, Stanley J. *Theology for the Community of God*. Nashville: Broadman & Holman, 1994.

Hallonsten, Gösta. "Theosis in Recent Research: A Renewal of Interest and a Need for Clarity." In *Partakers of the Divine Nature*, edited by Michael J. Christensen and Jeffery A. Wittung, 281–93. Grand Rapids: Baker Academic, 2008.

Hart, David Bentley. *The Beauty of the Infinite: The Aesthetics of Christian Truth*. Grand Rapids: Eerdmans, 2003.

———. *The Doors of the Sea: Where Was God in the Tsunami?* Grand Rapids: Eerdmans, 2011.

Hegel, Georg Wilhelm Friedrich. *Hegel's Logic: Being Part One of the Encyclopaedia of the Philosophical Sciences (1830)*. Edited by William Wallace. Oxford: Clarendon, 1975.

———. *Hegel's Science of Logic*. Translated by A. V. Miller. Muirhead Library of Philosophy. New York: Humanities, 1969.

Heine, Ronald E. *Classical Christian Doctrine: Introducing the Essentials of the Ancient Faith*. Grand Rapids: Baker Academic, 2013.

———. *Origen: Scholarship in the Service of the Church*. New York: Oxford University Press, 2010.

———. *Reading the Old Testament with the Ancient Church: Exploring the Formation of Early Christian Thought*. Grand Rapids: Baker Academic, 2007.

Hemmer, Ryan. "'After All, What Is a Man in Nature?' Technology, Nihilism, and the Meaning of Man." *Stone-Campbell Journal* 15.2 (2012) 205–16.

Herbert, George. *The English Poems of George Herbert: With a Priest to the Temple and His Collection of Proverbs Called Jacula Prudentium*. New York: Dutton, 1800.

Hesiod. *Theogony; Works and Days; Shield*. Translated by A. Athanassakis and N. Apostolos. Baltimore: Johns Hopkins University Press, 1983.

Hesselink, I. John. "The Reformed View: The Real Presence of Christ." In *Understanding Four Views on the Lord's Supper*, edited by J. Armstrong, 59–74. Grand Rapids: Zondervan, 2007.

Hicks, John Mark. *Come to the Table: Revisioning the Lord's Supper.* Orange, CA: New Leaf, 2002.

Hippolytus of Rome. *The Treatise on the Apostolic Tradition of St. Hippolytus of Rome, Bishop and Martyr.* London: SPCK, 1968.

Hoekema, Anthony A. *The Bible and the Future.* Grand Rapids: Eerdmans, 1979.

Holsinger-Friesen, Thomas. *Irenaeus and Genesis: A Study of Competition in Early Christian Hermeneutics.* Winona Lake, IN: Eisenbrauns, 2009.

Howells, William Dean. "Earliest Spring." In *The Oxford Book of English Verse*, edited by A. Quiller-Couch, 812. Oxford: Clarendon, 1919.

Hunsinger, George. *Disruptive Grace: Studies in the Theology of Karl Barth.* Grand Rapids: Eerdmans, 2000.

Hurtado, Larry W. "New Testament Studies in the 20th Century." *Religion* 39.1 (2009) 43–57.

Ignatius of Antioch. *The Epistle of Ignatius to the Philippians.* No pages. Online: http://www.ccel.org/ccel/schaff/anf01.v.xvii.html.

Inwood, Michael. "Sublation." In *A Hegel Dictionary*, edited by M. Inwood, 283–85. Oxford: Blackwell, 1992.

Irenaeus of Lyons. *Against Heresies.* No pages. Online: http://www.ccel.org/ccel/schaff/anf01.ix.html.

———. *Demonstration of the Apostolic Preaching.* No pages. Online: http://www.ccel.org/ccel/irenaeus/demonstr.toc.html.

———. *St. Irenaeus of Lyons: Against the Heresies, Book 1.* Ancient Christian Writers. Edited by D. Unger and J. Dillon. Mahwah, NJ: Paulist, 1992.

Jensen, Richard A. "Theosis and Preaching: Implications for Preaching in the Finnish Luther Research." *Currents in Theology and Mission* 31.6 (2004) 432–37.

Jerome. *To Paulinius (Letter 53).* No pages. Online: http://www.ccel.org/ccel/schaff/npnf206.v.LIII.html.

John of the Cross. *The Flame of Living Love: Translated from St. John of the Cross.* Translated by R. Campbell. London: Longmans, Green & Co., 1949.

John Paul II. "Spirit Enables Us to Share in Divine Nature: At the General Audience of Wednesday, May 27, 1988." No pages. Online: http://www.vatican.va/jubilee_2000/magazine/documents/ju_mag_01061998_p-10_en.html#top.

Johnson, Adam J. "A Fuller Account: The Role of 'Fittingness' in Thomas Aquinas' Development of the Doctrine of the Atonement." *International Journal of Systematic Theology* 12.3 (2010) 302–18.

Jonas, Hans. *The Gnostic Religion: The Message of the Alien God and the Beginnings of Christianity.* Boston: Beacon, 1963.

Kant, Immanuel. *Religion within the Limits of Reason Alone.* New York: HarperOne, 2008.

Kaufmann, Walter Arnold. *Hegel: A Reinterpretation.* New York: Anchor, 1966.

Keenan, James F. "The Virtue of Prudence (IIa IIae, qq. 47–56)." In *Ethics of Aquinas*, edited by S. Pope, 259–71. Washington, DC: Georgetown University Press, 2002.

Keith, Chris, and Larry W. Hurtado. *Jesus among Friends and Enemies: A Historical and Literary Introduction to Jesus in the Gospels.* Grand Rapids: Baker Academic, 2011.

Kelly, Eugene. *The Basics of Western Philosophy.* Amherst, NY: Humanity, 2007.

Kent, Matthew A. "Prime Matter according to St. Thomas Aquinas." PhD diss. New York: Fordham University, 2006.

Kierkegaard, Søren. *Concluding Unscientific Postscript to Philosophical Fragments.* 2 vols. Kierkegaard's Writings, 11 and 12. Edited and translated by H. Hong and E. Hong. Princeton: Princeton University Press, 1992.

———. *Discourses at the Communion on Fridays.* Edited by Sylvia Walsh. Bloomington, IN: Indiana University Press, 2011.

———. *Either/OR.* 2 vols. Kierkegaard's Writings, 3 and 4. Edited and translated by H. Hong and E. Hong. Princeton: Princeton University Press, 1987.

———. *Fear and Trembling.* Kierkegaard's Writings, 6. Edited and translated by H. Hong and E. Hong. Princeton: Princeton University Press, 1983.

———. *Kierkegaard's Attack upon "Christendom," 1854–1855.* Edited and translated by W. Lowrie. Princeton: Princeton University Press, 1991.

———. *Philosophical Fragments, Johannes Climacus.* Kierkegaard's Works, 7. Edited and translated by H. Hong and E. Hong. Princeton: Princeton University Press, 1985.

———. *Practice in Christianity.* Kierkegaard's Works, 20. Edited and translated by H. Hong and E. Hong. Princeton: Princeton University Press, 1991.

———. *The Sickness unto Death: A Christian Psychological Exposition for Upbuilding and Awakening.* Kierkegaard's Works, 19. Translated and edited by H. Hong and E. Hong. Princeton: Princeton University Press, 1983.

———. *Works of Love.* Kierkegaard's Works, 16. Translated and edited by H. Hong and E. Hong. Princeton: Princeton University Press, 1998.

Kilcullen, John. "The Political Writings." In *The Cambridge Companion to Ockham*, edited by P. Spade, 302–25. Cambridge: Cambridge University Press, 1999.

King, Peter. "Ockham's Ethical Theory." In *The Cambridge Companion to Ockham*, edited by P. Spade, 227–44. Cambridge: Cambridge University Press, 1999.

Kobusch, Theo. "Grace (Ia IIae, qq. 109–14)." Translated by Grant Kaplan and Frederick G. Lawrence. In *Ethics of Aquinas*, edited by S. Pope, 207–18. Washington, DC: Georgetown University Press, 2002.

Kugel, James L. *The Idea of Biblical Poetry: Parallelism and Its History.* New Haven: Yale University Press, 1981.

Kuhn, Karl A. "The 'One Like a Son of Man' Becomes the 'Son of God.'" *Catholic Biblical Quarterly* 69.1 (2007) 22–42.

Kurz, Joel. "The Gifts of Creation and the Consummation of Humanity: Irenaeus of Lyons' Recapitulatory Theology of the Eucharist." *Worship* 83.2 (2009) 112–32.

Lamont, John R. T. "The Justice and Goodness of Hell." *Faith And Philosophy* 28.2 (2011) 152–73.

Lawrence, Frederick G. "The Fragility of Consciousness: Lonergan and the Postmodern Concern for the Other." In *Communication and Lonergan*, 173–211. Kansas City, MO: Sheed & Ward, 1993.

———. "The Human Good and Christian Conversation." In *Communication and Lonergan*, 248–68. Kansas City, MO: Sheed & Ward, 1993.

———. "Between Capitalism and Marxism: Introducing Lonergan's Economics." *Revista Portuguesa de Filosofia* 63.4 (2007) 941–59.

———. "The Hermeneutic Revolution and the Future of Theology." In *Between the Human and the Divine: Philosophical and Theological Hermeneutics*, edited by Andrzej Wierciński, 326–54. Toronto: Hermeneutic, 2002.

———. "Philosophy, History, and Apocalypse in Voegelin, Strauss, and Girard." In *Politics & Apocalypse*, edited by Robert Hamerton-Kelly, 95–137. East Lansing, MI: Michigan University Press, 2007.

Leff, Gordon. *William of Ockham: The Metamorphosis of Scholastic Discourse.* Totowa, NJ: Rowman and Littlefield, 1975.

Leithart, Peter J. *Athanasius.* Grand Rapids: Baker Academic, 2011.

Levering, Matthew. *The Theology of Augustine: An Introductory Guide to His Most Important Works.* Grand Rapids: Baker Academic, 2013.

Lewis, Clive Staples. "Dogma and the Universe." In *God in the Dock*, edited by W. Hooper, 108–13. Grand Rapids: Eerdmans, 1972.

———. "The Grand Miracle." In *God in the Dock*, edited by W. Hooper, 80–88. Grand Rapids: Eerdmans, 1972.

———. *A Grief Observed.* Edited by M. L'Engle. New York: HarperOne, 2009.

———. *God in the Dock: Essays on Theology and Ethics.* Edited by W. Hooper. Grand Rapids: Eerdmans, 1970.

———. *The Grand Miracle, and Other Selected Essays on Theology and Ethics from God in the Dock.* Edited by W. Hooper. New York: Ballantine, 1983.

———. "Man or Rabbit." In *God in the Dock*, edited by W. Hooper, 38–47. Grand Rapids: Eerdmans, 1972.

———. *Mere Christianity.* 3rd ed. San Francisco: HarperSanFrancisco, 2001.

———. *The Problem of Pain.* San Francisco: HarperSanFrancisco, 2001.

Liddell, H. G., et al. *A Greek-English Lexicon.* 9th rev. ed. Oxford: Clarendon, 1996.

Lonergan, Bernard. "Analysis of Faith." In *Early Latin Theology*, edited by Robert M. Doran and H. Daniel Monsour, 413–82. Toronto: University of Toronto Press, 2011.

Lonergan, Bernard. *Collection.* Collected Works of Bernard Lonergan, 4. Edited by Frederick E. Crowe and Robert M. Doran. Toronto: University of Toronto Press, 1988.

———. "Dimensions of Meaning." In *Collection*, edited by Frederick E. Crowe and Robert M. Doran, 232–43. Toronto: University of Toronto Press, 1988.

———. *The Divine Redeemer: A Supplement to De Verbo Incarnato.* Translated by Michael Shields from *De bono et malo.* Toronto: Lonergan Research Institute, 2000.

———. *Early Latin Theology.* Collected Works of Bernard Lonergan, 19. Edited by Robert M. Doran and H. Daniel Monsour. Translated by Michael G. Shields. Toronto: University of Toronto Press, 2011.

———. *"Existenz* and *Aggiornamento."* In *Collection*, edited by Frederick E. Crowe and Robert M. Doran, 222–31. Toronto: Toronto University Press, 1988.

———. "Finality, Love, Marriage." In *Collection*, edited by Frederick E. Crowe and Robert M. Doran, 17–52. Toronto: Toronto University Press, 1988.

———. *The Incarnate Word.* Translated by Charles Hefling *from De Verbo Incarnato*, 3rd ed. Toronto: Lonergan Research Institute, 2006.

———. *For a New Political Economy.* Collected Works of Bernard Lonergan, 21. Edited by P. McShane. Toronto: University of Toronto Press, 1998.

———. *Grace and Freedom: Operative Grace in the Thought of St. Thomas Aquinas.* Collected Works of Bernard Lonergan, 1. Edited by Frederick E. Crowe and Robert M. Doran. Toronto: University of Toronto Press, 1988.

————. *Insight: A Study of Human Understanding.* Collected Works of Bernard Lonergan, 3. Edited by Frederick E. Crowe and Robert M. Doran. Toronto, University of Toronto Press, 1992.

————. *Macroeconomic Dynamics: An Essay in Circulation Analysis.* Collected Works of Bernard Lonergan, 15. Edited by Patrick Byrne and Frederick Lawrence. Toronto: University of Toronto Press, 1999.

————. *Method in Theology.* Toronto: University of Toronto Press, 2003.

————. "Moral Theology and the Human Sciences." In *Philosophical and Theological Papers, 1965–1980*, 301–12. Toronto: University of Toronto Press, 2004.

————. "The Notion of Sacrifice." In *Early Latin Theology,* edited by Robert M. Doran and H. Daniel Monsour, 3–52. Toronto: University of Toronto Press, 2011.

————. "On Redemption." In *Philosophical and Theological Papers, 1958–1964*, 3–28. Toronto: University of Toronto Press, 1996.

————. *Philosophical and Theological Papers, 1958–1964.* Collected Works of Bernard Lonergan, 6. Edited by Robert C. Croken, Frederick E. Crowe, and Robert M. Doran. Toronto: University of Toronto Press, 1996.

————. *Philosophical and Theological Papers, 1965–1980.* Collected Works of Bernard Lonergan, 17. Edited by Robert C. Croken and Robert M. Doran. Toronto: University of Toronto Press, 2004.

————. "Self-Transcendence: Intellectual, Moral, Religious." In *Philosophical and Theological Papers, 1965–1980*, edited by Robert C. Croken and Robert M. Doran, 313–31. Toronto: University of Toronto Press, 2004.

————. "The Subject." In *A Second Collection: Papers by Bernard J. F. Lonergan, S.J.,* edited by William F. J. Ryan and Bernard J. Tyrrell, 69–86. Toronto: University of Toronto Press, 1974.

————. "The Supernatural Order." In *Early Latin Theology,* edited by Robert M. Doran and H. Daniel Monsour, 53–256. Toronto: University of Toronto Press, 2011.

————. *The Triune God: Systematics.* Collected Works of Bernard Lonergan, 12. Edited by Robert M. Doran and H. Daniel Monsour. Translated by Michael Shields. Toronto: University of Toronto Press, 2007.

————. *Understanding and Being.* Edited by E. A. Morelli and M. D. Morelli. Collected Works of Bernard Lonergan, 5. Toronto: University of Toronto Press, 1990.

Lossky, Vladimir. *The Mystical Theology of the Eastern Church.* Crestwood, NY: St. Vladimir's Seminary Press, 1976.

————. *Orthodox Theology: An Introduction.* Crestwood, NY: St. Vladimir's Seminary Press, 1978.

Louth, Andrew. *Maximus the Confessor.* New York: Routledge, 1996.

Lovejoy, Arthur O. *The Great Chain of Being: A Study of the History of an Idea.* New Brunswick, NJ: Transaction, 2009.

Lowery, Robert A. *Revelation's Rhapsody: Listening to the Lyrics of the Lamb: How to Read the Book of Revelation.* Joplin, MO: College, 2006.

Luther, Martin. *The Large Catechism.* No pages. Online: http://bookofconcord.org/lc-1-intro.php.

————. *Selections from His Writings.* Edited by J. Dillenberger. Garden City, NY: Doubleday, 1961.

————. *Works.* 69 vols. Edited and translated by J. Pelikan et al. Saint Louis: Concordia, 1955–86.

Marshall, Bruce D. "*Quod Scit Una Uetula*: Aquinas on the Nature of Theology." In *The Theology of Thomas Aquinas*, edited by Rik Van Nieuwenhove and Joseph Wawrykow, 1–35. Notre Dame: University of Notre Dame Press, 2005.

Maximus the Confessor. *Ad Thalassium 2*. In *The Cosmic Mystery of Jesus Christ*, edited by R. Wilken and P. Blowers, 99–102. Crestwood, NY: St. Vladimir's Seminary Press, 2003.

———. *Ad Thalassium 22*. In *The Cosmic Mystery of Jesus Christ*, edited by R. Wilken and P. Blowers, 115–18. Crestwood, NY: St. Vladimir's Seminary Press, 2003.

———. *Ad Thalassium 6*. In *The Cosmic Mystery of Jesus Christ*, edited by R. Wilken and P. Blowers, 103–4. Crestwood, NY: St. Vladimir's Seminary Press, 2003.

———. *Ad Thalassium 61*. In *The Cosmic Mystery of Jesus Christ*, edited by R. Wilken and P. Blowers, 131–44. Crestwood, NY: St. Vladimir's Seminary Press, 2003.

———. *Ambiguum 10*. In *Maximus the Confessor*, edited by A. Louth, 94–154. New York: Routledge, 1996.

———. *Ambiguum 41*. In *Maximus the Confessor*, edited by A. Louth, 155–62. New York: Routledge, 1996.

———. *Ambiguum 42*. In *The Cosmic Mystery of Jesus Christ*, edited by R. Wilken and P. Blowers, 119–22. Crestwood, NY: St. Vladimir's Seminary Press, 2003.

———. *Ambiguum 7*. In *The Cosmic Mystery of Jesus Christ*, edited by R. Wilken and P. Blowers, 45–74. Crestwood, NY: St. Vladimir's Seminary Press, 2003.

———. *Ambiguum 71*. In *Maximus the Confessor*, edited by A. Louth, 163–68. New York: Routledge, 1996.

———. *Chapters on Knowledge*. In *Selected Writings*, edited by George C. Berthold, 127–80. Mahwah, NJ: Paulist, 1985.

———. *Commentary on the Our Father*. In *Selected Writings*, edited by George C. Berthold, 99–126. Mahwah, NJ: Paulist, 1985.

———. *The Four Hundred Chapters on Love*. In *Selected Writings*, edited by George C. Berthold, 33–98. Mahwah, NJ: Paulist, 1985.

———. *Mystagogia*. In *Selected Writings*, edited by George C. Berthold, 181–226. Mahwah, NJ: Paulist, 1985.

———. *Selected Writings*. Classics of Western Spirituality. Edited by George C. Berthold. Mahwah, NJ: Paulist, 1985.

———. *St. Maximus the Confessor's Questions and Doubts*. Edited by D. Prassas. DeKalb, IL: Northern Illinois University Press, 2009.

———. *Various Texts on Theology, the Divine Economy, and Virtue and Vice*. In *The Philokalia, Volume 2: The Complete Text; Compiled by St. Nikodimos of the Holy Mountain & St. Markarios of Corinth*, edited by G. Palmer et al., 164–284. London: Faber & Faber, 1981.

McDonnell, Kilian, and George T Montague. *Christian Initiation and Baptism in the Holy Spirit: Evidence From the First Eight Centuries*. Collegeville, MN: Liturgical, 1991.

McGrath, Alister E. *Christian Theology: An Introduction*. 5th ed. Malden, MA: Wiley-Blackwell, 2011.

———. *Theology: The Basics*. 3rd ed. Malden, MA: Wiley-Blackwell, 2012.

McGuckin, John A. "The Strategic Adaptation of Deification in the Cappadocians." In *Partakers of the Divine Nature*, edited by Michael J. Christensen and Jeffery A. Wittung, 95–114. Grand Rapids: Baker Academic, 2008.

McLaughlin, Michael T. *Knowledge, Consciousness, and Religious Conversion in Lonergan and Aurobindo.* Rome: Editrice Pontificia Università Gregoriana, 2003.

Meconi, David Vincent. *The One Christ: St. Augustine's Theology of Deification.* Washington, DC: Catholic University of America Press, 2013.

Melchin, Kenneth R. *Living with Other People: An Introduction to Christian Ethics Based on Bernard Lonergan.* Collegeville, MN: Liturgical, 1998.

Merriell, D. Juvenal. "Trinitarian Anthropology." In *The Theology of Thomas Aquinas,* edited by Rik Van Nieuwenhove and Joseph Wawrykow, 123–42. Notre Dame: University of Notre Dame Press, 2005.

Meyendorff, John. *Byzantine Theology: Historical Trends and Doctrinal Themes.* New York: Fordham University Press, 1983.

Milbank, John. *Theology and Social Theory: Beyond Secular Reason.* 2nd ed. Malden, MA: Blackwell, 2006.

Miller, Mark. "Why the Passion?: Bernard Lonergan on the Cross as Communication." PhD diss. Chestnut Hill, MA: Boston College, 2008.

Minns, Denis. *Irenaeus.* Washington, DC: Georgetown University Press, 1994.

Moore, Russell, ed. *Understanding Four Views on the Lord's Supper.* Grand Rapids: Zondervan, 2007.

Mudd, Joseph. "Eucharist and Critical Metaphysics: A Response to Louis-Marie Chauvet's Symbol and Sacrament Drawing on the Works of Bernard Lonergan." PhD diss. Chestnut Hill, MA: Boston College, 2010.

Newbigin, Lesslie. *The Open Secret: An Introduction to the Theology of Mission.* Grand Rapids: Eerdmans, 1995.

———. *Signs Amid the Rubble: The Purposes of God in Human History.* Edited by Geoffrey Wainwright. Grand Rapids: Eerdmans, 2003.

Niebuhr, Reinhold. *Christian Realism and Political Problems.* New York: Scribner, 1953.

Nietzsche, Friedrich Wilhelm. *On the Genealogy of Morality.* Edited by K. Ansell-Pearson and C. Diethe. Cambridge: Cambridge University Press, 2007.

Nil, Sorsky. *Nil Sorsky: The Authentic Writings.* Edited by. David M. Goldfrank. Kalamazoo, MI: Cistercian, 2008.

Noll, Mark A. *Jesus Christ and the Life of the Mind.* Grand Rapids: Eerdmans, 2011.

Norman, R. Stanton. "Human Sinfulness." In *A Theology for the Church,* edited by D. Akin, 409–78. Nashville: B. & H. Academic, 2007.

Numbers, Ronald L. *The Creationists: From Scientific Creationism to Intelligent Design.* Cambridge, MA: Harvard University Press, 2006.

Oden, Thomas. *Classic Christianity: A Systematic Theology.* New York: HarperOne, 2009.

———. *The Rebirth of Orthodoxy: Signs of New Life in Christianity.* New York: HarperOne, 2002.

O'Keefe, John J. "The Suffering of the Impassible God: The Dialectics of Patristic Thought." *Pro Ecclesia* 16.4 (2007) 462–65.

Origen. "Commentary on Matthew." In *Ante-Nicene Fathers,* vol. 10, edited by Allen Menzies and translated by John Patrick, 411–512. Peabody, MA: Hendrickson, 1999.

———. *Commentary on the Epistle to the Romans.* Translated by T. Scheck. Washington, DC: Catholic University of America Press, 2001.

Osborn, Eric. *Irenaeus of Lyons.* Cambridge: Cambridge University Press, 2005.

Palm, Ralph. "Hegel's Concept of Sublation: A Critical Interpretation." PhD diss. Leuven: Catholic University of Leuven, 2009.

Palmer, John. "Parmenides." *The Stanford Encyclopedia of Philosophy* (Summer 2012 Edition). Edited by Edward N. Zalta. Online: http://plato.stanford.edu/archives/sum2012/entries/parmenides/.

Pascal, Blaise. *Pensées*. Translated by Roger Ariew Indianapolis, IN: Hackett, 2005.

Pearson, Birger A. *Ancient Gnosticism: Traditions and Literature*. Minneapolis, MN: Fortress, 2007.

Peters, James R. *The Logic of the Heart: Augustine, Pascal, and the Rationality of Faith*. Grand Rapids: Baker Academic, 2009.

Petillo, Matthew. "The Experience of Grace in the Theologies of Karl Rahner and Bernard Lonergan." PhD diss., Chestnut Hill, MA: Boston College, 2009.

Pickstock, Catherine. *After Writing: On the Liturgical Consummation of Philosophy*. Malden, MA: Blackwell, 1998.

———. "Liturgy, Art and Politics." *Modern Theology* 16.2 (2000) 159–80.

Pieper, Josef. *A Brief Reader on the Virtues of the Human Heart*. San Francisco: Ignatius, 1991.

Plato. *Gorgias*. Translated by W. C. Helmbold. London: Pearson, 1952.

———. *The Republic of Plato*. Translated and edited by Allan David Bloom. New York: Basic, 1991.

———. *Timaeus and Critias*. Translated by H. D. P. Lee. Baltimore: Penguin, 1971.

Plotinus. *Enneads*. 7 vols. Plotinus: In Seven Volumes. Cambridge: Harvard University Press, 1979.

Pope, Stephen J., editor. *The Ethics of Aquinas*. Washington, DC: Georgetown University Press, 2002.

Porter, Jean. "Right Practical Reason: Aristotle, Action, and Prudence in Aquinas." *Journal Of Religious Ethics* 26.1 (1998) 191–215.

———. "Right Reason and the Love of God: The Parameters of Aquinas' Moral Theology." In *The Theology of Thomas Aquinas*, edited by Rik Van Nieuwenhove and Joseph Wawrykow, 167–91. Notre Dame: University of Notre Dame Press, 2005.

Potts, Michael. "Aquinas, Hell, and the Resurrection of the Damned." *Faith and Philosophy* 15.3 (1998) 341–51.

Presley, Stephen. "Irenaeus and the Gnostics on 1 Corinthians 15:53–54." No pages. Online: http://bible.org/article/irenaeus-and-gnostics-1-corinthians-1553–54#P89_25511.

Pseudo-Dionysius, the Areopagite. *Pseudo-Dionysius: The Complete Works*. Edited and translated by Colm Luibhéid and Paul Rorem. New York: Paulist, 1987.

Quiller-Couch, Arthur Thomas. *The Oxford Book of English Verse 1250–1900. Volume 2 of the Oxford Book of English Verse, 1250–1900*. Oxford: Clarendon, 1919.

Rea, Robert Floyd. "Grace and Free Will in John Cassian." PhD diss. St. Louis, MO: St. Louis University, 1991.

Reese, William L. "Hegel." In *Dictionary of Philosophy and Religion: Eastern and Western Thought*, 2nd ed., edited by W. Reese, 286–87. Atlantic Highlands, NJ: Humanities, 1996.

Ruether, Rosemary Radford. *Introducing Redemption in Christian Feminism*. Cleveland, OH: Pilgrim, 2000.

Russell, Norman. *The Doctrine of Deification in the Greek Patristic Tradition*. Oxford: Oxford University Press, 2006.

Scheler, Max. *Ressentiment.* Edited by Manfred S. Frings. Milwaukee: Marquette University Press, 1994.

Schockenhoff, Eberhard. "The Theological Virtue of Charity (IIa IIae, qq. 23–46)." Translated by Grant Kaplan, and Frederick G. Lawrence. In *Ethics of Aquinas*, edited by S. Pope, 244–58. Washington, DC: Georgetown University Press, 2002.

Schwager, Raymund. "Christ's Death and the Prophetic Critique of Sacrifice." *Semeia* 33 (1985) 109–23.

Scotus, John Duns. "Ordinatio I, dist. 44." In *Duns Scotus on the Will and Morality: Selected and Translated with an Introduction by Allen B. Wolter, O.F.M.*, edited by Allen B. Wolter, 191–94. Washington, DC: Catholic University of America Press, 1997.

Second Council of Orange. No pages. Online: http://www.fordham.edu/halsall/basis/orange.txt.

Simpson, Christopher Ben. *Deleuze and Theology.* London: T. & T. Clark, 2012.

———. *Religion, Metaphysics, and the Postmodern: William Desmond and John D. Caputo.* Indiana Series on the Philosophy of Religion. Bloomington, IN: Indiana University Press, 2009.

———. "Theology, Philosophy, God and the Between." *Radical Orthodoxy: Theology, Philosophy, Politics,* 1.1–2 (2012) 262–79.

———. *The Truth Is the Way: Kierkegaard's* Theologia Viatorum. Eugene, OR: Cascade, 2011.

Sire, James W. *Naming the Elephant: Worldview as a Concept.* Downers Grove, IL: InterVarsity Press, 2004.

Smith, Gary V. *Isaiah 40–66.* New American Commentary Series, 15B. Nashville, TN: B. & H., 2007

Smith, J. Warren. "Suffering Impassibly: Christ's Passion in Cyril of Alexandria's Soteriology." *Pro Ecclesia* 11 (2002) 463–83.

Smith, James K. A. *Desiring the Kingdom: Worship, Worldview, and Cultural Formation.* Grand Rapids: Baker Academic, 2009.

———. *Imagining the Kingdom How Worship Works.* Grand Rapids: Baker Academic, 2013.

Snell, R. J. *Through a Glass Darkly: Bernard Lonergan & Richard Rorty on Knowing Without a God's-eye View.* Milwaukee: Marquette University Press, 2006.

Snell, R. J., and Steven D. Cone. *Authentic Cosmopolitanism: Love, Sin, and Grace in the Christian University.* Eugene, OR: Pickwick, 2013.

Sokolowski, Robert. *Christian Faith & Human Understanding: Studies on the Eucharist, Trinity, and the Human Person.* Washington, DC: Catholic University of America Press, 2006.

———. *The God of Faith and Reason: Foundations of Christian Theology.* Washington, DC: Catholic University of America Press, 1995.

Stebbins, J. Michael. *The Divine Initiative: Grace, World-order, and Human Freedom in the Early Writings of Bernard Lonergan.* Toronto: University of Toronto Press, 1995.

Steenberg, M. C. *Irenaeus on Creation the Cosmic Christ and the Saga of Redemption.* Boston: Brill, 2008.

———. *Of God and Man: Theology As Anthropology From Irenaeus to Athanasius.* London: T. & T. Clark, 2009.

Stump, Eleonore. *Aquinas.* New York: Routledge, 2003.

———. "The Problem of Evil." *Faith And Philosophy* 2.4 (1985) 392–423.

Sullivan, Francis A. "The Development of Doctrine about Infants Who Die Unbaptized." *Theological Studies* 72.1 (2011) 3–14.

The Symbol of Chalcedon. No pages. Online: http://www.ccel.org/ccel/schaff/creeds2. iv.i.iii.html.

Te Velde, Rudi A. "Evil, Sin, and Death: Thomas Aquinas on Original Sin." In *The Theology of Thomas Aquinas*, edited by Rik Van Nieuwenhove and Joseph Wawrykow, 143–66. Notre Dame, IN: University of Notre Dame Press, 2005.

Thiselton, Anthony C. *The Two Horizons: New Testament Hermeneutics and Philosophical Description with Special Reference to Heidegger, Bultmann, Gadamer, and Wittgenstein.* Exeter, UK: Paternoster, 1980.

Thunberg, Lars. *Microcosm and Mediator: The Theological Anthropology of Maximus the Confessor.* 2nd ed. Chicago: Open Court, 1995.

Twain, Mark. *Adventures of Huckleberry Finn.* New York: Dover, 1994.

U. S. Congress of Catholic Bishops. *Catechism of the Catholic Church: With Modifications from the Editio Typica.* New York: Doubleday, 1997.

Van Bavel, Tarsicius J. "Church *(ecclesia)*." In *Augustine through the Ages: An Encyclopedia*, edited by A. Fitzgerald, 168–76. Grand Rapids: Eerdmans, 2009.

Van Nieuwenhove, Rik, and Joseph Wawrykow, Joseph. *The Theology of Thomas Aquinas.* Notre Dame: University of Notre Dame Press, 2005.

VanArragon, R. L. "Is It Possible to Freely Reject God Forever?" In *The Problem of Hell: A Philosophical Anthology*, edited by Joel Buenting, 29–43. Burlington, VT: Ashgate, 2010.

Vishnevskaya, Elena. "Divinization as Perichoretic Embrace in Maximus the Confessor." In *Partakers of the Divine Nature*, edited by Michael J. Christensen and Jeffery A. Wittung, 132–45. Grand Rapids: Baker Academic, 2008.

Volk, John. "Lonergan on the Historical Causality of Christ: An Interpretation of 'The Redemption: A Supplement to *De Verbo Incarnato*.'" PhD diss. Milwaukee: Marquette University, 2012.

Von Balthasar, Hans Urs. *The Cosmic Liturgy: The Universe according to Maximus the Confessor.* Translated by B. Daley. San Francisco: Ignatius, 2003.

———. *Dare We Hope "That All Men Be Saved"? With a Short Discourse on Hell.* San Francisco: Ignatius, 1988.

Vööbus, Arthur. "Theological Reflections on Human Nature in Ancient Syrian Traditions." In *Doctrines of Human Nature, Sin, and Salvation in the Early Church*, edited by E. Ferguson, 31–50. London: Garland, 1993.

Walsh, Sylvia. "Introduction." In *Discourses at the Communion on Fridays*, edited by S. Walsh, 1–36. Bloomington, IN: Indiana University Press, 2011.

Warfield, Benjamin Breckinridge. *Evolution, Scripture, and Science.* Edited by Mark A. Noll, and David N. Livingstone. Grand Rapids: Baker, 2000.

Wawrykow, Joseph. "Grace." In *The Theology of Thomas Aquinas*, edited by Rik Van Nieuwenhove and Joseph Wawrykow, 192–221. Notre Dame, IN: University of Notre Dame Press, 2005.

Weaver, J. Denny. "Violence in Christian Theology." *Cross Currents* 51.2 (2001) 150–76.

Webber, Robert. *Ancient-future Time: Forming Spirituality through the Christian Year.* Grand Rapids: Baker, 2004.

———. *Ancient-future Worship: Proclaiming and Enacting God's Narrative.* Grand Rapids: Baker, 2008.

Wesley, John. "On Visiting the Sick (Sermon 98)." No pages. Online: http://wesley.nnu.edu/john-wesley/the-sermons-of-john-wesley-1872-edition/sermon-98-on-visiting-the-sick/.

———. "The Scripture Way of Salvation (Sermon 43)." No pages. Online: http://www.umcmission.org/Find-Resources/John-Wesley-Sermons/Sermon-43-The-Scripture-Way-of-Salvation.

Westphal, Merold. *Becoming a Self: A Reading of Kierkegaard's Concluding Unscientific Postscript.* West Lafayette, IN: Purdue University Press, 1996.

Wieland, Georg. "Happiness (Ia IIae, qq 1–5)." Translated by Grant Kaplan. In *Ethics of Aquinas*, edited by S. Pope, 57–68. Washington, DC: Georgetown University Press, 2002.

Wilkins, Jeremy D. "Trinitarian Missions and the Order of Grace according to Thomas Aquinas." In *Philosophy and Theology in the Long Middle Ages*, edited by K. Emery et al., 689–708. Leiden: Brill, 2011.

———. "Why Two Divine Missions? Development in Augustine, Aquinas, and Lonergan." *Irish Theological Quarterly* 77.1 (2012) 37–66.

Willard, Dallas. *The Spirit of the Disciplines: Understanding How God Changes Lives.* San Francisco: HarperSanFrancisco, 1990.

Williams, A. N. *The Ground of Union: Deification in Aquinas and Palamas.* New York: Oxford University Press, 1999.

Williams, Rowan. *Resurrection: Interpreting the Easter Gospel.* Cleveland, OH: Pilgrim, 2002.

Wilson, Henry S. "Luther on Preaching as God Speaking." *Lutheran Quarterly* 19.1 (2005) 63–76.

World Council of Churches. *Baptism, Eucharist and Ministry.* Geneva: World Council of Churches, 1982.

Wright, Christopher J. H. *The Mission of God: Unlocking the Bible's Grand Narrative.* Downers Grove, IL: InterVarsity, 2006.

Wright, N. T. *Jesus and the Victory of God.* Christian Origins and the Question of God, 2. London: SPCK, 1996.

———. *Justification: God's Plan & Paul's Vision.* Downers Grove, IL: InterVarsity, 2009

———. *The New Testament and the People of God.* Christian Origins and the Question of God, 1. London: SPCK, 1992.

———. *The Resurrection of the Son of God.* Christian Origins and the Question of God, 3. London: SPCK, 2003.

———. *Surprised by Hope: Rethinking Heaven, the Resurrection, and the Mission of the Church.* New York: HarperOne, 2008.

Wybrew, Hugh. *The Orthodox Liturgy: The Development of the Eucharistic Liturgy in the Byzantine Rite.* Crestwood, NY: St. Vladimir's Seminary Press, 1990.

Zizioulas, Jean. *The Eucharistic Communion and the World.* New York: T. & T. Clark, 2011.

Name Index

Scripture Index

⤶

NEW TESTAMENT